# Organizing in the Digital Age

# PERSPECTIVES ON PROCESS ORGANIZATION STUDIES

Series Editors: Ann Langley and Haridimos Tsoukas

*Perspectives on Process Organization Studies* is an annual series, linked to the International Symposium on Process Organization Studies, and is dedicated to the development of an understanding of organizations and organizing at large as processes in the making. This series brings together contributions from leading scholars, which focus on seeing dynamically evolving activities, interactions, and events as important aspects of organized action, rather than static structures and fixed templates.

**Volume 1: Process, Sensemaking, and Organizing**
Editors: Tor Hernes and Sally Maitlis

**Volume 2: Constructing Identity in and around Organizations**
Editors: Majken Schultz, Steve Maguire, Ann Langley, and Haridimos Tsoukas

**Volume 3: How Matter Matters: Objects, Artifacts, and Materiality in Organization Studies**
Editors: Paul R. Carlile, Davide Nicolini, Ann Langley, and Haridimos Tsoukas

**Volume 4: Language and Communication at Work: Discourse, Narrativity, and Organizing**
Editors: François Cooren, Eero Vaara, Ann Langley, and Haridimos Tsoukas

**Volume 5: The Emergence of Novelty in Organizations**
Editors: Raghu Garud, Barbara Simpson, Ann Langley, and Haridimos Tsoukas

**Volume 6: Organizational Routines: How They Are Created, Maintained, and Changed**
Editors: Jennifer Howard-Grenville, Claus Rerup, Ann Langley, and Haridimos Tsoukas

**Volume 7: Skillful Performance: Enacting Capabilities, Knowledge, Competence, and Expertise in Organizations**
Editors: Jörgen Sandberg, Linda Rouleau, Ann Langley, and Haridimos Tsoukas

**Volume 8: Dualities, Dialectics, and Paradoxes in Organizational Life**
Editors: Moshe Farjoun, Wendy Smith, Ann Langley, and Haridimos Tsoukas

**Volume 9: Institutions and Organizations: A Process View**
Editors: Trish Reay, Tammar B. Zilber, Ann Langley, and Haridimos Tsoukas

**Volume 10: Time, Temporality, and History in Process Organization Studies**
Editors: Juliane Reinecke, Roy Suddaby, Ann Langley, and Haridimos Tsoukas

# Organizing in the Digital Age

## *A Process View*

*Edited by*
Michael Barrett
Emmanuelle Vaast
Ann Langley
and
Haridimos Tsoukas

OXFORD
UNIVERSITY PRESS

OXFORD
UNIVERSITY PRESS

Great Clarendon Street, Oxford, OX2 6DP,
United Kingdom

Oxford University Press is a department of the University of Oxford.
It furthers the University's objective of excellence in research, scholarship,
and education by publishing worldwide. Oxford is a registered trade mark of
Oxford University Press in the UK and in certain other countries



Published in the United States of America by Oxford University Press
198 Madison Avenue, New York, NY 10016, United States of America

British Library Cataloguing in Publication Data

Data available

Library of Congress Control Number: 2023948644

ISBN 9780198899457

DOI: 10.1093/oso/9780198899457.001.0001

Printed and bound in the UK by
Clays Ltd, Elcograf S.p.A.

# Contents

# List of Figures

# List of Tables

# List of Editors and Contributors

## Volume Editors

**Michael Barrett** is Professor of Information Systems and Innovation Studies at Cambridge Judge Business School, University of Cambridge, UK. He is also Academic Director of Cambridge Digital Innovation and Distinguished Visiting Professor of Innovation at the Stockholm School of Economics. He has published in many top-tier IS (information systems) and organization journals and has won several best paper awards at EGOS and the Academy of Management (AOM). In 2016, Michael was awarded the Distinguished Scholar award by the OCIS division of the AOM. Michael Barrett is currently Editor-in-Chief of the *Information & Organization* journal and is on the Advisory Board of the *Journal of the Association of Information Systems*. He has held several editorial responsibilities including: Senior Editor of *MIS Quarterly*, Associate Editor of *Information Systems Research*.

**Emmanuelle Vaast** is Professor of Information Systems and Associate Dean of Research at the Desautels Faculty of Management of McGill University. Her research examines how social practices emerge and change with the implementation and use of new technologies and how these new practices are associated with organizational and change dynamics. She has in particular investigated the learning and knowledge dynamics taking place at different levels (communities and networks of practice, for instance) and the boundary spanning involved in these dynamics when new Information Systems get implemented and used. She has served as Senior Editor at *Information Systems Research*.

**Ann Langley** is Emerita Professor of Management at HEC Montréal, Canada and Distinguished Research Environment Professor at Warwick Business School. Her research focuses on strategic change, leadership, innovation, and the use of management tools in complex organizations with an emphasis on processual research approaches. She has published over 80 articles and several books including *Strategy as Practice: Research Directions and Resources* with Gerry Johnson, Leif Melin, and Richard Whittington (Cambridge University Press, 2007). She is Coeditor of the journal of *Strategic Organization*, and has edited two handbooks, *SAGE Handbook of Process Organization Studies* (2016) with Haridimos Tsoukas and *Oxford Handbook of Organizational Paradox* with Wendy Smith, Marianne Lewis, and Paula Jarzabkowski.

**Haridimos Tsoukas** (www.htsoukas.com) holds the Columbia Ship Management Chair in Strategic Management at the University of Cyprus, Cyprus and is a Professor of Organization Studies at Warwick Business School, University of Warwick, UK. He obtained his PhD at the Manchester Business School (MBS), University of Manchester, and has worked at MBS, the University of Essex, the University of Strathclyde, and the

ALBA Graduate Business School, Greece. He has published widely in several leading academic journals, including the *Academy of Management Review, Strategic Management Journal, Organization Studies, Organization Science, Journal of Management Studies,* and *Human Relations.* He was the Editor-in-Chief of *Organization Studies* (2003–2008). His research interests include: knowledge-based perspectives on organizations; organizational becoming; the management of organizational change and social reforms; the epistemology of practice; and epistemological issues in organization theory. He is the editor (with Christian Knudsen) of *The Oxford Handbook of Organization Theory: Meta-theoretical Perspectives* (Oxford University Press, 2003). He has also edited *Organizations as Knowledge Systems*, Palgrave Macmillan, 2004 (with N. Mylonopoulos) and *Managing the Future: Foresight in the Knowledge Economy*, Blackwell, 2004 (with J. Shepherd). His book *Complex Knowledge: Studies in Organizational Epistemology* was published by Oxford University Press in 2005. He is also the author of the book *If Aristotle Were a CEO* (in Greek, Kastaniotis, 2004).

## Contributors

**Shaz Ansari** is a Professor of Strategy and Innovation at Judge Business School, University of Cambridge. He holds a PhD from University of Cambridge. He serves on the Editorial Boards of several leading journals, *Academy of Management Journal, Administrative Science Quarterly, Strategic Management Journal, Academy of Management Review, Strategic Management Journal, Organization Science, Journal of Management, Journal of Management Studies, Organization Studies and Research in the Sociology of Organizations,* where he has also published. His research interests include framing theory, social movements and new market development, institutional processes and diffusion of practices, technology management, disruptive innovation, platform ecosystems, social and environmental issues in management, commons, reputation management.

**Bijan Azad** is a Professor and Director of Darwazah Center for Innovation Management & Entrepreneurship, Olayan School of Business, American University of Beirut. His latest publication is titled, 'How Digital Visualizations Shape Strategy Work on the Frontlines', in *Long Range Planning.* A previous book contribution of his is on technology materiality, and affordances, appearing in *Materiality and Organizing: Social Interaction in a Technological World* (2012) Oxford University Press. He earned his PhD and Master's degrees from Massachusetts Institute of Technology, Cambridge, Massachusetts, USA. He is a regular attendee at the International Process Symposium PROS.

**Dubravka Cecez-Kecmanovic** is Emeritus Professor at the UNSW Business School, Sydney, Australia. She employs critical, sociomaterial, and process-oriented research perspectives to study and theorize dynamic entanglements of the social and the technological and their performative effects in organizational and broader societal contexts. She is Senior Editor of the *Journal of AIS* and *Information & Organization.*

**Kenneth Frank** received his PhD in measurement, evaluation, and statistical analysis from the School of Education at the University of Chicago in 1993. He is

MSU Foundation Professor of Sociometrics, Professor in Counseling, Educational Psychology and Special Education; and adjunct (by courtesy) in Fisheries and Wildlife and Sociology at Michigan State University. His substantive interests include the study of schools as organizations, social structures of students and teachers and school decision-making, and social capital.

**Raghu Garud** is Farrell Chair in Innovation and Entrepreneurship, and Professor of Management & Organization, Pennsylvania State University. Raghu's research explores the emergence and adoption of novelty. He is the Academy of Management TIM Division's 2020 distinguished scholar.

**Dirk S. Hovorka** is Professor of Systems and Design in the Business Information Systems Discipline at the University of Sydney. His current research addresses how scientific and societal practices bring forth 'worlds' through theory, design, and conceptualizations of 'the future'. Recognizing that the future has an implacable resistance to prediction and control, and that increasing rates of societal change render our knowledge about the past less indicative of future states, his research focuses on speculative approaches to 'knowing' in regard to technology, society, and biophysical environments. He is the recipient of multiple teaching awards and coauthor of the AIS 2011 Best Paper 'Secondary Design: A Case of Behavioral Design Research'. He is Senior Editor of JAIS Research Perspectives and co-chairs conference tracks and workshops on making futures a site of inquiry.

**Lotta Hultin** is a Postdoctoral Research Fellow at the House of Innovation, Stockholm School of Economics. Her research focuses on technology, work, and organization from a management studies perspective, exploring in particular the role of technologies and, more broadly, materiality, in organizational practices. Her work has appeared in *Organization Studies*, *Human Relations*, and *Information & Organization*, and she has presented frequently at major international conferences and workshops.

**Tim Ingold** is Professor Emeritus of Social Anthropology at the University of Aberdeen. He has carried out fieldwork among Saami and Finnish people in Lapland and has written on environment, technology, and social organization in the circumpolar North, on animals in human society, and on human ecology and evolutionary theory. His more recent work explores environmental perception and skilled practice. Ingold's current interests lie on the interface between anthropology, archaeology, art, and architecture. His recent books include *The Perception of the Environment* (2000), *Lines* (2007), *Being Alive* (2011), *Making* (2013), *The Life of Lines* (2015), *Anthropology and/as Education* (2018), *Anthropology: Why It Matters* (2018), *Correspondences* (2020), *Imagining for Real* (2022) and *The Rise and Fall of Generation Now* (2023). Ingold is a Fellow of the British Academy and the Royal Society of Edinburgh. In 2022 he was made a CBE for services to Anthropology.

**Lucas D. Introna** is Professor of Organization, Technology and Ethics at Lancaster University Management School. His research focuses on theorizing social/technical entanglements, especially with regard to the ethics and politics implicated in such entanglements. He has published widely on topics such as: sociomateriality, phenomenology of technology, information and power, privacy, surveillance, IT and post-modern ethics, and virtuality.

**Matthew Jones** is Reader in Information Systems at the Judge Business School, University of Cambridge. His work focuses on the relationship between information technology and organizational and social change. The main focus of his research in recent years has been in the healthcare sector, particularly acute hospitals, but he has previously undertaken studies in the press and broadcasting media, management consultancy, and the photographic industry. His research tends to involve engaged fieldwork in organizations and he has published on methodological and theoretical issues in such research.

**Inkyu Kim** is a doctoral candidate in Business Information Systems in the Broad College of Business at Michigan State University.

**Nelson King** has a PhD in Industrial and Systems Engineering from the University of Southern California and post-doctoral work in the Imaging and Informatics Lab at the University of Southern California. His research explores the socio-organizational implications of emerging digital systems that impact society, such as digital healthcare, using process-oriented research genres and the principles of organizational ergonomics. He uses his 20 years of experience in industry to bring together academia and practice insights that address industrial challenges. Dr King was Co-editor in-Chief of *Health Systems* (a journal of The OR Society) and a member of the IEEE Systems Council Human System Integration Technical Committee.

**Moritz J. Kleinaltenkamp** is a Postdoc at Freie Universität Berlin, and a Fellow at the Hertie School's Centre for Digital Governance. His research focuses on processes of innovation, entrepreneurship, and strategy, particularly in the context of emerging technologies. His work has received multiple recognitions from the Organization and Management Theory division of the Academy of Management. Since 2023, he is also serving as member of the European Commission's Innovation-Friendly Regulations Advisory Group.

**Arun Kumaraswamy** is a Professor in the Department of International Business at Florida International University's College of Business. Arun studies management of innovation and technology catch-up in emerging economies. He has co-authored articles in management and international business journals, and co-edited two special issues and the book *Managing in the Modular Age: Architectures, Networks and Organizations.* He serves on the editorial review boards of *Journal of International Business Studies, Journal of International Management*, and *Journal of World Business.*

**Magnus Mähring** is the Erling Persson Professor of Entrepreneurship and Digital Innovation at the Stockholm School of Economics, Chair of the House of Innovation and the Department of Entrepreneurship, Innovation and Technology, Co-director of the Swedish Center for Digital Innovation, and a Fellow at Cambridge University. His research focuses on organizational transformation processes, often involving digital technologies. He has published in a range of journals including *Organization Studies, Human Relations, MIS Quarterly, Information Systems Research*, and *California Management Review.*

**Alice Pentland,** MD is the James H. Sterner Professor and Chair of the Department of Dermatology at the University of Rochester, Rochester, NY.

**Brian T. Pentland** is the Main Street Capital Partners Endowed Professor in the Department of Accounting and Information Systems at Michigan State University. He received his PhD in Management from the Massachusetts Institute of Technology in 1991.

**Philipp Tuertscher** is Professor of Collaborative Innovation at the KIN Center for Digital Innovation, School of Business and Economics, Vrije Universiteit Amsterdam. His research explores organizational mechanisms and social practices for collaborative innovation in a variety of settings. Besides studying innovation processes on collaborative crowdsourcing platforms and online communities, such as Linux, Wikipedia, and Threadless, Philipp has been studying innovation and the creation of digital infrastructure in large-scale scientific collaborations at CERN. He published his research in the *Academy of Management Annals*, *Information Systems Research*, *Journal of Management Studies*, *Organization Science*, *Organization Studies*, and *Strategic Organization*, among others.

**Julie Ryan Wolf** is an Associate Professor in Dermatology and Radiation Oncology at the University of Rochester. She received her PhD in Pathology from UNC-Chapel Hill, and her MPH from University of Rochester.

**Yunna Xie** is a doctoral candidate in Health Services Research and Policy at the University of Rochester. She received her Bachelor's degree in Dentistry from West China School of Stomatology, Sichuan University, and Master of Science degree in Health Economics from Heidelberg University.

**Tim Ingold,** Department of Anthropology, University of Aberdeen, Aberdeen AB25 2DA, Scotland, UK, tim.ingold@abdn.ac.uk

**Lotta Hultin,** Stockholm School of Economics, Stockholm, Sweden, lotta.hultin@hhs.se

**Lucas Introna,** Lancaster University Management School, Lancaster, UK, l.introna@lancaster.ac.uk

**Magnus Mähring,** Stockholm School of Economics, Stockholm, Sweden, magnus.mahring@hhs.se

**Dubravka Cecez-Kecmanovic,** Information Systems and Technology Management, UNSW Business School, Sydney, Australia, dubravka@unsw.edu.au

**Matthew Jones,** Judge Business School, University of Cambridge, Trumpington Street, Cambridge CB2 1AG, UK, mrj10@cam.ac.uk

**Brian T. Pentland,** 632 Bogue St, Michigan State University, East Lansing, 48824 USA, pentland@broad.msu.edu,

**Julie Ryan Wolf,** PhD, 601 Elmwood Ave, Box 697, Rochester, NY 14642, julie_ryan@urmc.rochester.edu, Yunna Xie: Yunna_Xie@URMC.Rochester.edu

**Inkyu Kim,** 632 Bogue St, Michigan State University, East Lansing, 48824 USA, kiminky1@broad.msu.edu

**Ken Frank,** Room 462 Erickson Hall, 620 Farm Lane, Michigan State University, East Lansing, MI 48824-1034, kenfrank@msu.edu Alice Pentland, MD, 601 Elmwood Ave, Box 697, Rochester, NY 14642

**Raghu Garud,** Pennsylvania State University, Smeal College of Business, 431 Business Building University Park PA 16802. USA, (814) 863-4534, rug14@psu.edu

**Arun Kumaraswamy,** Florida International University, College of Business, Department of International Business, 11200 SW 8th Street, MANGO 441, Miami FL 33199. USA, (305) 348-3780, akumaras@fiu.edu

**Philipp Tuertscher,** Vrije Universiteit Amsterdam, School of Business and Economics, KIN Center for Digital Innovation, de Boelelaan 1105, 1081 HV Amsterdam, The Netherlands, +31 (0)20 59 85988, philipp.tuertscher@vu.nl

**Moritz J. Kleinaltenkamp,** Freie Universität Berlin (Berlin, Germany), moritz.kleinaltenkamp@fu-berlin.de

**Shahzad (Shaz) Ansari,** Judge Business School, University of Cambridge (Cambridge, UK), s.ansari@jbs.cam.ac.uk

**Bijan Azad** *, Ph.D., Associate Professor, Business Decision and Information Systems, Director of Darwazah Center for Innovation Management & Entrepreneurship, Olayan School of Business, American University of Beirut, Email: ba20@aub.edu.lb

**Nelson King,** Ph.D., Higher Education Consultant, Los Angeles, California, Email: king2know@gmail.com

- Dubravka Cecez-Kecmanovic: dubravka@unsw.edu.au
- Alice Pentland: (please contact Brian Pentland instead: Pentland@broad.msu.edu
- Michael Barrett: m.barrett@jbs.cam.ac.uk
- Emma Vaast: Emmanuelle.Vaast@mcgill.ca
- Ann Langley: ann.lnagley@hec.ca
- Hari Tsoukas: Hari.Tsoukas@wbs.ac.uk
- Dirk S. Hovorka: dirk.hovorka@sydney.edu.au

# Series Editorial Structure

# Series Endorsements

As we become more willing to convert reified entities into differentiated streams, the resulting images of process have become more viable and more elusive. Organization becomes organizing, being becomes becoming, construction becomes constructing. But as we see ourselves saying more words that end in 'ing', what must we be thinking? That is not always clear. But now, under the experienced guidance of editors Langley and Tsoukas, there is an annual forum that moves us toward continuity and consolidation in process studies. This book series promises to be a vigorous, thoughtful forum dedicated to improvements in the substance and craft of process articulation.

*Karl E. Weick*, Rensis Likert Distinguished University Professor of Organizational Behavior and Psychology, University of Michigan, USA

In recent years process and practice approaches to organizational topics have increased significantly. These approaches have made significant contributions to already existing fields of study, such as strategy, routines, knowledge management, and technology adoption, and these contributions have brought increasing attention to the approaches. Yet because the contributions are embedded in a variety of different fields of study, discussions about the similarities and differences in the application of the approaches, the research challenges they present, and the potential they pose for examining taken for granted ontological assumptions are limited. This series will provide an opportunity for bringing together contributions across different areas so that comparisons can be made and can also provide a space for discussions across fields. Professors Langley and Tsoukas are leaders in the development and use of process approaches. Under their editorship, the series will attract the work and attention of a wide array of distinguished organizational scholars.

*Martha S. Feldman*, Johnson Chair for Civic Governance and Public Management, Professor of Social Ecology, Political Science, Business and Sociology, University of California, Irvine, *USA*

*Perspectives on Process Organization Studies* will be the definitive annual volume of theories and research that advance our understanding of process questions dealing with how things emerge, grow, develop, and terminate over time. I applaud Professors Ann Langley and Haridimos Tsoukas for launching this important book series, and encourage colleagues to submit their process research and subscribe to PROS.

*Andrew H. Van de Ven*, Vernon H. Heath Professor of Organizational Innovation and Change, University of Minnesota, USA

The new series—*Perspectives on Process Organization Studies*—is a timely and valuable addition to the organization studies literature. The ascendancy of process perspectives in recent years has signified an important departure from traditional perspectives on organizations that have tended to privilege either self-standing events or discrete entities. In contrast, by emphasizing emergent activities and recursive relations, process perspectives take seriously the ongoing production of organizational realities. Such a performative view of organizations is particularly salient today, given the increasingly complex, dispersed, dynamic, entangled, and mobile nature of current organizational phenomena. Such phenomena are not easily accounted for in traditional approaches that are premised on stability, separation, and substances. Process perspectives on organizations thus promise to offer powerful and critical analytical insights into the unprecedented and novel experiences of contemporary organizing.

*Wanda J. Orlikowski*, Alfred P. Sloan Professor of Information Technologies and Organization Studies, Massachusetts Institute of Technology, USA

The recent decades witnessed conspicuous changes in organization theory: a slow but inexorable shift from the focus on structures to the focus on processes. The whirlwinds of the global economy made it clear that everything flows, even if change itself can become stable. While the interest in processes of organizing is not new, it is now acquiring a distinct presence, as more and more voices join in. A forum is therefore needed where such voices can speak to one another, and to the interested readers. The series *Perspectives on Process Organization Studies* will provide an excellent forum of that kind, both for those for whom a processual perspective is a matter of ontology, and those who see it as an epistemological choice.

*Barbara Czarniawska*, Professor of Management Studies, School of Business, Economics and Law at the University of Gothenburg, Sweden

We are living in an era of unprecedented change; one that is characterized by instability, volatility, and dramatic transformations. It is a world in which the seemingly improbable, the unanticipated, and the downright catastrophic appear to occur with alarming regularity. Such a world calls for a new kind of thinking: thinking that issues from the chaotic, fluxing immediacy of lived experiences; thinking that resists or overflows our familiar categories of thought; and thinking that accepts and embraces messiness, contradictions, and change as the *sine qua non* of the human condition. Thinking in these genuinely processual terms means that the starting point of our inquiry is not so much about the *being* of entities such as 'organization', but their constant and perpetual *becoming*. I very much welcome this long overdue scholarly effort at exploring and examining the fundamental issue of *process* and its implications for organization studies. Hari Tsoukas and Ann Langley are to be congratulated on taking this very important initiative in bringing the process agenda into the systematic study of the phenomenon of organization. It promises to be a path-breaking contribution to our analysis of organization.

*Robert Chia*, Professor of Management, University of Strathclyde, UK

This new series fits the need for a good annual text devoted to process studies. Organization theory has long required a volume specifically devoted to process research that can address process ontology, methodology, research design, and analysis. While many authors collect longitudinal data, there are still insufficient methodological tools and techniques to deal with the nature of that data. Essentially, there is still a lack of frameworks and methods to deal with good processual data or to develop process-based insights. This series will provide an important resource for all branches of organization, management, and strategy theory. The editors of the series, Professors Ann Langley and Hari Tsoukas are excellent and very credible scholars within the process field. They will attract top authors to the series and ensure that each paper presents a high quality and insightful resource for process scholars. I expect that this series will become a staple in libraries, PhD studies, and journal editors' and process scholars' bookshelves.

*Paula Jarzabkowski*, Professor of Strategic Management,
Aston Business School, UK

# 1

# Organizing in the Digital Age: A Process View

## An Introduction

*Michael Barrett, Emma Vaast, Ann Langley, and Haridimos Tsoukas*

Digital technologies are transforming every aspect of our organizing, whether this be within organizations, across industries, or the way we live in society. This represents a step change in the speed, scale, and scope of change associated with digitalization over the last few decades, and an increased need for process perspectives to understand the relationship between technology and organizing.

Earlier research adopted contingency theory and variance-based studies to explore and classify organization structures related to variables such as organizational size (Woodward 1958; Thompson 1967) and focused on technology as an outcome rather than a process in its use across industries. With the growth of information technologies and the Internet, research studies began to adopt process-based approaches to understand how technology was transforming work practices within organizations (Orlikowski and Robey 1991), within occupational communities (Vaast and Walsham 2009), and across industries and markets (Barrett and Walsham 1999). These studies drew on meta-theories such as structuration theory (Giddens 1984, 1991), Actor-Network Theory (ANT) (Latour 1987; Walsham and Sahay 1999), and other Science, Technology, and Society (STS) theories (Pickering 1993; Barrett, Oborn, Orlikowski, and Yates 2012), while adopting qualitative approaches such as ethnography (Zuboff 1988) and in-depth interpretive case studies (Walsham 1995, 2006).

With the rise of artificial intelligence (AI) and a proliferation of digital technologies transforming the business and work landscape (Brynjolfsson and McAfee 2014), there has been increasing recognition and interest in the study of digitalization. This process is spurred on by digital innovations

Michael Barrett et al., *Organizing in the Digital Age: A Process View.* In: *Organizing in the Digital Age.* Edited by: Michael Barrett, Emmanuelle Vaast, Ann Langley, and Haridimos Tsoukas, Oxford University Press. © Oxford University Press (2024). DOI: 10.1093/oso/9780198899457.003.0001

(Yoo et al. 2012), which are having a profound effect on customer expectations, service innovation (Barrett et al. 2015), new forms of collaboration, and transformed digital operating and business models (Ansari and Garud, 2009; Schwab 2017). The ensuing digital transformation associated with a wide array of digital innovations (e.g. mobile, AI, Internet of Things (IoT), and other technologies) are radically influencing the potential for the speed, scale, and scope of change associated with work practices, industries, and ecosystems (Hinings Gegenhuber and Greenwood 2018), though there are significant challenges related to its successful implementation (Wessel et al. 2021).

Scholars adopting a process view have gradually embraced a wider sociomaterial perspective on organizing (Zammuto et al. 2007; Orlikowski and Scott 2008). The Covid-19 crisis has magnified the importance of digital technologies in contemporary processes of organizing and accelerated the role of digital transformation in work-life (Marabelli et al. 2021). Rapid use of digital technologies in unprecedented and often creative ways has been a hallmark of improvisational responses to the Covid pandemic (Orlikowski and Scott 2021). The time is ripe for evolving process-based theories to further our understanding of organizing in the digital age (Gkeredakis, Lifshitz-Assaf, and Barrett 2021). Our hope is that the chapters presented in this book will help us towards this goal as digital technologies increasingly influence how we organize our work and social life.

## 1.1 The Puzzle: Questioning Digital Work, Agency, and Temporality in Process Studies of Organizing in the Digital Age

The central themes underpinning most of the chapters in this volume concern the becoming of digital work, the conceptualization of agency in digital work, and the role of temporality in contemporary organizing, together constituting the key puzzle of organizing in the digital age as viewed from a process perspective. While information technology (IT) and changes in work practices have long been studied from a process perspective (Barrett and Walsham 1999), this earlier work tended to adopt an actor-centric approach (Hayes 2001; Vaast and Walsham 2009). As a result, the conceptualization of IT and work adopted a social practice approach, which, while recognizing the need for understanding the duality between technology and people in the design and use of technology in the workplace, tended to privilege the role of human agency in these dynamics (Mousavi Baygi et al. 2021).

As Hultin et al. note (this volume), an actor-centric vocabulary suggests that the governing agency is located within—or in the interaction between—separate entities or actors (social or material). In this way they 'forfeit the possibility to account for how these actors are always governed by being already positioned in certain ways within the performative flow of material-discursive practices' (p. 40).

However, scholars have gradually started to better account for the increasing complexity and entwinement or imbrication of digital technologies in work practices (Leonardi and Barley 2008; Jones 2014). This has led to a groundswell in research focused on conceptualizing materiality, technology, and organizing through sociomaterial perspectives on work practices (Orlikowski and Scott 2008; Barrett et al. 2012; Cecez-Kecmanovic et al. 2014). The increasing entanglement of digital technologies and work accelerated through the pandemic calls into question the need for understanding digital work happening at scale (Barrett and Orlikowski 2021). It also highlights the critical need to examine and expose inequalities related to digital innovation emerging during the pandemic (Faraj et al. 2021; Gkeredakis et al. 2021; Zheng and Walsham 2021). These developments reinforce the 'dark side of information and communication technologies', related to privacy, the security of personal data, misinformation and fake news, cybercrime, and the use of AI and data for surveillance capitalism (Zuboff 2019). There is increasingly a need to focus on ethical goals and engage in more critical research approaches (Sahay, Mukherjee, Walsham, and Erickson 2022) as we consider whether we are making a better world with these technologies (Walsham 2012).

While being mindful of these critical concerns, this book highlights a process view for organizing in a digital age and draws together practice perspectives some of which are widely accepted (e.g. sociomaterial perspectives) while others are gaining increasing attention (e.g. an Ingoldian perspective). The way we conceptualize agency and the becoming of digital work is critical for understanding processes of organizing and shapes how we view and relate to organizational phenomena surrounding IT and work practices. As briefly noted above, there have been decades of inquiry and re-conceptualization of the positioning of human and material agency which has highlighted the intrigue of this ongoing puzzle. With an increasing focus on entanglement, the dichotomy implied by *working digitally*, for example, is not useful (Orlikowski and Scott 2016) in distinguishing different kinds of work in contemporary organizing in our digital age (Orlikowski and Scott 2021). Further, the digital shaping of work has never been more evident than during the pandemic lockdowns as work-from-home online practices are being enacted the world over through a myriad of technologies (Barrett and Orlikowski 2021) including: email communication, distributed collaboration tools, mobile chat, online transactions, AI and robotics, digital twins, and social media interactions. The spaces associated with work have long been important to understand how organizing literally takes place (de Vaujany and Vaast 2014). The pandemic and the new order of work that has emerged from it, as well as from increased digitalization, have drastically changed the physical and virtual spaces in which work takes place and the ways in which these spaces connect with each other (Richardson 2021; Vayre 2022). For example, technological innovation during the pandemic has accelerated new ways of working and further integrated spatiotemporal, technological, and socio-cultural dimensions of work-life (Aroles, Cecez-Kecmanovic, Dale, Kingman, and Mitev 2021). Similarly, there has been a dramatic growth of digital health during Covid, which has accelerated opportunities to transform how healthcare is provided and where it is delivered. Emerging digital technologies, including remote patient monitoring, telehealth, and AI-based predictive diagnostics, have boosted the shift towards digital home services (Oborn et al., 2021). The rapid growth in digitally enabled hybrid care models is being facilitated by novel uses of technologies such as digital twins to provide operational coordination and control (Croatti et al., 2020).

This becoming of digital work enacted by a multiplicity of digital technologies draws attention to the ongoing need for reflection as to how we might best conceptualize agency in digital work. As Hultin et al. suggest (this volume), the issue may be framed as *centring of human agency and backgrounding of materiality*. This means that some studies, while acknowledging that human subjects are embedded in a material environment and use material artifacts in their work (e.g. Nicolini et al. 2012; Stigliani and Ravasi 2012), they typically remain at the centre of this work as constructors of practices and authors of discourse. Thus, to the extent that it is recognized that social discourse is embedded in material relationships, 'non-humans' are attended to mainly in terms of their structuring, conditioning, or intermediating role (e.g. Swan et al. 2007; Nicolini et al. 2012; Jones and Massa 2013; Farquharson et al. 2014; Monteiro and Nicolini 2015). In these accounts, the materiality of objects clearly matters, yet mostly as external props and tools in a structuring, conditioning, or intermediating role (e.g. Swan et al. 2007; Nicolini et al. 2012).

Furthermore, concern with the role of agency in digital work reaches new heights when we consider the rapid and pervasive development and implementation of Artificial Intelligence (AI). The intended replacement of knowledge workers with the march of AI is unprecedented (Cecez-Kecmanovic this volume). It has sparked much recent debate (Raisch and Krakowski 2021) on conceptualizing agency through processes of automation or augmentation, the latter recognizing that humans may collaborate closely with AI in accomplishing digital work tasks. Furthermore, Raisch and Krakowski (2021) highlight the need to deal with the tension brought about by these different agencies to achieve complementarities of AI in organizations. As work processes change and increasingly rely upon algorithms, questions associated with how people and algorithms interact with one another (Shaikh and Vaast 2023 and with how algorithmic management disrupts control and flows in organizations (Kellogg et al. 2020, Pachidi, Berends, Faraj, and Huysman 2021) have become pressing. More examinations of the specific features and affordances of different digital technologies are also warranted to understand better diverse digitalization-related phenomena. Blockchain technologies, IoT applications, machine learning algorithms for instance represent some of the many digital technologies that are (re-)shaping organizational processes. Care should be taken to understand what digital technologies may or may not do and to distinguish the myths from the realistic potentials associated with them.

Focusing on AI, Cecez-Kecmanovic (this volume) notes that its current promise is that powerful learning algorithms will enable automation of knowledge work which will result in better outcomes—more objective and even fairer decisions—than that achieved through human performance (Faraj et al. 2018, Holford 2019). She challenges the fundamental assumptions underlying these AI systems, which tend to reduce knowledge work to a bounded, self-contained mechanism, which is somehow detached from practice. The underlying ontological and epistemological stance is that of a 'blob' world of knowledge work that is self-contained and disinterested in the harmful social consequences that can occur. More specifically, in AI-powered automated knowledge systems, objects of work as *blobs* are not individuals but instead *datafied individuals* (data sets)—compiled from social media posts, health records, purchasing transactions, search history, crime records, etc. Rules developed from past data are applied to these datafied individuals to calculate the outcomes on job selection or credit risk scores that typically have material effects on the *actual* individuals.

The latter emphasizes the *ethical and moral dimension of agency* with the use of AI systems in this approach to automation of knowledge work. As Jones (this volume) argues, the use of digital data in conducting process research requires a detailed and critical analysis of the particular types of data that might be drawn on, how they are produced, how they are used, and how they contribute to the organizational phenomena being studied.

This implies an understanding of data as a process (Jones 2019; Jones et al. 2019) in conducting digital work, especially that performed by AI.

Cecez-Kecmanovic (this volume) proposes a different world of knowledge work. Following Ingold (2015, 2017), she suggests a different conceptualization of digital work and agency in which human knowledge workers and AI technologies *co-respond* to each other and work in harmony. In this more positive viewpoint, AI and knowledge workers are bounded in sympathy as they cooperatively attend to and examine problems, investigate possible solutions and their implications, make proposals or decisions, and, in the process, learn together.

The third and final part of our puzzle questions the role of temporality which is at the heart of agency (Emirbayer and Mische 1998; Orlikowski and Yates 2002; Reinnecke, Suddaby, Langley, and Tsoukas 2021) within digital work. Hultin et al. (this volume) highlight that traditional views of time in digital work are as a quantity that can be identified in space, but that this constrains us from studying temporal qualities, such as timings, rhythms, and tempos and more generally the ongoing flow of practices. An alternative perspective (Emirbayer and Mische 1998) is that we view agency situated within the flow of time, how agency is informed by the past, but also oriented towards the future and towards the present.

Conceptualizing temporal flows of organizing are both foundational and challenging (Reinecke, Suddaby, Langley, and Tsoukas 2021). Within the domain of digital work, should we understand the relationship of temporality and agency to be how time (past data) shapes agency (AI-biased decision-making) or how agency shapes conceptions of time. Drawing from Ingold (2011, 2015, 2017), Hultin et al. (this volume) suggest that a temporal flow of agency implies a view of agency as something that is not inherent and belonging to any one actor or as a serial chain of consequences set in motion by an initial force. Rather, agency is an ongoing temporal flow, always inheriting from previous practices, imparting to subsequent practices, while being always subject to the contingent possibilities of the present.

Within our rapidly accelerating era of digital work, where firms seek to leverage a multiplicity of digital innovations in enabling digital transformation (Hinings et al. 2018, Gegenhuber, T., et al. 2022), creative agency related to digital innovation is of ever-increasing importance (Yoo et al. 2012). A key issue therefore is to better understand the temporal dimensions of creativity, especially in the late modern context of an accelerating world, something that Ingold (this volume) helps us address from a philosophical perspective. Closer to the specific challenges of digital work, Simpson et al (2020) highlights the important relationship between temporality and creative agency for hi-tech organizations engaged in innovation. Hi-tech firms such as Apple and Google not only realize that new ideas take time to develop and mature, but they need to protect employee's time to be creative in developing and implementing innovations for digital transformation. In our contemporary context with the acceleration of digital innovation during the Covid crisis this relationship is even more important as witnessed by firms undergoing high levels of experimentation (Gkeredakis et al. 2021) and improvisation during this period of liminal innovation (Orlikowski and Scott 2021).

Adopting processual approaches to understanding the unfolding of creative practice which recognize the flow of agency are of increasing importance for digital transformation in a post-Covid business landscape. As Simpson et al. (2020) illustrates in the classic case of Post-It Notes at 3M, the creative agency involved more than just *timeless* immersion in the flow of experimentation or having much needed blocks of time set aside for innovative thinking. It was also *timefully* resourced by the simultaneity of recollections of the past (Silver's glue) and imagining of futures (dependable page markers). This timefulness is fundamentally grounded in ongoing practice and emphasizes temporal experience as an important complement to timelessness in understanding the temporal organizing of creative practice.

## 1.2 Contributions to This Volume: Exploring Digital Technologies and Organizing in Process Studies

In his piece, 'Creation beyond Creativity: From the Novelty of Ends to the Renewal of Life', Timothy Ingold sets the scene for our exploration of organizing in the digital age by challenging us to continue to (re)consider the age-old questions related to creative agency which are ever more critical in a digital age where the potential for combinatorial innovation (Yoo et al. 2012) may arguably never have been greater. The question remains as to whether creativity, such as needed to fuel one's digital strategy, necessarily involves the recombination of elements already to hand. Drawing eclectically from Dewey, Bergson, and Whitehead, across fields of philosophy, religion, and art, Ingold elaborates on the distinction between novelty and newness, and the nature of creative agency as going beyond what he terms the proliferation of ends to focus on the promise of a perpetual beginning. Ingold's extensive body of thought on temporality, creativity, and agency serves as foundational inspiration for the two following chapters in the volume.

In their contribution 'On Thinking Movement: Theorizing Flows of Organizing in a Digital Age', Lotta Hultin, Lucas Introna, and Magnus Mähring (this volume) challenge scholars adopting a process-based ontology of 'becoming' to experiment with a new vocabulary in thinking about movement. Specifically, their perspective focuses on temporal flow rather than a traditional spatial perspective in understanding transformation. They start by problematizing an actor-centric ontology, which they argue performatively enacts the world as consisting of boundaries, entities, actors, and categories. Further, they challenge the assumed qualities and intentionality of important actors and artifacts in the 'here and now', and subsequently highlight the importance of tracing the multiplicity of (agentic) flows that already enact them. Their theoretical approach draws on Ingold (2007, 2011, 2015), who describes the flow of agency as 'agentic lines' as trails along which life is lived, and which are knotted together to form a 'meshwork'. By foregrounding the temporal flow of practices, they illustrate the value of their approach through an analysis of empirical studies conducted at the Swedish Migration Board. They conclude by reflecting on how organizational scholars could benefit from experimenting with temporally oriented vocabularies in their research.

In her chapter, 'Algorithmic Automation of Knowledge Work—A Sketch for Exploring the Becoming of Knowledge Work', Dubravka Cecez-Kecmanovic (this volume) challenges the primacy and privilege given to AI-powered automation of knowledge work in contemporary times. AI powered by learning algorithms, viewed as both superior to humans in performance as well as being more objective and fairer, is increasingly displacing knowledge workers across a wide range of sectors. However, this promise often touted for AI-based knowledge work does not take responsibility for its emerging harmful organizational and social consequences. Cecez-Kecmanovic problematizes the fundamental ontological and epistemological assumptions about the nature of knowledge and knowledge work underpinning algorithmic automation of work. Again drawing from Ingold (2015, 2017), she suggests that instead of adopting a 'blob' world of work enacted by the AI automation of knowledge work, we could productively imagine a different world of knowledge work in which human knowledge workers and AI technologies *co-respond* to each other and work in harmony. Together, knowledge workers and their technologies can cooperatively attend to and examine problems, investigate possible solutions and their implications, make proposals or decisions, and, in the process, learn.

Dirk Hovorka's chapter, 'Utopias as Borderlands: Reconceptualizing Post-pandemic Future(s)' (this volume), highlights how, among many disruptions, during the Covid-19 pandemic we collectively became participants in a '*natural experiment*' involving growing reliance upon digital technologies for work. This has challenged established ways of working without providing full clarity on what the future of work might actually entail. This has also challenged researchers to rethink the status quo of our understanding of what work involves and to engage critically with what the future may hold. For instance, how is work tied to particular workplaces? Encouraging us to imagine what may be, Hovorka's chapter relies upon utopia as a '*speculative engagement*' that views the future as a '*digital geography*' to critique the present, consider multiple potentials for the future, and radically reconsider what we think we know. Utopias and dystopias of the work future do not predict what the future will entail. They enable us to navigate between past practices and potential new ones with a deeper view of what hopes and challenges may emerge tomorrow.

Matthew Jones' chapter, 'Physics or Archaeology? Process Organization Studies in the Age of Data Abundance' (this volume), asks original questions regarding what process researchers in the digital world may actually be able to study and conclude from their work. As digital trace data have become increasingly available and processing abilities have drastically improved, what kinds of new investigations may researchers undertake? The abundance of data has led some researchers to think that all research might reach closer to a physics ideal. Computational social science, for instance, has thrived from the growing availability of data. However, as Jones astutely reminds us, all data, including digitally produced ones, do not simply reflect reality. They are constructed and thus provide a partial perspective on the phenomena they concern. Rather than the physics model, then, Jones instead recommends that researchers of the digital follow archaeologists who have long constructed and reconstructed social phenomena on the basis of their existing knowledge as well as of changing and fragmented data.

Like Jones' chapter, the chapter by Brian Pentland, Julie Ryan Wolf, Yunna Xie, Inkyu Kim, Kenneth Frank, and Alice Pentland, 'Processual Shadows: What Can We See with Digital Trace Data?' (this volume), focuses on the potential and limitations of digital trace data as a resource for the study of organizing processes. Specifically, using digital trace data from a clinical information system in four dermatology clinics and the *Threadnet* software (specially designed for process analysis), the authors show that they were able to detect shifts in routine dynamics that were unnoticed by the participants in the routines themselves. Yet the authors also warn that the 'processual shadows' visible from digital data traces may be difficult to interpret without in-person observational data such as that obtained from ethnography. Indeed, both types of methods (digital traces and ethnographic observation) offer distinctive and complementary strengths and weaknesses that suggest their use in combination. The authors conclude with a preliminary analysis of how the Covid-19 pandemic affected digital data traces from the clinics, confirming the need for complementary methods.

The chapter by Raghu Garud, Arun Kumaraswamy, and Philipp Tuertscher, 'Collaborating Using Digital Technologies: The Use of Generative Memory' (this volume), elaborates on our understanding of how digital traces may contribute to organizing processes, this time in the context of distributed collaboration. Building on an in-depth qualitative study of Wikipedia posts, the authors are able to track the way in which individual participants in the definition of key concepts were able to coordinate their work over time, by drawing on past digital traces as a kind of generative memory. The records of who contributed what, when, and why, enabled participants to appreciate the track records of contributors over time, and make decisions about which adjustments could be accepted and confirmed, helping to avoid conflict that might arise from distributed and asynchronous co-creation. The particular nature of the digital traces, that included not only quantitative decontextualized information, but a rich verbal accounting available from past article discussions and versions of the articles themselves contribute to the generative character of these traces. The authors argue that the multi-layered digital traces created by this technology shape interactions among actors with different perspectives, but do not determine them completely, enabling emergent outcomes.

Moritz Kleinaltenkamp and Shahzad Ansari in their chapter, 'Blockchain and the Performativity of Emerging Technology Theories' (this volume), alert us to the performativity of digital technologies, emphasizing how emerging technologies may be producing a new social reality such as organizational change. Relying upon the emerging technology of the controversial technology of blockchain and building upon performativity theories, their chapter revisits the important question of the impact of new technologies in organizations. It explains how emerging technologies require theories ascribing value and impact to them. Their insights onto the roles of the actors doing such theorizing as well as onto the ways in which this theorizing amplifies the potential impact of emerging technologies will be of interest to organization and technology researchers alike.

Finally, in their chapter, 'Computer Workarounds or Expediting Work?', Bijan Azad and Nelson King (this volume) provide a processual understanding of the why and how of IT computer workarounds within an organizational work practice. In so doing, they go beyond traditional conceptualizations which are often focused narrowly on user intent and IT use. Drawing on a framework that links pragmatism, interactionism, phenomenology, and ecological psychology they develop a more holistic view of how users face anomalies in work practice and dynamically implement a set of workarounds to restore workflow. In so doing, they seek to move away from characterizing attempts to bypass IT as workarounds, and instead examine the specific entwinement of medical practice and IT-enabled workflow. Their study explores a case study of a medication dispensing system and demonstrates why and how computer workarounds can emerge endogenously in response to work practice anomalies. The findings uncover three distinctive types of compensatory actions: *performative procedures*, ad hoc *role crafting*, and *gaming the system*, which are characterized by the logics of *expedience* and *satisficing* in what they term *expediting work*.

## 1.3 Process Organization Studies and Organizing in a Digital Age

As the contributions of this volume as well as the wealth of related current research attest, digital technologies and the ways in which people, organizations, and institutions (Faik et al. 2020) adjust and build upon them remain a fertile ground for scholarship. We encourage scholars of organization and technology to pursue more work in this domain. Especially, we invite research that both recognizes and seeks to reconcile the utopian and dystopian futures associated with digital technologies and that would engage creatively with digital trace data in process theorizing.

Regarding the utopian and dystopian aspects associated with digital technologies, dialectical approaches (Farjoun 2016; Putnam et al. 2016) are essential to bring together seemingly contradictory perspectives on the current and future situations associated with digital technologies. Scholarship has touched upon the *future of work* (Malone 2018) and has, for instance, probed how the emergence of new digital technologies lead to obsolescence and to transformations of work (Vaast and Pinsonneault 2021). Process researchers are particularly well-suited to examine such digitally enabled transformations in work and organizing. They can highlight and unpack the specific processes of transformation of work and occupations associated with new digital technologies (Wang et al. 2020; Mousavi Baygi et al. 2021). As Hovorka (this volume) indicates, current processes of change associated with digital technologies have blurred the boundaries of work and life, making the future equally '*utopian*' and '*dystopian*'. In a related manner, Cecez-Kecmanovic (this volume) goes beyond unrealistic expectations associated with the promise of AI for knowledge work. Instead, she impresses upon us the importance of considering in a realistic and ongoing manner the expected and unexpected changes that come from new digital technologies. In a way, these contributions pay homage to Winner's (1986, 1993, 2006) seminal and sceptical take on the revolutionary character of new technologies, and their pro-bias for innovation. At the same time, recent work has gone beyond stories of both gloom and doom and of utopia and techno-optimism to develop stories of hope around how information technologies are contributing to making the world better (Sahay et al. 2022). While it is important to be reflective and critical and expose the dark side, there is also a need for bold new visions which can imagine how digital technologies can contribute to positive social outcomes without being shackled to the failures of digital which have haunted our past.

Regarding digital trace data and their potential for process theorizing, as indicated in notable contributions in this volume (see Garud et al. this volume; Jones this volume; Pentland et al. this volume, in particular), the growing reliance upon digital echnologies has also opened new possibilities to collect digital trace data and to develop empirical analyses (e.g. netnographies, innovative social network analyses) that can be illuminating for process researchers (Whelan et al. 2016; McKenna et al. 2017). For researchers studying digital organizing this has indeed meant that there is greater availability and access to digital trace data, which is automatically produced in actions and activities.

These digital developments have created a unique opportunity for innovation and creativity by process researchers. They can complement existing organizational studies of processes, which while often theoretically rich, tend to rely upon partial data. Researchers can thus bring together two so far separate '*islands*' of process scholarship to deepen their understanding of processes (Pentland et al. 2021). Process scholarship that has traditionally been theoretically deep (Langley 1999; Langley et al. 2013) may now be combined with process modelling techniques that have been technically sophisticated (Van Der Aalst et al. 2011; Maaradji et al. 2016). In the bridging of these two islands of knowledge is great potential for new theorizing.

At the same time, however, the unprecedented access to new data and methods leads to new ethical and epistemological questions for researchers. We need to acknowledge the potential risks for privacy of the people involved in the activities captured by digital trace data. That these data are available and accessible does not negate but, instead, enhances the accountability and responsibility of researchers (Schultze and Mason 2012; Vaast and Walsham 2013). Researchers of digital trace data should rethink what the negative unanticipated consequences of their work may be. This can lead them to questions such as: How could researchers design original methods that are respectful of people and the phenomena they investigate? How do we redefine human and process research in an age of unmatched access to data and of heightened responsibility for researchers?

Pentland et al. (this volume) propose a solution to these questions by advocating for complementary methods within the same project (e.g. process modelling and qualitative analysis of interviews and participant observation). We encourage process researchers to continue reflecting upon these important issues and to engage, critically, rigorously, and ethically with digital trace data. We also hope that these ethical and moral dimensions will be in the forefront of reader's minds as they engage with the chapters of this volume that aim to demonstrate the value of creating a dialogue between digital technologies and organizing in process organization studies.

## References


Ansari, S., and Garud, R. (2009). 'Inter-generational Transitions in Socio-technical Systems: The Case of Mobile Communications', *Research Policy* 38/2: 382–392.

Aroles, J., Cecez-Kecmanovic, D., Dale, K., Kingma, S. F., and Mitev, N. (2021). 'New Ways of Working (NWW): Workplace Transformation in the Digital Age', *Information and Organization* 31/4: 10378.

Barrett, M., and Orlikowski, W. (2021). 'Scale Matters: Doing Practice-Based Studies of Contemporary Digital Phenomena', *MIS Quarterly* 45/1: 467–472.

Barrett, M., Davidson, E., Prabhu, J., and Vargo, S. L. (2015). 'Service Innovation in the Digital Age', *MIS Quarterly* 39/1: 135–154.

Barrett, M., Oborn, E., Orlikowski, W. J., and Yates, J. (2012). 'Reconfiguring Boundary Relations: Robotic Innovations in Pharmacy Work', *Organization Science* 23/5: 1448–1466.

Barrett, M., and Walsham, G. (1999). 'Electronic Trading and Work Transformation in the London Insurance Market', *Information Systems Research* 10/1: 1–22.

Brynjolfsson, E., and McAfee, A. (2014). The second machine age: Work, progress, and prosperity in a time of brilliant technologies. WW Norton & Company.

Cecez-Kecmanovic, D., Galliers, R. D., Henfridsson, O., Newell, S., and Vidgen, R. (2014). 'The Sociomateriality of Information Systems', *MIS Quarterly* 38/3: 809–830.

Croatti, A., Gabellini, M., Montagna, S., and Ricci, A. (2020). 'On the Integration of Agents and Digital Twins in Healthcare', *Journal of Medical Systems* 44: 1–8.

De Vaujany, F.-X., and Vaast, E. (2014). 'If These Walls Could Talk: The Mutual Construction of Organizational Space and Legitimacy', *Organization Science* 25/3: 713–731.

Emirbayer, M., and Mische, A. (1998). 'What is agency?', *American Journal of Sociology* 103/4: 962–1023.

Faik, I., Barrett, M., and Oborn, E. (2020). 'How Information Technology Matters in Societal Change: An Affordance-based Institutional Logics Perspective', *MIS Quarterly* 44/3.

Faraj, S., Pachidi, S., and Sayegh, K. (2018). 'Working and Organizing in the Age of the Learning Algorithm', *Information and Organization* 28/1: 62–70.

Faraj, S., Renno, W., and Bhardwaj, A. (2021). 'Unto the Breach: What the COVID-19 Pandemic Exposes About Digitalization', *Information and Organization* 31/1: 100337.

Farjoun, M. (2016). 'Contradictions, Dialectics', in A. Langley and H. Tsoukas (eds), *The Sage Handbook of Process Organization Studies*, Sage, 87–109.

Farquharson M., Ortenblad A., and Hsu S. W. (2014). Trusting local translation: Experience from transplanting a 'Made in Britain' entrepreneurship course in China. *Management Learning* 45/2: 182–199.

Gegenhuber, T., Logue, D., Hinings, C. R., and Barrett, M. (Eds.). (2022). *Digital Transformation and Institutional Theory*. Emerald Publishing Limited.

Gkeredakis, M., Lifshitz-Assaf, H., and Barrett, M. (2021). 'Crisis as Opportunity, Disruption and Exposure: Exploring Emergent Responses to Crisis Through Digital Technology', *Information and Organization* 31/1: 100344.

Giddens, A. (1984). *The Constitution of Society. Outline of the Theory of Structuration*. Berkeley: University of California Press.

Giddens, A. (1991). *Modernity and Self-Identity*. Cambridge: Polity Press.

Hayes, N. (2001). 'Boundless and Bounded Interactions in the Knowledge Work Process: The Role of Groupware Technologies', *Information and Organization* 11: 79–101.

Hinings, B., Gegenhuber, T., and Greenwood, R. (2018). 'Digital Innovation and Transformation: An Institutional Perspective', *Information and Organization* 28/1: 52–61.

Holford, W. D. (2019). 'The Future of Human Creative Knowledge Work within the Digital Economy', *Futures* 105: 143–154.

Ingold, T. (2007). 'Materials Against Materiality', *Archaeological Dialogues* 14/1: 1–16.

Ingold, T. (ed.). (2011). *Redrawing anthropology: Materials, movements, lines*. Ashgate Publishing, Ltd.

Ingold, T. (2015). *The life of lines*. Routledge.

Ingold, T. (2017). 'On Human Correspondence', *Journal of the Royal Anthropological Institute* 23/1: 9–27.

Jones, M. (2014). 'A Matter of Life and Death', *MIS Quarterly* 38/3: 895–A6.

Jones, M. (2019). 'What We Talk About When We Talk About (Big) Data', *The Journal of Strategic Information Systems* 28/1: 3–16.

Kellogg, K. C., Valentine, M. A., and Christin, A. (2020). 'Algorithms at Work: The New Contested Terrain of Control', *Academy of Management Annals* 14/1: 366–410.

Langley, A. (1999). 'Strategies for Theorizing Process Data', *Academy of Management Review* 24/4: 691–710.

Langley, A., Smallman, C., Tsoukas, H., and Van de Ven, A. H. (2013). 'Process Studies of Change in Organization and Management: Unveiling Temporality, Activity, and Flow', *Academy of Management Journal* 56/1: 1–13.

Latour, B. (1987). *Science in Action: How to Follow Scientists and Engineers through Society*. Cambridge: Harvard University Press.

Leonardi, P. M., and Barley, S. R. (2008). 'Materiality and Change: Challenges to Building Better Theory About Technology and Organizing', *Information and Organization* 18/3: 159–176.

Maaradji, A., Dumas, M., La Rosa, M., and Ostovar, A. (2016). 'Fast and Accurate Business Process Drift Detection', in *International Conference on Business Process Management*. Springer, 406–422.

Malone, T.W. (2018). 'How Human-Computer "Superminds" Are Redefining the Future of Work', *MIT Sloan Management Review* 59/4: 34–41.

Marabelli, M., Vaast, E., and Li, J. L. (2021). 'Preventing the Digital Scars of Covid-19', *European Journal of Information Systems* 30/2: 176–192.

McKenna, B., Myers, M. D., and Newman, M. (2017). 'Social Media in Qualitative Research: Challenges and Recommendations', *Information and Organization* 27/2: 87–99.

Mousavi Baygi, R., Introna, L. D., and Hultin, L. (2021). 'Everything Flows: Studying Continuous Sociotechnological Transformation in a Fluid and Dynamic Digital World', *MIS Quarterly* 45/1:423–452.

Nicolini, D., Mengis, J., & Swan, J. (2012). Understanding the role of objects in cross-disciplinary collaboration. *Organization science*, 23/3, 612–629.

Oborn, E., Pilosof, N. P., Hinings, B., and Zimlichman, E. (2021). 'Institutional Logics and Innovation in Times of Crisis: Telemedicine as Digital "PPE"', *Information and Organization* 31/1: 100340.

Orlikowski, W. J., and Robey, D. (1991). 'Information Technology and the Structuring of Organizations', *Information Systems Research* 2/2: 143–169.

Orlikowski, W. J., and Scott, S. V. (2008). Sociomateriality: Challenging the Separation of Technology, Work and Organization. *Academy of Management Annals* 2/1: 433–474.

Orlikowski, W. J., and Scott, S. V. (2016). Digital Work: A Research Agenda. In B. Czarniawska (ed.). *A Research Agenda for Management and Organization Studies.* Cheltenham, UK: Edward Elgar, 88–95.

Orlikowski, W. J., and Scott, S. V. (2021). 'Liminal Innovation in Practice: Understanding the Reconfiguration of Digital Work in Crisis', *Information and Organization* 31/1: 100336.

Pachidi, S., Berends, H., Faraj, S., and Huysman, M. (2021). 'Make Way for the Algorithms: Symbolic Actions and Change in a Regime of Knowing', *Organization Science* 32/1: 18–41.

Pentland, B. T., Vaast, E., and Wolf, J. R. (2021). 'Theorizing Process Dynamics with Directed Graphs: A Diachronic Analysis of Digital Trace Data', *MIS Quarterly* 45/2: 939–956.

Pickering, A. (1993). 'The Mangle of Practice: Agency and Emergence in the Sociology of Science'. *American Journal of Sociology* 99/3: 559–589.

Putnam, L. L., Fairhurst, G. T., and Banghart, S. (2016). 'Contradictions, Dialectics, and Paradoxes in Organizations: A Constitutive Approach', *Academy of Management Annals* 10/1: 65–171.

Raisch, S., and Krakowski, S. (2021). 'Artificial Intelligence and Management: The Automation–Augmentation Paradox', *Academy of Management Review* 46/1: 192–210.

Reinecke, J., Suddaby, R., Tsoukas, H., and Langley, A. (eds.). (2021). *Time, temporality, and history in process organization studies.* Oxford: Oxford University Press.

Richardson, L. (2021). 'Coordinating Office Space: Digital Technologies and the Platformization of Work', *Environment and Planning D: Society and Space* 39/2: 347–365.

Sahay, S., Mukherjee, A., Walsham, G., and Erickson, T. (2022). *Digital Development Stories of Hope from Health and Social Development.* Practical Action Publishing.

Schultze, U., and Mason, R. O. (2012). 'Studying Cyborgs: Re-Examining Internet Studies as Human Subjects Research', *Journal of Information Technology* 27/4: 301–312.

Schwab, K. (2017). The fourth industrial revolution. Currency.

Shaikh, M., and Vaast, E. (2023). 'Algorithmic Interactions in Open Source Work', *Information Systems Research* 34/2: 744–765.

Simpson, B., Tracey, R., and Weston, A. (2020). 'The Timefulness of Creativity in World. *Time, Temporality and History in Process Organization Studies* 69.

Stigliani, I., and Ravasi, D. (2012). 'Organizing Thoughts and Connecting Brains: Material Practices and the Transition from Individual to Group-Level Prospective Sensemaking. *Academy of Management Journal* 55/5: 1232–1259.

Swan, J., M. Bresnen, S. Newell, M. Robertson. (2007). 'The Object of Knowledge: The Role of Objects in Biomedical Innovation', *Human Relations* 60/12: 1809–1837.

Thompson, J. D. (1967). *Organizations in Action*. New York: McGrath - Hill.

Vaast, E., and Pinsonneault, A. (2021). 'When Digital Technologies Enable and Threaten Occupational Identity: The Delicate Balancing Act of Data Scientists', *MIS Quarterly* 45/3: 1087–1112.

Vaast, E., and Walsham, G. (2009). 'Trans-Situated Learning: Supporting a Network of Practice with an Information Infrastructure', *Information Systems Research* 20/4: 547–564.

Vaast, E., and Walsham, G. (2013). 'Grounded Theorizing for Electronically-Mediated Social Contexts', *European Journal of Information Systems* 22/1: 9–25.

Van Der Aalst, W., Adriansyah, A., De Medeiros, A. K. A., Arcieri, F., Baier, T., Blickle, T., Bose, J. C., Van Den Brand, P., Brandtjen, R., and Buijs, J. (2011). 'Process Mining Manifesto', in *International Conference on Business Process Management*. Springer, 169–194.

Vayre, E. (2022). *Digitalization of Work: New Spaces and New Working Times*. Wiley.

Walsham, G. (1995). 'Interpretive Case Studies in IS Research: Nature and Method', *European Journal of Information Systems* 4/2: 74–81.

Walsham, G., and Sahay, S. (1999). 'GIS for District-Level Administration in India: Problems and Opportunities'. *MIS Quarterly* 39–65.

Walsham, G. (2006). 'Doing Interpretive Research'. *European Journal of Information Systems* 15/3: 320–330.

Walsham, G. (2012). 'Are We Making a Better World with ICTs? Reflections on a Future Agenda for the IS Field', *Journal of Information Technology* 27/2: 87–93.

Wang, B., Schlagwein, D., Cecez-Kecmanovic, D., and Cahalane, M. C. (2020). 'Beyond the Factory Paradigm: Digital Nomadism and the Digital Future (S) of Knowledge Work Post-Covid-19', *Journal of the Association for Information Systems* 21/6:10.

Wessel, L., Baiyere, A., Ologeanu-Taddei, R., Cha, J., and Blegind-Jensen, T. (2021). 'Unpacking the Difference between Digital Transformation and IT-enabled Organizational Transformation', *Journal of the Association for Information Systems* 22/1: 102–129.

Whelan, E., Teigland, R., Vaast, E., and Butler, B. (2016). 'Expanding the Horizons of Digital Social Networks: Mixing Big Trace Datasets with Qualitative Approaches', *Information and Organization* 26/1–2: 1–12.

Winner, L. (1986). 'Myth Information: Romantic Politics in the Computer Revolution,' in *Philosophy and Technology* Ii. Springer, 269–289.

Winner, L. (1993). 'Upon Opening the Black Box and Finding It Empty: Social Constructivism and the Philosophy of Technology', *Science, Technology, & Human Values* 18/3: 362–378.

Winner, L. (2006). *The Whale and the Reactor: A Search for Limits in an Age of High Technology*. University of Chicago Press.

Woodward, J. (1958). *Management & Technology*. London: H.M.S.O.

Yoo, Y., Boland Jr, R. J., Lyytinen, K., & Majchrzak, A. (2012). 'Organizing for Innovation in the Digitized World', *Organization Science* 23/5: 1398–1408.

Zammuto, R. F., Griffith, T. L., Majchrzak, A., Dougherty, D. J., and Faraj, S. (2007). 'Information Technology and the Changing Fabric of Organization', *Organization Science* 18/5: 749–762.

Zheng, Y., and Walsham, G. (2021). 'Inequality of What? An Intersectional Approach to Digital Inequality under Covid-19', *Information and Organization* 31/1: 100341.

Zuboff, S. (1988). *In the Age of the Smart Machine*. Basic Books.

Zuboff, S. (2019). *The Age of Surveillance Capitalism: The Fight for a Human Future at the New Frontier of Power*. Profile Books.

# 2

# Creation beyond Creativity

## From the Novelty of Ends to the Renewal of Life

*Tim Ingold*

For the past two millennia, debates around creation and creativity have turned around the question of whether it is possible to create something from nothing, or whether creativity necessarily involves the recombination of elements already to hand. These debates divided theologians and philosophers from classical through medieval times. Following the Renaissance, however, and in the subsequent rise of modern science, creation came to be strongly associated with the recombinant power of intelligent design. This chapter charts how, from the mid-twentieth century, this association went on to underpin the burgeoning field of creativity research in psychology, leading to an exclusive focus on the novelty of ideas and products that left no room for the creativeness of life itself, in its intrinsic potential for renewal. Drawing on the thinking of John Dewey, Henri Bergson, and Alfred North Whitehead, on questions of philosophy, religion, and art, the chapter elaborates on the distinction between novelty and newness, and makes a plea for the restoration of the idea of creation not as the proliferation of ends but as the promise of perpetual beginning.

***

*At some point in its two-thousand-year history, the promise of creation took a wrong turn.*

## 2.1 Theology

The word 'creation' comes from the Greek κτίσις and Latin *creatio*, referring fundamentally to the act of bringing forth or begetting—as parents, for example, beget their children. It was used in just this sense, and often, by the Roman author Titus Lucretius Carus, in his prose-poem *De Rerum*

Tim Ingold, *Creation beyond Creativity*. In: *Organizing in the Digital Age*. Edited by: Michael Barrett, Emmanuelle Vaast, Ann Langley, and Haridimos Tsoukas, Oxford University Press. 
DOI: 10.1093/oso/9780198899457.003.0002

*Natura*, dating from the first century BCE. Addressing Nature, pointedly in the feminine, as 'the creatress of things' (*rerum natura creatrix*), Lucretius implicitly compared her generative capacity to that of giving birth. However, when, five centuries later, St Jerome chose to import *creatio* into his translation of the Old Testament from Hebrew into Latin, in what became known as the Vulgate Bible, the term took on an entirely new significance. For the Testament's opening words, 'in the beginning, God created heaven and earth' (*in principio creavit Deus caelum et terram*), implied the creation of something out nothing. Following this precedent, the doctrine of *creatio ex nihilo* went on to become foundational to the Christian theology of the time. It was a doctrine, however, that flew in the face of the long-accepted philosophical principle, as Lucretius had put it, that 'nothing's made of nothing' (*ex nihilo nihil fit*). Already in the fifth century BC the Greek philosopher Empedocles—whose poem *On Nature* Lucretius would later adopt as the model for his own work—was insisting that everything there is arises from the 'mixture and exchange of what was mixed'. Though subsequently expressed in many different ways, not least by Aristotle—for whom all coming-into-being involves the unification of form and matter—the idea that in substance the world is eternal, admitting only to processes of composition and corruption, was widely accepted.[1]

For many centuries, scholars grappled with the problem of how to reconcile theological and philosophical principle, and all sorts of distinctions were drawn. For example, Peter Lombard, Bishop of Paris in the twelfth century, distinguished 'to make' (*facere*) from 'to create' (*creare*) on the grounds that whereas the former means to fashion something out of present material, the latter is to produce something from nothing. Mortal beings can make, but God alone can create. Not long after, Boethius of Dacia went on to suggest that there is one kind of truth pertaining to nature, wherein everything comes from the rearrangement of materials already to hand, and another kind of truth pertaining to faith, according to which the world was indeed created *ex nihilo*—only to be condemned by the official Church for trafficking in 'double truth'. It was left to Thomas Aquinas, in the thirteenth century, to resolve the problem by giving the doctrine of *creatio ex nihilo* a firm foundation in philosophy. His masterstroke was to acknowledge that what is created out of nothing is not a universe of things, of one sort and another, but existence itself. With existence comes everything else: forms, materials, even time. It is thus absurd, argued Aquinas, to suppose that the Creator temporally preceded his Creation, with His plan for the world preformed and ready to roll. Rather—and this is the critical point—the Creator and the work of Creation *are one and the same*. Or to put it another way, for Aquinas, God the Creator is immanent as the generative power of His creation and is revealed in every part of it—in ant, tree, and stone, mountain and cloud, and of course in human beings.

It makes no more sense, then, to put God on one side, and the world on the other, of a division between creator and created, than it does to attribute the world's coming into being to a capacity such as we might attribute to a subject. The world according to Aquinas came into existence in an act of creation, not as the result of any plan, or through the exercise of any faculty, that paved the way for it. For who would be so foolish as to say: 'God must have been very creative to come up with all that'? In the fourteenth century William of Ockham—Franciscan friar, theologian, and philosopher—warned explicitly against mistaking an abstract, conceptual generalization, drawn from our retrospective evaluation of acts of creation, for a pre-installed capacity deemed responsible for bringing them about in the first place. To put creatures down to the 'creativity' of their maker, Ockham argued, is no less absurd than putting laughter down to a faculty of 'risibility', with which the laugher is allegedly pre-endowed. Creation, like laughter, exists only in the act.[2] And if it has its reasons, they are reasons that think themselves out in the creative process itself, rather than preceding it. Creation is not so much the product of reason as reason at work.

However, the onset of the Renaissance, in the fifteenth century, heralded a shift in attitudes towards creation that would prove to be decisive. For while medieval commentators would often compare God to a painter, sculptor, or architect—yet one so masterly as to will his creatures into existence not just in part but in the entirety of their being—Renaissance artists would appeal to divine creation as the measure of their own virtuosity, expressed not just in the excellence of their workmanship but in the perfection of their design.[3] While claiming godlike powers for themselves, they would also see in their work the realization of a mental capacity to conceive of forms in advance of their realization in the material. With that, creation 'jumped the fence', as it were, from world to mind. It came to be identified with a faculty of intelligence. And the will of God, by the same token, was transformed into a capacity for intelligent design. He really had thought it all up in advance. The world itself, by contrast—the world He created—was left on the other side of the fence. Godless and mechanical, it revealed nothing of the will of the Creator, offering but silent testimony to His handiwork.[4] Yet by the same token, it presented a suitable field of inquiry for the natural sciences, whose flourishing marked the onset of what we now call modernity. For as Newton would go on to show, the universe—having once been created—can be left to run by itself, with the precision of clockwork.

It is no wonder, then, that the theologian William Paley, writing at the turn of the nineteenth century, would point to the intricacy of design of living creatures, by comparison to the far more rudimentary mechanism of a man-made watch, as proof of the existence of an intelligence of infinitely greater power than anything to which a mortal mind could aspire.[5] Nor does it come as any surprise that the science of evolution, after Darwin, would claim an equivalent power for natural selection. Indeed, only a fine line divides advocates of intelligent design, nowadays branded by their scientific opponents as 'creationists', from neo-Darwinian fundamentalists for whom natural selection offers a necessary and sufficient explanation for the phenomena of life. For both, the design—whether written by God or natural selection—precedes its material instantiation, and for both it is in the design, not in the instantiation, that the creativity is to be found. This, however, is to understand creativity as a faculty underwriting acts of creation in a sense dismissed by Ockham as absurd and which would have been unrecognizable to Aquinas and indeed to the theologians and philosophers of earlier centuries. Yet, following its migration from philosophy by way of theology, this was the sense in which the concept of creativity finally fetched up in what was then—in the early decades of the twentieth century—the relatively young discipline of psychology.

## 2.2 Psychology

Though the term cropped up from time to time in earlier writings, the minting of 'creativity' as a key concept in psychology owes much to the efforts of one individual, Joy Paul Guilford. A pioneer in the study and measurement of human intelligence, Guilford first introduced his idea of creativity in a chapter on 'Invention', included in his comprehensive survey of the field, *General Psychology*, published in 1939. He began the chapter with a parable of what the world would be like, were it not for the inventive capacity of human beings:

> There would disappear from the world all cities, towns, and country homes, and even the crudest dwellings of primitive man. All means of transportation, including the ships of the air and the seas, trains and motor cars, railroads and highways would vanish. All these things, and many more, are creations of the human brain. *They were present in thought before they appeared in tangible form.*
>
> (Guilford 1939: 461, my emphasis)

In short, without invention there would have been no history, no arts or culture, no civilization worthy of the name. Humankind would have remained at the level of the brutes, stuck where they have always been, doing what they have always done, confined to the slow lane of biological evolution. In Guilford's worldview, nature, left to her own devices, brings forth nothing without precedent, only more of the same. And God isn't even in the picture. Instead, all the creative work is left to humankind. More specifically, it is left to the human brain, the seat of intelligence, and is accomplished before a hand is even lifted in its physical execution. Moreover, in the absence of divine agency, there can be no creation *ex nihilo*. Echoing the philosophy of the ancients, if not their humility when it comes to human powers of creation, Guilford assumed that nothing could come from nothing, and therefore that new ideas or patterns of thought could only come from breaking down old ones and remixing them in novel combinations.[6] There could be no composition without disintegration.

Following the intervention of the Second World War, Guilford returned to the theme of creativity in a presidential address delivered in 1950 to the American Psychological Association. In an absurdly sycophantic account of the occasion, psychologist Robert Keith Sawyer sets the scene:

> As the applause swelled, Dr. Guilford took a deep breath, smoothed his tie and jacket, and began to walk to the podium. It was Sept. 5, 1950, and Dr. Guilford was at the peak of his long and industrious career. He had dedicated his life to psychological research. He's played a key leadership role during World War II, helping the U.S. military carry out the most massive testing program in history. And now, he had attained the highest honor that the discipline of psychology can give—he had been elected president of the American Psychological Association. ... As Dr. Guilford began to talk, the hundreds of assembled psychologists in the room were shocked when they realised the topic he had chosen: the APA president had chosen to talk about creativity.
>
> **(Sawyer 2012: 15)**

So what did Guilford say? Not much. His concern was principally to bring to the fore what he saw as a neglected and unresearched topic of inquiry. Today, now that the concept of creativity has spilled over from psychology into a host of other disciplines from arts education to management and business studies, when the sheer number of research publications on the subject is so great that they can only be reviewed through a sampling procedure,[7] and when the c-word has been so thoroughly absorbed into the fast-talking, shallow-thinking patter of legions of advertisers, market consultants, and business analysts that it has ceased to raise any eyebrows, it is hard to believe that only seventy years ago, the topic was so novel as to surprise the audience at Guilford's presidential address. Any listeners hoping for a clear definition of creativity, however, would have been disappointed. Instead, they were treated to such circularities as the following: 'creativity refers to the abilities that are most characteristic of creative people'; 'creative behavior ... includes such activities as inventing, designing, contriving, composing, and planning'; 'people who exhibit these types of behavior to a marked degree are recognized as being creative'. The search is on, then, for some X-factor—or more likely, as Guilford admits, a combination of factors unique to each individual—capable of magnifying an intelligence common to all to this higher degree. Not many make it. Of all the people who have ever lived in historical times, Guilford estimates, only about two in a million have any claim to genius (Guilford 1950: 444).

Whatever Guilford may or may not have said, his presentation certainly had an impact, for in the following two decades, of the 1950s and '60s, creativity research took off to the point that it soon became an unstoppable bandwagon. Looking back on developments since then, Sawyer is confident that 'after decades of research, we're closer than ever to an explanation of creativity' (2012: 4). Complete explanation will come, however, only when creativity is finally reduced to what Sawyer thinks it is, namely a capacity for the recombination of ideas. For thought—in his view, as in that of most cognitive psychologists—cannot surpass itself. It can only endlessly reshuffle its elementary materials in a kaleidoscopic array of novel permutations and combinations. All thoughts and concepts, Sawyer tells us, are combinations of pre-existing ones. Hence creativity, as he defines it, 'involves a combination of two or more thoughts or concepts that have never been combined before' (2012: 7). It follows that to explain creativity, all you have to do is to show how the human mind is capable of this kind of cognitive dissection and reassembly. It is a matter of revealing the construction and operation of the kaleidoscope.

Yet if thought-combinations are deemed creative only when they are new, then how are we to tell them apart from combinations that merely repeat what has gone before? After all, what is new to me may be old hat to everyone else. Philosopher and cognitive scientist Margaret Boden deals with the problem by introducing a distinction between two kinds of creative ideas: psychological and historical, P-creative and H-creative. An idea is P-creative, she says, when it is novel with respect to the individual who had it. But if it is novel with respect to the *whole of human history*, then it is H-creative (Boden 1990: 32). Others have expressed the same contrast in terms of a distinction between 'little c' and 'big C' creativity: on the one hand those solutions to everyday problems that represent a 'first' for each of us, but which thousands if not millions of people have come up with before; on the other hand those flashes of eminent genius, unique to the history of the world, that 'drive civilisation forward' (Hennessey and Amabile 2010: 570, 572; Sawyer 2012: 8–9).[8] Every C- or H-creative event, to recite the mantra of lunar exploration, is 'one small step for man, one giant leap for mankind'. These events, as they happen, are the steps of history, forged by exceptional genius, while all the individual c- or P- creative events allow the rest of us to catch up by recapitulating the same steps for ourselves. Thus does genius, poised at the cutting edge of historical advance, pull the rest of humanity in its wake.

## 2.3 History

What, then, can history be? It can only be a record of world-leading innovations. Yet if this is what history is, then it can play no part in the formation of creative ideas themselves. For a cognitive scientist like Boden, or a psychologist of innovation like Sawyer, minds are completely outside of history, as are the fundamental materials of thought. New thought-combinations, we are led to believe, simply pop up, with apparent spontaneity, in the mind of the creative individual. Paradoxically, the ideas that Boden calls historical, or H-creative, are distinguished by the fact that they arise *de novo*, independently of any historical influence whatsoever. By the same token, history itself has nothing to do with the origination of ideas, only with their recognition and dissemination. It is history that determines whether an idea, having come to the mind of an individual, will be judged by society to be appropriate, useful or valuable, such that it enters into wider circulation. Ideas that fail to find any purchase in society merely fall by the wayside and are lost to history. But in coming up with creative ideas in the first place, every mind is on its own, cut off from the world of persons, things, and relations in which it necessarily subsists. As Boden states, quite categorically, 'the mind's creations must be produced with the mind's resources' (Boden 1990: 29). Only *after* they have been created do ideas enter history.

But if we are to regard history as a record of innovations, then how are we to tell whether something is new or not? Perhaps it might be possible to determine if an idea is new in the life of some particular individual: indeed creativity researchers, according to Sawyer, have devised all sorts of clever experiments to do exactly that (Sawyer 2012: 8). But determining whether the idea is new *in the history of the world* is another matter altogether. Suppose that an idea has occurred to me and I want to know whether it is truly historical, in Boden's terms. The only way to find out would be by doing a search to see whether anyone has had it previously. The probability is a million to one that someone has. So then: no history; just a bit more of the same, another turn of the wheel of perpetual reinvention. I thought for a moment that it might have been a historical idea, that it was genuinely without precedent, but no, it was merely psychological. But suppose that I found, in my researches, that actually no-one had had it before, then indeed, history was made with my idea—or at least potentially made, since the idea has no chance of actually *entering* into history unless it is communicated to others, and thereby added to the pool of ideas already in circulation.

Events, in this view—and it is one that is widely held, albeit more implicitly than explicitly—can only be historical if they are truly unprecedented. A thing is novel, it is historical, only when it makes its first appearance. With every subsequent iteration its quotient of creativity, so to speak, wears thinner until the normality of its repetition comes to mark nothing more than the passage of time. As the art historian George Kubler argued, in an essay on history and time penned over 50 years ago, time is beaten out in the repetition of events, against which history stands out as the incidence of the unique. Here's what he wrote:

> Our actual perception of time depends on regularly recurrent events, unlike the awareness of history, which depends on unforeseeable change and variety. Without change there is no history; without regularity there is no time. Time and history are related as rule and variation: time is the regular setting for the vagaries of history.
>
> **(Kubler 1962: 71–72)**

This is why art historians typically get so exercised over the question of whether a work is an original or a copy. Originals belong to history, but copies do not: they sink back into time. In this sense, Kubler suggests (1962: 39), historical events are analogous to prime numbers: they cannot be factored as multiples of what has already happened. Yet if the analogy holds, then more must be at stake in the creative process than the mere combination and recombination of pre-existing elements. It suggests, rather, a creation whose primacy lies precisely in a coming-into-existence that surpasses any compound of what had gone before. Something, it seems, is missing from the account of creativity as recombination: something wherein time, creativity, and history come together as one.

To get at what this is, we will need to retrace our steps from where it all began, with the idea of creation as a bringing forth, epitomized in the birth of a child to its parents. Can there be any more creative process than that by which a baby—as the Biblical psalm has it—is 'knit together' in its mother's womb? On greeting the baby when it first comes into the world, would we say: 'that is indeed novel, we have never seen the like before?', or, conversely, 'Oh, just another one: babies, they are all the same.' In truth the latter remark, which one might imagine coming from the lips of a fatigued and disgruntled midwife, was set down in writing as a statement of scientific fact by the evolutionary psychologists John Tooby and Leda Cosmides. 'Infants', they say, 'are everywhere the same', in that they all come into the world already equipped with a universal cognitive architecture primed for the acquisition of culture (Tooby and Cosmides 1992: 33). But supposing that unlike these scientists, we admit that this baby, at least, was creatively fashioned, rather than a mere replica run off from a universal human genotype in advance of its encounter with a cultural environment, would we then credit the happy parents with having brought about an unprecedented creative event at the moment when they conceived the child, whose blessed realization is now cradled before them? Does the creativity of conception lie wholly in accidents of genetic recombination?

For the child herself, after all, this is only a start. Her life begins in the womb, and proceeds, after birth, through infancy, childhood, youth, and maturity, and eventually into old age. Is this not a creative process in itself? There is surely more to it than the mere expression, over time, of a design laid down at the outset. For in both growing and being grown, human beings undergo histories of development and maturation within fields of relationships, established through the presence and activities of others. And critically, this growth is not just in strength and stature but also in knowledge, in the work of the imagination and the formation of ideas. For the latter is just as much a full-bodied knitting together of materials and experience as is the former. Ideas, after all, don't just pop up, ready-formed, from nowhere. They too have lives. Every idea is like a place you visit. You can return to it over and over again, but each time it is a little different, enriched by the memories of your previous stay, and by what has transpired since. Or to echo the aphorism of the philosopher Heraclitus, you cannot step twice into exactly the same idea, which is why the notion of checking through the record of the past to see whether anyone has had it before—and thereby to determine whether it is of truly historic significance, rather than a mere milestone in the life of the individual—is not just impracticable but ludicrous.

## 2.4 Philosophy

What is omitted from the equation of creativity with recombination, then, is growth, becoming, the actual forming or making of persons and ideas, or in a word, *ontogenesis*. Many years ago, in the course of writing a book on the meaning of evolution, I came across a succinct statement of this absent dimension in the work of the American theologian Henry Nelson Wieman. For me, it was a seminal discovery. There are two senses of creativity, Wieman argued, and it is important to distinguish them (Wieman 1961: 63–66). In one sense, he says, creativity is a characteristic doing of the human person. A human being is creative in this sense 'when he constructs something according to a new design that has already come within reach of his imagination' (1961: 65). This is a sense already familiar to us from our discussion of the power of intelligent design and is most commonly invoked whenever creativity is identified with innovation. It is found by looking back from a final product—what Wieman calls a 'created good'—to an unprecedented idea in the mind of an agent, in whose doing or making it was actualized. The origination of the idea is extraordinary, but the product follows from the idea, in its realization, with an ordinary, even mechanical inevitability.

But in the second sense, according to Wieman, creativity is *what a person undergoes but cannot do* (1961: 65–66). His argument is that behind the contingencies of what people do, and the miscellany of products or created goods to which these doings give rise, is the 'creative good' that is intrinsic to human life itself, in its capacity to generate persons in relationships. This is the kind of creativity that does not begin here, with an idea in mind, and end there, with a completed object. Rather, it *carries on through*, without beginning or end. It is, for Wieman, 'what progressively creates personality in community' (1961: 66). Consider again the example of the infant, progressing through childhood and adolescence within the nurturing environment of family and kin. To be sure, he or she may create many things in the course of growing up, and many more in later life: things imagined, and subsequently made or done. But there is surely more to the creativity of a life than the sum total of a lifetime's achievements. For every act carries its own burden of suffering: every doing is also an undergoing. And it is precisely in Wieman's second sense, in the undergoing rather than the doing, that the creativity of the life process itself is to be found. This is a sense, however, that has been largely eclipsed by contemporary discourses in psychology, and in the other human sciences that have drawn on it. The question is: what would it take to bring it back?

Three philosophers of the early twentieth century can help us in this enterprise: Henri Bergson, Alfred North Whitehead, and John Dewey, and it comes as no surprise to find that Wieman had been strongly influenced by all three. It was almost certainly from Dewey that Wieman took the key distinction between doing and undergoing, for Dewey himself had placed it at the centre of his reflections on *Art and Experience*, published in 1934. Every experience, Dewey had argued, entails its quotients of doing and of undergoing, and the key question for him was to figure out the relation between them (Dewey 1987: 50). They cannot simply alternate, he thought, for otherwise there could be no continuity from one doing to the next, and life would fragment into a scatter of disconnected episodes. What happens in reality, to the contrary, is that undergoing always overflows doing, to the extent that whatever you do next takes into itself something of the experience of what you did before.[9] Thus, while in our doings we fashion a world, in our undergoings we are the creatures of our own self-fashioning. Or as Bergson had written in his *Creative Evolution* of 1911: 'It is ... right to say that what we do depends on what we are; but it is necessary to add also that we are, to a certain extent, what we do, and that *we are creating ourselves continually*' (Bergson 1911: 7, my emphasis). This endless creation of ourselves—this becoming—corresponds precisely to Wieman's idea of a creativity undergone rather than done.

Now to understand creativity in this sense is to read it forwards, in the unfolding of the relations and processes that actually give rise to worldly beings, rather than back, in the retrospective attribution of final products to initial designs. It is to recognize, with Bergson, that ontogenesis not only takes time but is also irreversible. Its time is duration: not a succession of instants but the prolonging of the past into the actual. 'Duration', Bergson wrote, 'is the continuous progress of the past which gnaws into the future and which swells as it advances' (1911: 4–5). This, in his terms, distinguishes creation from mere fabrication. For fabrication, Bergson argued, 'even when it invents, it proceeds, or imagines itself to proceed, by a new arrangement of elements already known'. In the combination and recombination of preexisting materials, nothing comes into existence that was not there before: in the endless production of novelties, nothing ever truly begins. Creation, however, is the wellspring of existence itself, bringing forth new life and time. 'If everything is in time', Bergson continued, 'everything changes inwardly, and the same concrete reality never recurs' (1911: 48). There is no going back. What follows, then, cannot be factored into any multiple or combination of that which preceded it: before and after are truly incommensurable. It is as if in every breath, we open our eyes on the world for the first time.

Like Bergson, Whitehead was also keen to emphasize the difference in perspective that comes from relinquishing our view of the world from the outside, as a fait accompli, for a position from the inside of its coming-into-being. From the outside you see creatures, each the living embodiment of a design, and each set apart from all the others and the environment to which it is adapted. But from the inside the creature turns out to be none other than the process of its own self-creation, a process that, at each and every moment, enfolds an entire universe into a singular nexus. Already in his Lowell lectures of 1925, subsequently published as *Science and the Modern World*, Whitehead had been at pains to distinguish these outside and inside perspectives, reserving what he called 'creativeness' for the latter.[10] A year later he returned to the same theme in a series of lectures, *Religion in the Making*, in which he attempted to apply the same ideas to religion that he had previously applied to science. Again, he distinguishes the two sides, or perspectives, positing the creature on the one side as an 'emergent fact', and on the other 'as the cause of itself, its own creative act' (Whitehead 1926: 101–102).

Yet in truth, Whitehead concludes, there are not two things, the creativity and the creature: 'There is only one entity which is the self-creating creature' (Whitehead 1926: 102). This is a key move which, with one stroke, demolishes the wall between creator and created that, as we have already seen, had had the effect of reducing creativity to a faculty of intelligent design. Indeed, in his insistence that creator and creation are one and the same, Whitehead is of the same mind as Aquinas, and indeed as Okham. For Aquinas, as Maryniarczyk puts it, 'the Creator is existence' (2016: 257). For Ockham, too, 'neither God nor his creating represents anything caused by the intellect'; rather, creation signifies God himself, 'as divine essence, really creating' (Leff 1975: 463–464). What is coming into being with creation, then, is nothing less than existence, life itself, refracted in the prolific forms of its worldly creatures. To bear witness to this becoming is to join in a moment of creation that, apperceived from the inside, stretches to eternity. And for Whitehead, a man of deep religious conviction, this is what it meant to enter into the presence of God.

## 2.5 Art

Let me take a step back. It was in the Renaissance, as we have seen, that the idea took root of the artist, and also the architect, as a mortal second only to God in powers of intellect and skills of execution. Ever since, at least in the Western world, this idea has formed a central plank in art's rhetoric of self-promotion. An entire mythology has grown up around the figure of the artist as a creative genius. Even today, now that art has been incorporated within the ambit of so-called 'creative industries', artists are regarded as prime innovators, celebrated for their capacity to come up with designs that are unprecedented in their imaginative reach. A key motif in the myth of genius is that artists are ahead of their time. Always on the cusp, they are the premier exemplars of H- or C-creativity. Yet while artists themselves, in the interests of patronage and promotion, have often and willingly connived in the myth, they have also had to wrestle with an ever-present tension between the public persona they present to the world, and their actual experience of artistic creation. For whereas the art world, in thrall to the market in high-end, luxury commodities, is looking for completed works ripe for both monetary and aesthetic evaluation by dealers and critics alike, in the experience of the artist no work is ever finished. 'The work of art', wrote the painter Paul Klee in his notebooks, 'is first of all genesis; it is never experienced purely as a result' (Klee 1961: 78). For the artist the *work* goes on, even as life does; what the market eagerly gobbles up are but the cast-offs of the daily struggle to begin afresh. And it is in this struggle, in the undergoing, that true artistic creation lies.

Once again, we can turn to Bergson for inspiration. He invites us to picture an artist, whom he presumes to be male, positioned before a canvas, his colours already on the palette, the model seated before him. Do we not know already what will appear? Perhaps in an abstract way we do, as we can expect a portrait that will bear some resemblance to the model. For the artist the presence of the model is a problem, to which the portrait will eventually emerge as a solution. Yet this solution, writes Bergson, 'brings with it that unforeseeable nothing which is everything in a work of art' (1911: 360). And this nothing that is everything *takes time*. It has a duration that is unshrinkable.[11] It is this, he says, that makes the difference between the work of art and, say, a jigsaw puzzle. Let's suppose that the original portrait, having subsequently achieved iconic status, is reproduced as a puzzle, available for sale in the gallery. Having bought one for yourself, you set to work to assemble the pieces. With the completion of the portrait the problem is solved. Yet comparing your completion of the reproduction and the painter's completion of the original, the relation between problem and solution in the two scenarios could not be more different. For with the puzzle the solution is already at hand before the work begins. With practice, you can speed up the assembly; in principle it takes no time at all. Not so, however, for the painter of the original work. For him the creation would have evolved even as he worked on it. 'The time taken up by the invention', as Bergson puts it, 'is one with the invention itself' (2011: 359). Enfolded into it is the duration of the artist's very life and soul.

For the artist, in short, the solution overflows the problem. And it is precisely in the overflow that its creative quotient lies. Like a prime number, it is a quotient that is in no wise reducible to any function of its original conditions. The artist does not live to execute thoughts that think themselves in him, as rearrangements of the fragments of earlier ones. For the thinking of artistic invention always surpasses thought, precisely as undergoing—as we have already seen—surpasses doing. Thinking as undergoing, as Dewey realized, surrenders to existence, yet this is not a passive surrendering but an active 'taking in', akin to inhalation, which readies the thinker for further release into activity, just as breathing in prepares a body for breathing out (Dewey 1987: 59). Every breath is new, of course, *but it is not a novelty.* Though it might sound like splitting hairs, there is an important distinction to be made here between newness and novelty, just as there is between creation and creativity. There is a newness to artistic invention that goes beyond the recombination of thought, in its ever-shifting patterns. For whereas the latter delivers only endings, the former ushers in perpetual beginning. Newness, again to borrow Bergson's words, is a 'ceaseless upspringing' (2011: 49). To apprehend newness is to inhabit the cusp, the moment of incipience in which the world is on the point of revelation. In novelty, however, that moment is already past, congealed into objects that present themselves to our attention, retrospectively, as candidates for appropriation.

The composer Manuel de Falla once observed that to write a piece of music is to give birth to a new life. In the throes of creation, the composer allows himself to be taken over by the work, to have it inhabit his very being as it swells within him. Eventually, after a period of gestation, the composition bodies forth, and goes on to live a life of its own in the world. It is not as though the work was finished, at the moment when the composer laid down his pen. Its life, unless cut short by the calamity of stillbirth, is only just beginning. It is a life lived in its performances. In this sense the musical work is crescent, not created, continually coming into being for as long as it lives. It is a thing that carries on, or *perdures* (Ingold 2014: 129). While you can return to the same piece over and over again, just as you can to an idea, it is different with every performance. You can never step twice into the same work, any more than you can into the same idea. What is true of music, moreover, applies equally to visual art, even if shown rather than performed. For showing, too, is a modality of presence, and the present never repeats. Even the work of art, then, is not fixed, despite the interventions of conservationists, armed with sophisticated technology, to preserve for eternity an imagined state of completion. The work of art, like music, is always crescent. And to compose or respond to any work of art, visual or musical, means participating in the creative process that Bergson called *invention*: 'the continual elaboration of the absolutely new' (1911: 11).

This is to understand invention, however, in a sense that could not be more different from that invoked by the psychologist Guilford, for whom—as you will recall—it denotes a capacity of the human brain to preconfigure, in thought, 'what never existed before'. By and large, the scientific study of creativity, following Guilford's lead, remains locked into a consumerist logic, driven by the imperatives of problem-solving, product innovation, and marketing, which offers only a superabundance of ends (Hennessey and Amabile 2010: 572). With this logic every new thing, every novelty, is over even before it is begun. The creative idea is already configured in thought in advance of the product, the solution in advance of the problem to which it is to be applied. To follow Bergson's lead means turning this around, putting things before ends rather than ends before things. It means setting newness before novelty, creation before creativity. We can no longer be content, then, to regard invention as a power of mental representation, or intelligent design. Invention does not set things up, in thought, in advance of their realization in the world. It does not even belong to individual human beings, let alone to their brains. It belongs to the world, to existence, perchance to God. To invent, after Bergson, is not to create a world but actively to participate from the inside in the world's ceaseless creation of itself—and, since we belong to the world, of ourselves as well. It is once again to reunite creator and created in one act. And at a time of present crisis, with the world on a knife-edge, this step has never been more needed. For only by restoring faith and hope in the perpetuity of beginning—or, in a word, in *creation*—can we open a real future to coming generations.

***

*Perhaps then, after its two-thousand-year odyssey, the promise of creation can at last come home.*

## Notes

1. For this and the following paragraph, I have drawn extensively on the authoritative review of philosophical creationism by Andrzej Maryniarczyk (2016). The citation from Empedocles is on page 224 of this review. My source for Lucretius' *De Rerum Natura* is http://www.perseus.tufts.edu/hopper/text?doc=Perseus%3Atext%3A1999.02.0131 (accessed 29/01/2020).

2. Okham's parallel between creativity and risibility, and the fallacy of confusing a post-hoc abstraction for a real, generative capacity, are discussed in the magisterial work of medievalist Gordon Leff (1975: 148–149). Ockham himself addresses the senses of creation, and what it means for a thing simultaneously to be created by God and by a natural agent, in his *Second Quodlibet*, Question 8 (Ockham 1991: 123–126).
3. As art historian Irving Lavin writes, 'Whereas before the artist was used to illustrate God's creativity, now in the flood of sixteenth-century treatises on art, the artist's creativity was likened unto God's' (Lavin 1977–1978: 38).
4. In the words of historian of religion Peter Harrison, 'Nature is no longer an autobiographical text, in which direct references to the author may be found. It is more like a mathematical treatise, which has no meaning as such, and does not speak directly of its author, but from which we can make inferences about certain of the qualities of the person who produced it' (1998: 203). See also Bono (1995: 193).
5. William Paley's *Natural Theology* was first published in 1802 (Paley 2006).
6. 'The creative person must break down old ways of thinking in order to construct the new' (Guilford 1939: 474).
7. In a recent survey of the field, Beth Hennessey and Teresa Amabile (2010) asked 26 colleagues each to nominate 10 'must have' papers published since 2000. They ended up with a list of 110 publications, to which they added another 400 citations of significant work, drawn from an electronic survey of titles published between 1998 and 2008.
8. Ronald Beghetto and James Kaufman (2007) take this one stage further, arguing that besides big-C ('eminent') and little c ('everyday') creativity, there is also a 'mini-c' creativity involved in the construction of personal knowledge and understanding.
9. 'There is ... an element of undergoing, of suffering in its large sense, in every experience' (Dewey 1987: 50).
10. 'There are two sides to the machinery involved in the development of nature. On one side there is a given environment with organisms adapting themselves to it... The other side of the evolutionary machinery, the neglected side, is expressed by the word *creativeness*' (Whitehead 1929: 140, original emphasis).
11. For a wonderful account of what actually goes on in the artist's painting of a portrait, with all its hazards, frustrations and setbacks, see Lord (1965).

## References


Beghetto, R. A. and Kaufman, J. C. (2007). 'Toward a Broader Conception of Creativity: A Case for "mini-c" Creativity', *Psychology of Aesthetics, Creativity, and the Arts* 1/2: 73–79.

Bergson, H. (1911). *Creative Evolution*, trans. A. Mitchell. London: Macmillan.

Boden, M. (1990). *The Creative Mind: Myths and Mechanisms*. London: Weidenfeld and Nicolson.

Bono, J.J. (1995). *The Word of God and the Languages of Man: Interpreting Nature in Early Modern Science and Medicine.* Madison, WI: University of Wisconsin Press.

Dewey, J. (1987). 'Art as Experience', in J. A. Boydston (ed.), *John Dewey: The Later Works, 1925–1953, Vol. 10: 1934*. Carbondale: Southern Illinois University Press, 42–110.

Guilford, J. P. (1939). *General Psychology*. Princeton, NJ: D. Van Nostrand.

Guilford, J. P. (1950). 'Creativity', *American Psychologist* 5: 444–454.

Harrison, P. (1998). *The Bible, Protestantism and the Rise of Natural Science*. Cambridge: Cambridge University Press.

Hennessey, B. A. and T. M. Amabile (2010). 'Creativity', *Annual Review of Psychology* 61: 569–598.

Ingold, T. (2014). 'The Creativity of Undergoing', *Pragmatics and Cognition* 22/1: 124–139.

Klee, P. (1961). *Notebooks, Volume 1: The Thinking Eye*, ed. J. Spiller, trans. R. Manheim. London: Lund Humphries.

Kubler, G. (1962). *The Shape of Time: Remarks on the History of Things*. New Haven, NJ: Yale University Press.

Lavin, I. (1977-8). 'The Sculptor's "Last Will and Testament"', *Allen Memorial Art Museum Bulletin, Oberlin College* 35: 4–39.

Leff, G. (1975). *William of Ockham: The Metamorphosis of Scholastic Discourse*. Manchester: Manchester University Press.

Lord, J. (1965). *A Giacometti Portrait*. New York: Farrar, Straus and Giroux.

Maryniarczyk, A. (2016). 'Philosophical Creationism: Thomas Aquinas' Metaphysics of *Creatio ex Nihilo*', *Studia Gilsoniana* 5/1: 217–268.

Ockham, W. (1991). *William of Ockham, Quodlibidal Questions: Volume 1, Quodlibets 1-4*, trans. A. J. Freddoso and F. E. Kelley. New Haven, NJ: Yale University Press.

Paley, W. (2006). *Natural Theology; or Evidences of the Existence and Attributes of the Deity, Collected from the Appearances of Nature*. Oxford: Oxford University Press.

Sawyer, R. K. (2012). *Explaining Creativity: The Science of Human Innovation*. Oxford: Oxford University Press.

Tooby, J. and Cosmides, L. (1992). 'The Psychological Foundations of Culture', in J. H. Barkow, L. Cosmides, and J. Tooby (eds), *The Adapted Mind: Evolutionary Psychology and the Generation of Culture*. Oxford: Oxford University Press, 19–136.

Whitehead, A. N. (1926). *Religion in the Making: Lowell Lectures 1926*. Cambridge: Cambridge University Press.

Whitehead, A. N. (1929). *Science and the Modern World: Lowell Lectures 1925*. Cambridge: Cambridge University Press.

Wieman, H. N. (1961). *Intellectual Foundations of Faith*. London: Vision Press.

# 3

# On Thinking Movement

## Theorizing Flows of Organizing in a Digital Age

*Lotta Hultin, Lucas D. Introna, and Magnus Mähring*

### 3.1 The Challenges of Thinking Movement

Most people and organizations recognize constant change as a fundamental condition under which they live and work, a condition constantly challenging our sense of where we are, where we are going, who we are, and who we want to be. We may experience uncertainty, humility, and even resignation as we try to make decisions in a world in which the boundaries that separate, categorize, and identify what we do and who we are seem to blur and even dissolve. As digital technologies increasingly permeate our private and organizational lives, and as digital innovations are transforming almost every aspect of our contemporary societies, the experiences of living and working in a fluid, mobile, interconnected, complex, and boundless world intensify (Kallinikos et al. 2013; Scott and Orlikowski 2014; Nambisan et al. 2017; Mousavi Baygi et al. 2021). How can we as researchers account for this fluid, ever-transforming world and for the dynamics, experiences, and consequences of this transformative flow?

We find many different answers to these questions in the history of organizational research. One dominant approach is to view social and technological change as transitions from one state of stability to a new state of stability, as suggested by the Lewin (1947) change model of unfreeze, change, and refreeze. The ontological assumption behind this tradition is that stability is the primary ontological state of entities (e.g. organizations, individuals, technologies). That is, they are more or less bounded entities defined by stability, routine, and order that change in response to changes in their social and material environments or as a result of the implementation of new organizational strategies, innovations, or technologies. Another way to put this is to say that this stream of work operates with a 'being' ontology in which the

Lotta Hultin, Lucas D. Introna, and Magnus Mähring, *On Thinking Movement.* In: *Organizing in the Digital Age.* Edited by: Michael Barrett, Emmanuelle Vaast, Ann Langley, and Haridimos Tsoukas, Oxford University Press. © Oxford University Press (2024). DOI: 10.1093/oso/9780198899457.003.0003 world is constituted by, or comprised of, more or less stable ontologically distinct entities (social and technical) that interact or connect to produce organizational change.

This view of organizations as bounded, rational, and stable entities has increasingly been challenged by researchers who have produced accounts that emphasize multiplicity, fluidity, diversity, and mobility (Feldman 2000; Orlikowski 2000; Tsoukas and Chia 2002; Hernes and Maitlis 2010; Langley et al. 2013; MacKay and Chia 2013). In these accounts, change processes are not understood as separate from the everyday practices of organizing. They cannot be summarized in a stage model or fully controlled and managed by individuals. Rather, social and technological change constitutes the ontological state of the world, an ongoing transformation contingent upon the temporal and performative flow of practices. For researchers who assume this ontology, the primary task is not to understand why the stability of organizations is challenged or how organizations enter into and emerge out of processes of change. Rather, their task is to understand the specificities in how organizations continuously transform, the contingencies that condition these transformations, the repetitions and patterns that might emerge over time within these transformations, and the consequences of these repetitive movements.

In conducting this task, many scholars, including the authors of this chapter, have found themselves struggling. It has proven to be difficult to develop accounts that stay true to the underlying assumptions of a transformational becoming ontology. Researchers have observed that 'we are not good at thinking movement' (Chia 1999: 109); contrary to intentions to account for continuous transformation and flow, scholarly accounts often end up centred on seemingly distinct and bounded actors and things (Wagner, Newell, and Piccoli 2010; Cecez-Kecmanovic 2016; Hultin 2019; Hultin et al. 2021; Mousavi Baygi et al. 2021). These actors and things can and do, of course, move and change over time, but changes tend to become enacted in empirical terms rather than ontological terms. 'Things change', or, 'things move', rather than, 'things are change', or, 'things are movement'. Moreover, it has been argued that our tendency to centre more or less distinct actors and things and study how these change in relation to one another has made us overlook or resign to the background temporal relationality, that is, how actors and things transform in specific ways because of the ways they are relationally positioned in the temporal flow of practice (Langley et al. 2013; Sandberg and Tsoukas 2015; Hultin et al. 2021; Mousavi Baygi et al. 2021). How can we understand that despite a long tradition of process-oriented research in OS and IS research, and despite the many theoretical articles outlining the specificities of its underlying assumptions (Pettigrew et al. 2001;

Chia 2002; Tsoukas and Chia 2002; Feldman and Orlikowski 2011; Nayak and Chia 2011; Langley et al. 2013), process scholars still struggle to 'think movement' (Chia 1999, 2002; Nayak and Chia 2011). That is, how can we produce accounts that disclose transformation as ontological and foreground the conditioning qualities of the temporal flow of everyday life and work?

In this chapter, we take the position that we as scholars tend to be trapped within a vocabulary developed and/or appropriated within a being ontology and that this vocabulary tends to performatively enact the world as consisting of boundaries, entities, actors, and categories (Latour 1999a; Hultin et al. 2021; Mousavi Baygi et al. 2021). Thus, to stay true to the assumptions of a 'becoming' ontology, to deepen our understanding of the ongoing fluid, mobile, and boundless transformations of the world, and to be able to take responsibility for these transformations, we need to develop conceptual vocabularies truly rooted in an ontology of becoming. To do so, we believe that there is a need to experiment with novel concepts focusing on movement and experience their performative effects in our research.

We provide two illustrations of such experimentation based on two studies conducted at the Swedish Migration Board (Hultin and Introna 2019; Hultin et al. 2021). Each illustration explores different empirical phenomena and engages with different theoretical literatures, specifically the literature on translation of management ideas (Morris and Lancaster 2006; Bergström and Diedrich 2011; Bruce and Nyland 2011; Mueller and Whittle 2011; Spyridonidis et al. 2016) and the literature on subject positioning (Bisel and Barge 2011; Bardon et al. 2012; Rennstam 2012; Symon and Pritchard 2015; Harding et al. 2017; Paring et al. 2017). What these illustrations have in common is the ambition to move beyond actor-centric accounts and foreground the conditioning role of the temporal flow of practices. To do so, they draw on different conceptual vocabularies rooted in a becoming ontology and show how these concepts help us foreground the temporal conditioning of the continuous becoming of the world. We conclude the chapter with a discussion of how organizational scholars could benefit from continuing to experiment with temporally oriented vocabularies in their research.

## 3.2 Problems with an Actor-Centric Vocabulary

Before we present the concepts that we will work through in our illustrations, we have a few more words about what we mean by an 'actor-centric vocabulary' and about how a habitual adoption of it can be problematic for scholars researching social and technological transformation. Let's take actor-network theory (ANT) as an example. Despite one of its originator's insistence that ANT is *not* about actors and interrelated networks (Latour 1999, 2004), it includes a vocabulary and methodological prescriptions that tend to produce accounts that centre distinct human and non-human actors and their agency in assembling networks in pursuit of heterogeneous translations. For example, by using words such as 'actor', 'network', 'connection', and 'association', researchers tend to enact action as the co-constitutive movement of agency *between* actors, assumed to be more or less separate and distinct (Barad 2007; Introna 2013). Hence, Latour's (1999a) desire to 'recall' ANT and the argument that the slippage into a 'demiurgic version' of ANT (Latour 1996, 1999a, 2004)—in which actors seem to exist separately from each other and the relational whole that already enact them—can partly be explained by the vocabulary of ANT, which gives the notions of 'actor' and 'network' unintended significance (Latour 1999a).

The problem of an actor-centric vocabulary has also been acknowledged in the related stream of work on sociomateriality (Kautz and Jensen 2013; Cecez-Kecmanovic et al. 2014; Jones 2014; Mazmanian et al. 2014; Cecez-Kecmanovic 2016). For example, it has been argued that the notion of entanglement implies the idea that things are in some way in need of being 'entangled', which implies their prior ontological separation. A similar remark has been made about the notion of material-discursive practices where the juxtaposition of the adjectives 'material' and 'discursive' invites the idea that there might be 'material practices' on one side and 'discursive ones' on the other and that they sometimes come together (Mazmanian et al. 2014; Cecez-Kecmanovic 2016). As is the case with Latour, we are fully aware that this is not what Barad (or those that draw on her work) means by 'entanglement' and 'material-discursive practices'. Nevertheless, this seems to be where the enactment of the vocabulary takes those who deploy it, perhaps inadvertently. So, we ask, what are some of the performative consequences of the adoption of an actor-centric vocabulary, and how can its consequential ontological slippage be problematic for scholars researching social and technological transformation? Let us consider some of these interconnected entailments of an actor-centric vocabulary.

*Centring of human agency and backgrounding of materiality:* Although a broad range of studies in different research areas does not assume human subjects to be defined within strict boundaries, through an actor-centric vocabulary, they tend to enact these subjects in a way that transcends the very situated discursive practices in which they are entangled (Latour 2003; Barad 2007). This means that although studies acknowledge that human subjects are embedded in a material environment and use material artifacts as props or tools in their work (e.g. Korica and Molloy 2010; Nicolini et al. 2012; Stigliani and Ravasi 2012), they typically remain at the centre of this work as constructors of practices and authors of discourse. Thus, to the extent it is recognized that social discourse is embedded in material relationships, 'non-humans' are attended to mainly in terms of their structuring, conditioning, or intermediating role (e.g. Swan et al. 2007; Nicolini et al. 2012; Jones and Massa 2013; Farquharson et al. 2014; Monteiro and Nicolini 2015). In these accounts, the materiality of objects clearly matters, yet mostly as external props, tools, and regulators of assumed self-formation practices; they are thus enacted as some sort of bridging mechanism between the 'inside' and the 'outside'.

*Enacting ontological separation:* In taking account of more-than-human agency and emphasizing the interactive collaboration between the social and the material in the process of organizing, process-oriented studies have moved our understanding of different phenomena beyond our anthropocentric tendencies (Bisel and Barge 2011; Rennstam 2012; Symon and Pritchard 2015; Harding et al. 2017; Paring et al. 2017). However, this empirical inclusiveness of the more-than-human into our accounts enacts these diverse actors as being ontologically distinct and separate. This means that the relationality conditioning the enactment of heterogeneous actors can be seen as a weak form of relationality (Slife 2004) because the actors or entities involved only affect each other's nonessential properties; that is, they do not change what they actually are but 'act on' each other from the outside (Cecez-Kecmanovic et al. 2014). Although a weak form of relationality ascribes both people and materiality with agency in the process of organizing, it upholds a separation of human and material agency and tends to enact humans as actors, ultimately deciding how they will respond to materiality (Leonardi 2011).

*Backgrounding of ongoing action/movement:* Another important consequence of adopting and reproducing an actor-centric vocabulary is that in enacting the governing agency as located within—or in the interaction between—separate entities or actors (social or material), we forfeit the possibility to account for how these actors are always governed by being already positioned in certain ways within the performative flow of material-discursive practices. In other words, in centring our accounts on individual actors' sayings and doings, we fail to capture the flows of agency that provide them with their actions, intentionality, and subjectivity in the first instance. This is a form of reduction in which one assumes that action requires as its necessary condition (or cause) an already constituted (human or non-human) actor, who subsequently acts. This is problematic as it hides the process through which actors not only do changes in practices but also always and already *undergo change* (i.e. the ways in which they continuously become transformed as they are differently positioned and conditioned by the situated flows of mundane, everyday work practices; Latour 1996, 2004; Ingold 2008, 2011).

*Spatialization of time and backgrounding of temporal qualities:* As the use of an actor-centric vocabulary enacts relationality in spatial terms as interactions, connections, or integrations of actors and objects in different social and material contexts, it backgrounds temporal relationality, that is, how the qualities and contingencies of the temporal flows of practices condition possibilities for doing, thinking and becoming. Differently put, through an actor-centric vocabulary, time becomes a quantity that can be identified in space as points or events along a timeline, or a structural parameter. What is problematic with this enactment of time is that it constrains us from studying temporal qualities, such as timings, rhythms, and tempos and more generally the temporal conditionalities of the ongoing flow of practices (Mousavi Baygi, Introna, and Hultin 2021). As a consequence, we fail to include how our possibilities to transform ourselves, others, organizations, and societies are always and already conditioned by the qualities of these temporal flows.

In assuming that research practices and accounts do not simply represent reality but performatively enact it—in other words, in assuming that the production of knowledge is a creative process of co-construction (Law and Urry 2004; Introna 2013)—we argue that it is our responsibility as researchers to question dominant ontological and epistemological positions and to strive to increase the diversity of our approaches (Law 2004; Law and Urry 2004; Koro-Ljungberg and Mazzei 2012; Shotter 2014; Manning 2015). In the following, we present the underlying assumptions of a becoming ontology and the concepts grounded in this ontology that we work through in our illustrations.

## 3.3 Theorizing Temporal Flows of Organizing

If a being ontology assumes a view of actors as points or locations of original causes (which then need to be connected in some manner), an ontology of becoming implies an understanding of the world as fundamentally dynamic and emphasizes continuous movement, transformation, process, and the conceptualization of things, not as made but as 'continuously in the making' (Bergson 1999: 49). A key underlying assumption is that 'existence is action' (Latour 1999b: 179). That is, every action participates in the ontological (re)enactment of all actors implicated in, or associated with, such action. Thus, actors or points are not the origin of action; neither is it the case that they preexist and then interact, whether in terms of primary or secondary qualities (or properties; Latour 2013). Rather, the movement of a thing, idea, or practice always already emerges from some prior action or translation in the past, the origin of which cannot be located, so that contingency is a temporal phenomenon, not a spatial one. Thus, whatever 'things' may be under discussion are in the making rather than given a priori qualities, just as states are temporary outcomes rather than inputs to processes.

Within organization studies there is a long scholarly tradition advocating for the adoption of an ontology of becoming (Chia 1995, 1999; Tsoukas and Chia 2002; Clegg et al. 2005; Bakken and Hernes 2006; Cooper 2007; Hernes 2007). Studies in this tradition are often grounded in the work of Whitehead (1978), Foucault (1980), Deleuze and Guattari (1987), Butler (1993; 1997a, b), or Bergson et al., (2002). In the field of science and technology studies (STS), Latour (1988, 2005), Pickering (1995), Law (1999), Mol (2003), Barad (2007), and others have argued for an ontology of becoming. Also, social anthropology, in particular the work of Ingold (2007b, 2011), is significant for its articulation of what Ingold (2011) calls the animic ontology of life. Ingold (2007a, 2015) describes the flow of agency as 'agentic lines' and argues that to study 'things and people is to study the lines they are made of' (2007a: 5). Lines are thus not defined by the points or entities that they connect or by the points that may compose them. Rather, they are trails along which life is lived (2006: 13), knotted together to form a 'meshwork' (2007a, 2011, 2015). In the meshwork, lines as they flow disclose relations, not between one thing and another, such as between the organism 'here' and the environment 'there', but rather only in correspondence with other lines. Following the lines in the meshwork entails following, temporally, the transformative flow of agency rather than assumed 'actors'.

In the two illustrations provided below, we draw on specific concepts from Ingold, as well as concepts adopted by Barad (2007), and two of her major sources of inspiration, Foucault (1980, 1991) and Butler (1993, 1997a, b). While Foucault and Butler share a view of agency as a continuous flow through practices in which the 'who', the assumed subject or being, is constituted by the 'how' (the temporal flow of practice), Barad (2007) attempts to more carefully consider the intimate entanglement of non-human and human elements in this flow. In her post-humanist accounts she 'calls into question the givenness of the differential categories of "human" and "non-human", examining the practices through which these differential boundaries are stabilized and destabilized' (Barad 2003: 808). This means that in a post-humanist account, we do not primarily attend to what actors do, think, or say but to what provides them with their actions and intentionality (i.e. what are already assumed as appropriate and legitimate ways of acting by the circulating flow of agency through material-discursive practices).

*Temporal flow of agency:* Attending to the temporal flow of agency implies a view of agency as something that is not inherent and belonging to any one actor or functioning in the form of a serial chain of consequences set in motion by an initial force. Rather, in this view, agency is an ongoing temporal flow, always inheriting from previous practices (and imparting to subsequent practices) yet also always subject to the contingent possibilities of the present (Deleuze and Guattari 1987). In short, the temporal flow is the very condition of agency. But it is not, in itself, an agent (Ingold 2011).

*Temporal conditioning of possibilities:* In the temporal flow of agency, we cannot distinguish any actors or entities that move. Rather, in following the lines of flow, of action, we follow the transformative flow of agentic possibilities. This means that we follow how the flow inherits conditions of possibility from prior actions and imparts conditions of possibility to subsequent actions, with every translation engendering new possibilities for being and action (Deleuze and Guattari 1987).

*Agentic lines:* Ingold's (2007a, 2015) way to talk about actors, subjects, and things in a world where agency flows temporally is to talk about 'the lines they are made of' (2007a: 5). This implies a view of actors not as bounded entities surrounded by an environment but as 'an unbounded entanglement of lines in fluid space' (Ingold 2011: 64). The transforming becoming of agentic lines is not defined by the points that might compose them, or the points that they associate with. In contrast to the lines of an ANT network, they do not connect, assemble, or associate entities. Rather, they are trails along which life is lived in ongoing co-responding transformation (Ingold 2007a, 2015).

*Correspondence:* According to Ingold, lines transform by corresponding with other lines as they flow. Such a correspondence does not disclose relationality, between the actor 'here' and the context 'there', but rather a temporal co-responding or co-occurrences with other lines, as they continue to flow. Correspondence denotes a relationality along a 'path through the terrain of lived experience', where a line joins the confluence of other lines of flow, creating together the conditions of possibility for ongoing transformative becoming (Ingold 2011: 161).

*Attentionality and undergoing:* Ingold argues that our practices are both directed (intentional) and being-directed (attentional), something we do and something that is actively happening to us (Ingold 2017). In this view, the 'I' who acts is not put in front (of the verb, as conventions of grammar require), but rather in the midst of the experience undergone. As we go about our daily work practices, we also become transformed by undergoing our work as we attentionally co-respond to the flow of everyday practices. Attention here is not consciously directed by a subject but rather emergent in the corresponding event, 'activated by the force of the directionality the event calls forth' (Manning 2016: 154).

*Genealogy:* In studying lines, we do not primarily attend to what actors do, think, or say, but rather to what provides them with their actions and intentionality, namely ways of becoming already assumed as appropriate and legitimate ways of acting by the circulating flow of agency through material-discursive practices. To do so we adopt a genealogical approach. This means that we start in the present with what is already taken for granted as bounded actors with intentions, attributes, and the like and trace the multiplicity of lines of flows through a number of constitutive and contingent correspondences (or moments) of their coming into being.

*Material-discursive practices:* Rooted in the work of Barad (2007), this concept denotes an agential realist view of discourse and materiality as ontologically (and not only empirically) inseparable (Orlikowski and Scott 2014; Orlikowski and Scott 2015). In this view, there are no a priori distinctions made between the discursive and the non-discursive. They are not separate elements acting on each other through interactions. Rather, they are entangled, which means that they are continuously constituted through each other in the flow of practice.

*Subject/object positioning:* An ontology of becoming implies that human and material actors are not assumed to be the locus of agency, but are viewed as enactments within a circulating and performative flow (Introna 2015). This means that the flow is what animates or 'enables a subject and constitutes the temporal condition for the subject' (Butler 1993: 60) by transforming her positioning in the flow of practice. Thus, in this view, the subject emerges as a position that is both the effect of the a prior condition of possibility for agency and the conditioned form of agency—that is, as what is taken up and reiterated in the subject's 'own' acting (Butler 1997b).

*Interpellation and hailing:* Althusser (2006a) uses the term 'interpellation' to describe the hailing of a person into their social and ideological subject position; 'hailing' is the prospect that subjects can be subjected to an address by other subjects that constitutes the conditions of possibility for them to become subjects of a particular kind. In our work and our illustration below (Hultin and Introna 2019), we adopt an agential realist understanding of interpellation, in which it is not the actors, human or material, that hail, as such. Rather, hailing occurs as the flow of material-discursive practices constitute, collectively and continuously, conditions of possibility for certain subject (and object) positions to appear as obvious and legitimate ways to be and to act, implicitly governing (Dean 2009) the practices of self-formation of those implicated.

## 3.4 Towards Temporally Oriented Vocabularies: Two Illustrations

The two illustrations provided below are based on published studies, address different empirical phenomena, engage with different theories, and employ partly different vocabularies but with the common ambition to foreground temporal flow of practices and to adhere more closely to a temporally oriented ontology of becoming. We use the illustrations to show how temporally oriented concepts matter in creating accounts that foreground temporal rather than spatial relationality.

### 3.4.1 Illustration 1: Tracing the Translating Agency through Genealogies of Everyday Attentional Work

#### 3.4.1.1 Introduction to the Study

The first illustration is based on an ethnographic study (Hultin et al. 2021)[1] conducted at the Swedish Migration Board (SMB), the central authority for implementation of migration policy in Sweden, managing applications and making asylum decisions, defending decisions in appeals court, and managing integration and settlement for those granted asylum. Starting in 2009, Lean Management principles were implemented at all examination units countrywide. By prioritizing flow efficiency, the underlying aims and ideas included shortening the processing time for asylum cases by identifying value-creating practices, eliminating those steps that do not create value, and pursuing continuous improvement of the process (cf. Liker, 2004; Womack and Jones 1994). We followed this implementation over a period of two years, with a particular focus on how 'Lean' became translated in mundane, everyday work practices of case officers. Adopting a genealogical approach (Foucault 1991; Garland 2014), we were particularly interested in how certain practices that became considered as appropriate 'Lean practices' emerged, developed, and became accepted as such by the operational staff. We focused specifically on the transformation of the subject position 'case officer' and 'asylum seeker' as they became enacted in and through the 'examining meeting' practice, and the position of the 'team leader' relative to these practices. More specifically, we selected two practices that had transformed the most since the implementation of Lean and that the case officers most often referred to as 'Lean': the *scheduling practice* (the practice through which asylum cases are distributed to case officers) and the *performance monitoring practice* (the practice through which the operational status is measured and the operational work monitored and coordinated).

Theoretically, we positioned our study in the specific literature on translation of management ideas that adopts a Latourian view of translation. We contribute to this literature by offering a theoretical reading that decentres the human actor and attends to how management ideas become translated in the flow of situated, mundane, everyday work practices. Although we rooted our exploration in the work of process-oriented scholars, we drew specifically on the work of Tim Ingold (2007a, 2017).

#### 3.4.1.2 The Ongoing Translation of Subject/Object Positions into 'Lean' Practices

At the Migration Board, we genealogically traced how the translation of 'Lean' unfolded along the flow of two *corresponding lines*, the lines of the scheduling practice and of the performance monitoring practice. Our genealogical approach oriented us to focus our account on the temporal unfolding of these practices and on how certain actions temporally conditioned the possibilities for other actions. In doing so, the question of 'who?' (i.e. in the being sense: acting, talking, and translating) became backgrounded, as the question of 'how?' (i.e. how certain ways of acting and talking become enacted as appropriate and legitimate in certain situations) became foregrounded. In genealogically tracing the lines of flow of these practices, we were able to study the practices, subjects, and objects of the board's operations as *specific positionings*, continuously (re)produced through these temporal unfolding lines.

In tracing genealogically the two operational practices as corresponding lines (illustrated in Table 3.1), we capture both how the *doings* of these operational practices change—in the conditionality of the flow—and specifically how this flow translates (or enacts) the meaning of 'scheduling' and 'monitoring' differently over time. Within the corresponding flows of the lines, we see how mundane details of operational practices, such as specific assumed material functionalities of technologies (e.g. an Outlook Calendar and a whiteboard used for group meetings) become transformed/translated in and through the conditionalities of the corresponding lines of flow. We see how specific ways of being and acting become meaningful, while others do not, depending on how they inherit and impart certain ways of doing and thinking as they flow. For example, the scheduling practice inherited geographical specialization of the officers from the previous practice, and it imparted to the subsequent practice a particular understanding of officer 'availability' to be scheduled. Moreover, this understanding of 'availability' enacted by the Outlook Calendar function culminates in 'availability' as an algorithmic scheduling practice. In other words, in genealogically following the lines of the scheduling and monitoring practices, we make visible the ways in which the flow of practice establishes a set of constitutive conditions that render certain subject/object positions (as particular modes of being and acting) to be taken as obvious, meaningful, and legitimate.

Table 3.1 also shows how these different lines of flow correspond to enact what Lean has become at the SMB. By 'correspond', we mean the ways in which a confluence of agentic lines of flows constitutes each other's possibility to enact practices in which certain subject positions become taken as meaningful, obvious, and legitimate ways to be. Importantly, as we focus our analysis on the attentional responses and adjustments to the conditionality of corresponding flows, we see how actors not only do changes in practices but also *undergo* change: in doing the practice, the practices also enact them as such (Ingold 2017). In following the flow of lines, we see how subjects identify or take themselves to be positioned in the flow in specific ways as consultants, managers, change agents, team leaders, and case officers, as well as suggest what they take the non-human actors to be in the flow. The notion of subject/object positions emerges as particularly valuable here because it enables us to avoid a separation of human and material agency and a depiction of a causal flow between distinct human and material actors. Instead, we are able to account for the ongoing flow of material-discursive practices that constitute the temporal possibilities for the subject/object to act and become enacted in certain ways. This also enables us to avoid separating the translating subject/object and the idea (Lean) translated. In other words, it enables us to give an account of how every actor is not just translating but is also already being translated, positioning and being positioned along the temporal flow of agentic lines. This means that in our account, a case officer is not reduced to a dot in a network, and their conditions of possibility to become are not configured in relation to other assumed actors. They are transformed through the corresponding flows of doings and undergoings to become: a regional expert, member of an expert team, standardized production resource, improver of process, and a resource to be improved.

**Table 3.1** Translations of Lean through the temporal flow of agency (the meshwork of the Swedish Migration Board)

**COLOUR CODING:**

| | |
|---|---|
| The agentic line of the flow **scheduling practice** | ***Conditions of possibility*** *(CoP)* for certain *doings and thinking* to be taken as appropriate and legitimate as *inherited from prior practices and impart to subsequent practices* |
| The agentic line of the **performance monitoring** practice | |

| *Before* **implementation of Lean** | *First six months* **after implementation** | *Current* **operations** | *Continued* **translations** |
|---|---|---|---|
| Separate units and local coordinators with geographical focus allowing for ownership of cases by officers | ***CoP*** for trust in geographical expertise and evaluation | | |
| Coordinator paper lists, allowing for implicit and **local** monitoring of load | Outlook calendars, allowing team leader access to officers' schedules | ***CoP*** for digital coordination of teams | |
| ***CoP*** for being an automous expert | Visualization boards, allowing for the **monitoring** of process flow | Outlook functionality, allowing for algorithmic scheduling | ***CoP*** for focus on individual productivity |
| | ***CoP*** for temporal awareness of team and **individual** cases | Visualization **boards** and SKAPA functionality, allowing for team awareness and competition | ... |
| | | ***CoP*** for quantitative measures and competition | ... |

| ***Subject (Object) positions* enacted as legitimate within the meshwork** | | | |
|---|---|---|---|
| **Officer:** The professional, *autonomous and self-managed expert* | **Officer:** The team expert, *supervised by the team* **leader** | **Officer:** An administrator, a performing team **member** and *a standardized production resource* | … |
| **Asylum Seeker:** A unique **geographically** defined *individual case* | **Asylum Seeker:** Geographically defined *team case* | **Asylum Seeker:** The *standard production unit* for the team | |
| **Outlook:** is enacted as a **possibility** for *managing my time* | **Outlook:** is enacted as a possibility for *managing team time* | **Outlook** is enacted as a possibility for *programming officer's (or production unit) time* | … |
| **Whiteboards:** are enacted as a place to make notes and *organize my own time* | **Whiteboards:** are enacted as a place to *manage the flow of applicant cases* and *improve processes* | **Whiteboards:** are enacted as a place to manage the *team and individual productivity* | |

*Source:* adapted from Hultin et al. 2021.

Similarly, we see how materiality matters in the translation process—not as objects working to modify other objects or subjects, but as ongoing becomings along the lines of flow, continuously conditioning possibilities for action as they correspond (Ingold 2007a, 2015). In this vocabulary, an object's properties (or affordances) cannot be found in its 'nature', in its materiality, or in the relationality with the user (as affordance theory suggests; cf. Leonardi 2011). Rather, our account shows how, by focusing on the conditionality of corresponding lines of flows, we can restore objects and subjects to the flows of practices through which they came into being and continue to subsist (Ingold 2015). In other words, we show how we can attend to agentic flows of materiality, not by imbuing materiality with agency that either facilitates, triggers, or resists human intention (McCabe and Russell 2017), but rather by telling their stories, genealogically (Foucault 1991)—that is, by starting in present everyday work practices and showing how they come into being specifically and conditionally through many contingent correspondences in the flow of everyday organizational life. Thus, the approach we employ here not only enables us to move beyond the dichotomous view of subject and object, structure and agency, idea and translator but also recognizes how categories such as 'ideas' or 'identities' are radically unstable and open to modification and alteration. Because the 'idea' of Lean, in this account, is always enacted in situated practices, and because no one owns the agency to define its boundaries, it is not just transforming organizational practices to the extent that influential human or non-human translators allow and facilitate its ongoing translation. Rather, as management ideas are inseparable from the flow of everyday work practices, they become transformed coincidentally and contingently.

In sum, by following the flow of practices along multiple corresponding lines (Ingold 2007a, 2015), we made visible the translating or transformative agency, not as located in and owned by the subject or object positions we like to call actors, but rather as a temporal flow that inherits from previous practices and imparts to subsequent practices and, in so doing, creates the constitutive conditions for subjects and objects to become positioned in particular ways in the flow of everyday work practices. In our account, intentions, interests, and preferences do not originate in assumed actors. Thus, the ability to skilfully manipulate interests (Morris and Lancaster 2006), enrol and mobilize other actors (Bergström and Diedrich 2011), or reconstruct and repackage ideas or issues (Brès and Gond 2014) is not centred or primary in this understanding of translation, as is suggested by the translation literature. Rather, it is in the contingent corresponding flows that translation of management ideas finds its meaning and ongoing transformation, always on the move.

### 3.4.2 Illustration 2: Identity Working as a Process of Material-Discursive Interpellation

#### 3.4.2.1 Introduction to the Study

Our second illustration is also based on an ethnographic study at the Swedish Migration Board (SMB), specifically on ethnographic work conducted at three different sites at the SMB in Stockholm: an old reception area located in a former police station, a contemporary reception area located in an office building, and one of the new national service centres replacing existing reception sites across the country.

In this study, we were interested in how the work and the roles of the case officers at these three sites developed differently over time and how the materialities of the different sites were implicated in this development. Theoretically, we engaged with the literature on subject positioning, specifically with the argument that the constitutive role of material-discursive practices has not sufficiently been addressed in this literature or the associated identity working literature (Bisel and Barge 2011; Bardon et al. 2012; Rennstam 2012; Symon and Pritchard 2015; Harding et al. 2017; Paring et al. 2017). To contribute to this literature, we assumed an agential realist position (Barad 2007) and in addition to adopting some of the concepts presented above (i.e. flow of agency, material-discursive practices, and subject/object positions) we also worked through Althusser's (2006a) concept of interpellation.

#### 3.4.2.2 On Becoming Hailed into a Subject/Object Position

Employing a post-humanist understanding of interpellation, we were able to show how, at the three different types of sites at the Migration Board, the officer and the asylum seeker become interpellated in very different ways. These differences were possible to trace to the conditions of possibilities provided in and through different subject positions, which are enacted in and through the temporal flow of material-discursive practices. Table 3.2 summarizes our analysis, illustrating how, in the material-discursive practices of *assigning/taking turns* and *giving/receiving help*, objects and subjects become hailed differently at each site.

Table 3.2 summarizes how, in the old reception (Figure 3.1), the conditioning flow of the corresponding material-discursive practices (where separate, colour-marked tickets and glass windows are positioned as appropriate)

**Table 3.2** Interpellation practices in the three different material-discursive sites

| Site of material-discursive practices | | Material discursive practice of *assigning turns* | Material discursive practice of *giving/receiving help* |
|---|---|---|---|
| **Old reception** *(Figure 1—former police station)* | <u>*Object position*</u> | ***Coloured ticket:*** An authority on the identity and sequence cases | ***Booth with glass wall:*** A separator and protector that allows for inspection |
| | <u>*Subject position*</u> ***Asylum Seeker*** | A more or less legitimate case from a specific region (as an instance within a particular category) | A potential safety threat |
| | ***Case Officer*** | Specialist or expert of a specific region | Expert authority in need of protection |
| **Current reception** *(Figure 2—the reception lobby)* | <u>*Object position*</u> | ***Single ticketing system:*** An authority of the sequence of cases | ***Open, flexible reception counter:*** A separator and negotiator of proximity |
| | <u>*Subject position*</u> ***Asylum Seeker*** | A generic, equally important customer | Customer with the right to initiate contact and express needs and interests |
| | ***Case Officer*** | An available service provider | Flexible and collaborative service providers |
| **Service centre** *(Figure 3—the service centre main area)* | <u>*Object position*</u> | ***Floor walker meeting point:*** An individualizer of the welcoming gesture | ***Officer/service scheduling:*** A scheduler of officers, to be available according to individual convenience |
| | <u>*Subject position*</u> ***Asylum Seeker*** | A unique individual or guest | Unique and empowered individual |
| | ***Case Officer*** | An attentive personal service provider | An always available and flexible personal service provider |

*Source:* adapted from Hultin and Introna 2019.

**Figure 3.1** The old reception area
*Source:* Taken by author Lotta Hultin.

allows the applicant and the officer to become hailed into specific subject positions: that of the 'more or less legitimate case from a specific region', that of 'a potential safety threat' in the case of the asylum seeker, and that of a 'specialist' and 'authority in need of protection' in the case of the officer. In the current reception area (Figure 3.2), the conditioning flow of the corresponding material-discursive practices (where a single-ticket system and open and flexible reception counters are positioned as appropriate) hails the officer and the applicant into different subject positions: that of a 'generic, equally important customer' and a 'customer with the right to initiate contact and express needs and interests' in the case of the asylum seeker, and that of an 'available service provider' and 'flexible and collaborative service provider' in the case of the officer. Finally, in the service centre (Figure 3.3), the conditioning flow of the corresponding material-discursive practices, of floor walking, name tags, and the mobile ticket systems in open spaces, hails the applicant as a 'guest' and a 'unique individual' and the officials as 'always available and flexible personal service providers'.

In this account, the positioning of the subject has no original or given starting point or any clear dividing lines that demarcate an assumed boundary between the self and the other. That is, the positioning does not originate in any specific discursive practices, such as in talk about organizations or professions (Meriläinen et al. 2004; Kuhn 2009; Brown and Lewis 2011; Harding et al. 2014; Laine et al. 2016). This means that asylum seekers and officers (in our narratives above) do not behave differently in the former police station, the current reception area, or the new service centre because historically emergent structures such as the material-discursive properties

**Figure 3.2** The current reception, and the ticket machine in its waiting area
*Source:* Taken by author Lotta Hultin.

**Figure 3.3** The new national service centre
*Source:* Taken by author Lotta Hultin.

of the reception desks, glass windows, queue tickets, signs, gestures, and so forth *cause them* to behave differently, collectively. Rather, in our account, they act in certain ways (and not in other ways) because the ongoing situated flow of material-discursive practices already make such ways of speaking and doing appear as appropriate and meaningful ways to become. This means that once the officers and applicants become hailed into specific subject positions, they tend to be kept in these positions by appeals to 'common sense'. As such, they tend to accept their positioning and its implied grid of intelligibility as obvious and appropriate ways of being and acting. This means that the subject emerges as a relational enactment—not, however, between the 'I' and the 'other', in the interaction between two actors modifying each other, or as causal consequence of agents drawing upon some form of preexisting structures, such as critical realist accounts would suggest (Fleetwood 2014: 206). Rather, the subject emerges as the momentary and historical enactment of a confluence of specific and ongoing—always concrete and mattering—material-discursive practices as they flow.

Significantly, such ongoing subject positionings do not transcend their contingent and situated enactment. This does not mean that the doer (the subject) is *determined* by the flow of these material-discursive practices or that there is no room for individual attempts to form, repair, maintain, strengthen, or revise their sense of 'identity' (Sveningsson and Alvesson 2003) in order to create or maintain a sense of subjectivity and agency. Rather, it is to problematize such assumed 'identity work' and to reveal the conditions of possibility of such identity work—that of a subject that is always already becoming positioned. In other words, our account shows how one must not underestimate the degree to which individual attempts at repositioning are always and already governed by the flow of a multiplicity of material-discursive practices in the mundane flow of everyday life.

In this view, 'material agency' is not something that inheres in material objects, which then somehow imbricates with human agency (cf., Leonardi 2011; Paring et al. 2017). Neither is it something that emerges in the interaction between assumed separate subjects and objects (Rennstam 2012) or that may either 'be "captured by" ... or resist enrolment into identity work' (Symon and Pritchard 2015: 255). Rather, in our account, agency 'is the enactment of iterative changes to particular practices' (Barad 2007: 235), and what we call the 'material' matters as profoundly constitutive, historically contingent meshworks of material-discursive practices that hail subjects/objects by already conditioning their possibilities to be and act in the flow of mundane everyday practices. Just as there is no subject outside the positions enacted in material-discursive practices, there is no object that can act/work or resist acting/working outside such subject/object positions (Barad 2007; 150). Thus, subjectivity and objectivity are not opposed to one another; objectivity is not the antithesis of subjectivity. In accounting for how matter matters in this way, we show how we can include and account for materiality in the citational practice of interpellation without 'thingifying' it (Barad 2003: 812) and without acknowledging it solely as an effect or consequence of discursive practices, consequently restoring the equation between matter and passivity.

## 3.5 Some Concluding Thoughts and Implications

In recent years, there have been many calls for scholars to develop process theoretical contributions that consider the dynamic unfolding of phenomena over time (e.g. Cloutier and Langley 2020). In this chapter, we have argued that doing this requires that we consciously scrutinize and adapt the conceptual vocabularies we enact in our studies to guard against our tendency to habitually adopt actor-centric vocabularies. Otherwise, many of our important insights might be lost with significant consequences, both practically and theoretically: practically because our actor-centric orientation can lead us to overinflate the assumed agentic possibilities of actors while not appreciating the multiplicity of flows that already enact them as such; and theoretically because by adopting an actor-centric language we are likely to find ourselves producing results and insights which are surprisingly familiar. How, then, does a vocabulary-centring movement help us achieve a temporal orientation mean for how we theorize phenomena as temporal becomings?

*Decentring actors and following the agentic flow of practices:* In our research practices, a vocabulary centring flow and enacting a genealogical orientation encourages us to look 'upstream' and follow the flow wherever it takes us. This helps us decentre our gaze and trace carefully the temporal histories of the contingent agentic flows that corresponded to produce the necessary conditions for these subject/object positions to become possible as such. Thus, not asking 'what is a case officer?' but rather 'what were the necessary transformative flows that enacted the case officer as the particular "case officer" that we now take her to be?' In doing this, we refrain from centring our data collection, analysis, and theorization on what we might have supposed as the important actors and artifacts 'here and now', while also not focusing on their assumed qualities, intentionalities, and so on. We thus do not 'follow the actors', but rather trace of the agentic flows along which certain possibilities for being and action emerge.

*Attending to the temporal conditionalities and contingencies:* The necessary conditions for understanding flows are temporal, not spatial. As such, we must attend more carefully to how precisely the flow of agency (human and more-than-human) inherits conditions of possibility from prior actions and imparts conditions of possibility to subsequent actions, continuously engendering new possibilities for being and action. Of particular significance here are contingencies, as Foucault (1980) pointed out. One such example from our illustration above is the manner in which the contingent use of the 'old police station' imparted conditions of possibilities for the subjects/objects to become positioned specifically. Practically, this means that our vocabulary needs to help us forgo a priori distinctions that often orient our data collection and analysis, such as contingent/systematic, major/minor, coincidental/intentional. This might also imply a need to transform our analytical methods, such as from 'coding' to 'narrating'.

*Asking different questions:* The shift toward a temporal, processual, and flow-oriented approach not only transforms what we attend to, it also requires that we attend to it differently. This means that our vocabularies need to help us ask different questions that solicit the flow of unfolding stories and moments. Rather than asking, 'Why did you do X?' we might ask, 'What happened that made X seem like the right thing to do at the time?' Rather than asking, 'Why did X happen?' one might ask, 'What were the specific coincidences that made it possible for X to happen at that time?' This flow-oriented phrasing shapes the way phenomena become (re)enacted in and for our research practices.

In sum, we believe that productive correspondence with the approaches and vocabularies that we engage with in this chapter can provide additional opportunities for rethinking and reinterpreting flow and transformation in a range of settings related to organizing in our digital age. To develop a theoretical vocabulary that allows us to think of the world as an ever-transforming flow of events is a true challenge, and to meet this challenge continued experimentation with vocabularies will be fruitful in helping us to 'think movement'.

To conclude, we want to turn to the question of responsibility. If our epistemic practices do not describe the world but also participate in its ongoing transformative enactment, then we as scholars have an urgent responsibility to become more attuned to how we enact the world(s). We need to do so not by enclosing it (in our categories and theories) but rather by opening it up to different transformative possibilities. As Barad (2007: 182) says, 'Questions of responsibility and accountability present themselves with every possibility;

each moment [of theorizing] is alive with different possibilities for the world's becoming and different reconfigurings of what may yet be possible.'

## Note

1. An earlier version of this study was presented at the Eleventh International Symposium on Process Organization Studies (PROS) in 2019.

## References

Althusser, L. (2006a). 'Ideology and Ideological State Apparatuses (Notes Towards an Investigation)', *The Anthropology of the State: A Reader* 9/1: 86–98.

Bakken, T., and Hernes, T. (2006). Organizing is both a noun and a verb: Weick meets Whitehead. *Organization Studies* 27: 1599–1610.

Barad, K. (2007). *Meeting the Universe Halfway: Quantum Physics and the Entanglement of Matter and Meaning*. Duke University Press.

Barad, K. (2003). 'Posthumanist Performativity: Toward an Understanding of How Matter Comes to Matter', *Signs: Journal of Women in Culture and Society* 28: 801–832.

Bardon, T., Clegg, S., and Josserand, E. (2012). 'Exploring Identity Construction from a Critical Management Perspective: A Research Agenda', *Management* 15: 351–366.

Bergson, H. (1999). *An Introduction to Metaphysics*. Hackett Publishing.

Bergson, H., Ansell-Pearson, K., and Mullarhey, J. (2002). *Henri Bergson: Key Writings*. Continuum Press.

Bergström, O., and Diedrich, A. (2011). 'Exercising Social Responsibility in Downsizing: Enrolling and Mobilizing Actors at a Swedish High-Tech Company', *Organization Studies* 32/7: 897–919.

Bisel, R. S., and Barge, J. K. (2011). 'Discursive Positioning and Planned Change in Organizations', *Human Relations* 64: 257–283.

Brès, L., and Gond, J-P. (2014). 'The Visible Hands of Consultants in the Construction of the Markets for Virtue: Translating Issues, Negotiating Boundaries and Enacting Responsive Regulations', *Human Relations* 67/11: 1347–1382.

Brown, A. D., and Lewis, M. A. (2011). 'Identities, Discipline and Routines', *Organization Studies* 32: 871–895.

Bruce, K., and Nyland, C. (2011). 'Elton Mayo and the Deification of Human Relations', *Organization Studies* 32/3: 383–405.

Butler, J. (1993). *Bodies That Matter: On the Discursive Limits of 'Sex'*. Routledge.

Butler, J. (1997a). *Excitable Speech: A Politics of the Performative.* Routledge.

Butler, J. (1997b). *The Psychic Life of Power: Theories in Subjection.* Stanford University Press.

Cecez-Kecmanovic, D., Galliers, R. D., Henfridsson, O., Newell, S., and Vidgen, R. (2014). 'The Sociomateriality of Information Systems: Current Status, Future Directions'. *MIS Quarterly* 38/3: 809–830.

Cecez-Kecmanovic, D. (2016). 'IFIP International Federation for Information Processing', in L. Introna et al. (eds), *IS&O 2016, IFIP AICT* 489. Springer International, 35–57.

Chia, R. (1995). 'From Modern to Postmodern Organizational Analysis', *Organization Studies* 16: 579–604.

Chia, R. (1999). 'A "Rhizomic" Model of Organizational Change and Transformation: Perspective from a Metaphysics of Change', *British Journal of Management* 10: 209–227.

Chia, R. (2002). 'Essai: Time, Duration and Simultaneity: Rethinking Process and Change in Organizational Analysis', *Organization Studies* 23/6: 863–868.

Clegg, S. R., Kornberger, M., and Rhodes, C. (2005). 'Learning/Becoming/Organizing', *Organization* 12/2: 147–167.

Cloutier, C., and Langley, A. (2020). 'What Makes a Process Theoretical Contribution?' *Organization Theory* 1/1: 1–32.

Cooper, R. (2007). 'Organs of Process: Rethinking Human Organization', *Organization Studies* 28: 1547–1573.

Dean, M. (2009). *Governmentality: Power and Rule in Modern Society* (2nd ed.). Sage Publications.

Deleuze, G., and Guattari, F. (1987) *A Thousand Plateaus: Capitalism and Schizophrenia.* University of Minnesota Press.

Farquharson, M., Ortenblad, A., and Hsu, S. W. (2014). 'Trusting Local Translation: Experience from Transplanting a "Made in Britain" Entrepreneurship Course in China', *Management Learning* 45/2: 182–199.

Feldman, M. S., and Orlikowski, W. J. (2011). 'Theorizing Practice and Practicing Theory', *Organization Science* 22/5: 1240–1253.

Feldman, M. S. (2000). 'Organizational Routines as a Source of Continuous Change', *Organization Science* 11/6: 611–629.

Fleetwood, S. (2014). 'Bhaskar and Critical Realism', in P. Adler, P. Du Gay, G. Morgan, and M. Reed (eds), *The Oxford Handbook of Sociology, Social Theory and Organisation Studies: Contemporary Currents.* Oxford University Press, 182–219.

Foucault, M. (1980). *Power/Knowledge.* Harvester.

Foucault, M. (1991). 'On the Genealogy of Ethics: An Overview of Work in Progress', in P. Rabinow (ed.), *The Foucault Reader.* Penguin, 340–372.

Garland, D. (2014). 'What Is a History of the Present? On Foucault's Genealogies and Their Critical Preconditions', *Punishment & Society* 16/4: 365–384.

Harding, N. H., Ford, J., and Lee, H. (2017). 'Toward a Performative Theory of Resistance: Senior Managers and Revolting Subject(ivitie)s', *Organization Studies* 38/9: 1209–1232.

Harding, N., Lee, H., and Ford, J. (2014). 'Who Is the Middle Manager? On Constituting an Organizational Self', *Human Relations* 67/10: 1213–1237.

Hernes, T. (2007). *Understanding Organization as Process: Theory for a Tangled World*. Routledge.

Hernes, T., and Matlis, S. eds. (2010). *Process, Sensemaking and Organization*. Oxford: Oxford University Press.

Hultin, L. (2019). 'On Becoming a Sociomaterial Researcher: Exploring Epistemological Practices Grounded in a Relational, Performative Ontology', *Information & Organization* 29/2: 91–104.

Hultin, L., and Introna, L. (2019) 'On Receiving Asylum Seekers: Identity Working as a Process of Material-Discursive Interpellation', *Organization Studies* 40/9: 1361–1386.

Hultin, L., Introna, L. D., and Mähring, M. (2021). 'The Decentered Translation of Management Ideas: Attending to the Conditioning Flow of Everyday Work Practices', *Human Relations* 74/4: 587–620.

Ingold, T. (2006). Rethinking the animate, re-animating thought, Ethnos 71: 9–20.

Ingold, T. (2007a). *Lines: A Brief History*. Routledge.

Ingold, T. (2007b). 'Materials against Materiality', *Archaeological Dialogues* 14/1: 1–16.

Ingold, T. (2008). 'When ANT Meets SPIDER: Social Theory for Arthropods', in C. Knappett and L. Malafouris (eds), *Material Agency: Toward a Non-anthropocentric Approach*. Springer, 209–215.

Ingold, T. (2011). *Being Alive: Essays on Movement, Knowledge and Description*. Routledge.

Ingold, T. (2015). *The Life of Lines*. Routledge.

Ingold, T. (2017). 'On Human Correspondence', *The Journal of the Royal Anthropological Institute* 23/1: 9–27.

Introna, L. D. (2013). 'Epilogue: Performativity and the Becoming of Sociomaterial Assemblages', in F-X. de Vaujany and N. Mitev (eds), *Materiality and Space in Management and Organization Studies*. Palgrave Macmillan Press, 330–342.

Introna, L. (2015). 'Why Sociomateriality Matters: The Ontological Choreography of the Plagiarist/Original'. Working paper. University of Lancaster.

Introna, L. D. (2019). 'On the Making of Sense in Sensemaking: Decentred Sensemaking in the Meshwork of Life', *Organization Studies* 40/5: 745–764.

Jones, C., and Massa, F. G. (2013). 'From Novel Practice to Consecrated Exemplar: Unity Temple as a Case of Institutional Evangelizing', *Organization Studies* 34/8: 1099–1136.

Jones, M. (2014). 'A Matter of Life and Death: Exploring Conceptualizations of Sociomateriality in the Context of Critical Care', *MIS Quarterly* 38/3: 895–925.

Kallinikos, J., Aaltonen, A., and Marton, A. (2013). 'The Ambivalent Ontology of Digital Artifacts', *MIS Quarterly* 37/2: 357–370.

Kautz, K., and Jensen, T. B. (2013). 'Sociomateriality at the Royal Court of IS: A Jester's Monologue', *Information and Organization* 23: 15–27.

Korica, M., and Molloy, E. (2010). 'Making Sense of Professional Identities: Stories of Medical Professionals and New Technologies', *Human Relations* 63/12: 1879–1901.

Koro-Ljungberg, M., and Mazzei, L. A. (2012). 'Problematizing Methodological Simplicity in Qualitative Research Editors Introduction', *Qualitative Inquiry* 18/9: 728–731.

Kuhn, T. (2009). 'Positioning Lawyers: Discursive Resources, Professional Ethics and Identification', *Organization* 16/5: 681–704.

Laine, M., Meriläinen, S., Tienari, J., and Vaara, E. (2016). 'Mastery, Submission, and Subversion: On the Performative Construction of Strategist Identity', *Organization* 23/4: 505–524.

Langley, A., Smallman, C., Tsoukas, H., and Van de Ven, A. (2013). 'Process Studies of Change in Organization and Management: Unveiling Temporality, Activity, and Flow', *Academy of Management Journal* 56/1: 1–13.

Latour, B. (1988). 'The politics of explanation: An alternative', in S. Woolgar (ed.), *Knowledge and reflexivity*. London: Sage Ltd, 155–176.

Latour, B. (1996). 'On Actor-Network Theory: A Few Clarifications', *Soziale Welt* 47/4: 369–381.

Latour, B. (1999a). 'On Recalling ANT', *The Sociological Review* 47/S1: 15–25.

Latour, B. (1999b). *Pandora's Hope: Essays on the Reality of Science Studies*. Harvard University Press.

Latour, B. (2004). 'On Using ANT for Studying Information Systems: A (Somewhat) Socratic Dialog', in C. Avgerou, C. Ciborra, and F. Land (eds), *Social Study of ICT*. Cambridge University Press, 62–76.

Latour, B. (2005). *Reassembling the Social: An Introduction to Actor Network Theory*. Oxford University Press.

Latour, B. (2003). 'The Promises of Constructivism', in D. Ihde and E. Selinger (eds), *Chasing Technoscience: Matrix for Materiality*. Indiana University Press, 27–46.

Latour B. (2013). *An Inquiry into Modes of Existence: An Anthropology of the Moderns*. Cambridge, MA: Harvard University Press.

Law, J., and Urry, J. (2004). 'Enacting the Social', *Economy and Society* 33/3: 390–410.

Law, J. (1999). 'After ANT: Complexity, Naming and Topology', *Sociological Review* 47/1: 1–14.

Law, J. (2004). *After Method Mess in Social Science Research*, London: Routledge.

Leonardi, M. (2011). 'When Flexible Routines Meet Flexible Technologies: Affordance, Constraint, and the Imbrication of Human and Material Agencies', *MIS Quarterly* 35/1: 147–167.

Lewin, K. (1947). 'Frontiers in Group Dynamics: I. Concept, Method and Reality in Social Science; Social Equilibria', *Human Relations* 1/1: 5–41.

Liker, J. K. (2004). *The Toyota Way: 14 Management Principles from the World's Greatest Manufacturer*. McGraw-Hill.

MacKay, R. B., and Chia, R. (2013). 'Choice, Chance and Unintended Consequences in Strategic Change: A Process Understanding of the Rise and Fall of Northco Automotive', *Academy of Management Journal* 56/1: 208–230.

Manning, E. (2015). 'Against Method', in Vannini, P. (ed.), *Non-representational methodologies: Re-envisioning research*. New York, NY: Routledge, 52–71.

Manning, E. (2016). *The Minor Gesture*. Duke University Press.

Mazmanian, M., Cohn, M., and Dourish, P. (2014). 'Dynamic Reconfiguration in Planetary Exploration: A Sociomaterial Ethnography', *MIS Quarterly* 38/3: 831–848.

McCabe, D., and Russell, S. (2017). '"The Costumes Don't Do It for Me": Obstacles to the Translation of "New" Management Ideas', *Management Learning* 48/5: 566–581.

Meriläinen, S., Tienari, J., Thomas, R., and Davies, A. (2004). 'Management Consultant Talk: A Cross-Cultural Comparison of Normalizing Discourse and Resistance', *Organization* 11/4: 539–564.

Mol, A. (2003). *The Body Multiple: Ontology in Medical Practice*. Duke University Press.

Monteiro, P., and Nicolini, D. (2015). 'Recovering Materiality in Institutional Work: Prizes as an Assemblage of Human and Material Entities', *Journal of Management Inquiry* 24/1: 61–81.

Morris, T., and Lancaster, Z. (2006). 'Translating Management Ideas', *Organization Studies* 27/2: 207–233.

Mousavi Baygi, R., Introna, L. D., and Hultin, L. (2021). 'Everything Flows: Studying Continuous Socio-Technological Transformation in a Fluid and Dynamic Digital World', *MIS Quarterly* 45/1: 423–452.

Mueller, F., and Whittle, A. (2011). 'Translating Management Ideas: A Discursive Devices Analysis', *Organization Studies* 32/2: 187–210.

Nambisan, S., Lyytinen, K., Majchrzak, A., Song, M. (2017). 'Digital innovation management: reinventing innovation management research in a digital world', *MIS Quarterly* 41/1: 223–238.

Nayak, A., and Chia, R. (2011). 'Thinking Becoming and Emergence: Process Philosophy and Organization Studies', *Research in the Sociology of Organizations* 32: 281–309.

Nicolini, D., Mengis, J., and Swan, J. (2012). 'Understanding the Role of Objects in Cross-Disciplinary Collaboration', *Organization Science* 23/3: 612–629.

Orlikowski, W. J. (2000). 'Using Technology and Constituting Structures: A Practice Lens for Studying Technology in Organizations', *Organization Science* 11/4: 404–428.

Orlikowski, W. J., and Scott, S. V. (2014). 'Exploring Material-Discursive Practices', *Journal of Management Studies* 52/5: 697–705.

Orlikowski, W. J., and Scott, S. V. (2015). 'Exploring Material-Discursive Practices', *Journal of Management Studies* 52/5: 697–705.

Paring, G., Pezé, S., and Huault, I. (2017). '"Welcome to the Whiteboard, the New Member of the Team": Identity Regulation as a Sociomaterial Process', *Organization* 24/6: 844–865.

Pettigrew, A. M., Woodman, R. W., and Cameron, K. S. (2001). 'Studying Organizational Change and Development: Challenges for Future Research', *Academy of Management Journal* 44/4: 697–713.

Pickering, A. (1995). *The Mangle of Practice: Time, Agency, and Science*. University of Chicago Press.

Rennstam, J. (2012). 'Object-Control: A Study of Technologically Dense Knowledge Work', *Organization Studies* 33/8: 1071–1090.

Sandberg, J., and Tsoukas, H. (2015). 'Making Sense of the Sensemaking Perspective: Its Constituents, Limitations, and Opportunities for Further Development', *Journal of Organizational Behavior* 36/S1: S6–S32.

Scott, S. V., and Orlikowski, W. J. (2014). 'Entanglements in Practice: Performing Anonymity through Social Media', *MIS Quarterly* 38/3: 863–893.

Shotter, J. (2014). 'Agential Realism, Social Constructionism, and Our Living Relations to Our Surroundings: Sensing Similarities Rather than Seeing Patterns', *Theory & Psychology* 24/3: 305–325.

Slife, B. D. (2004). 'Taking Practice Seriously: Toward a Relational Ontology', *Journal of Theoretical and Philosophical Psychology* 24/2: 157–178.

Spyridonidis, D., Currie, G., Heusinkveld, S., et al. (2016). 'The Translation of Management Knowledge: Challenges, Contributions and New Directions', *International Journal of Management Reviews* 18/3: 231–235.

Stigliani, I., and Ravasi, D. (2012). 'Organizing Thoughts and Connecting Brains: Material Practices and the Transition from Individual to Group-Level Prospective Sensemaking', *Academy of Management Journal* 55/5: 1232–1259.

Swan, J., Bresnen, M., Newell, S., et al. (2007). 'The Object of Knowledge: The Role of Objects in Biomedical Innovation', *Human Relations* 60/12: 1809–1837.

Sveningsson, S., and Alvesson, M. (2003). 'Managing Managerial Identities: Organizational Fragmentation, Discourse and Identity Struggle', *Human Relations* 56/10: 1163–1193.

Symon, G., and Pritchard, K. (2015). 'Performing the Responsive and Committed Employee through the Sociomaterial Mangle of Connection', *Organization Studies* 36/2: 241–263.

Tsoukas, H., and Chia, R. (2002). 'On Organizational Becoming: Rethinking Organizational Change', *Organization Science* 13/5: 567–582.

Wagner, E. L., Newell, S. M., and Piccoli, G. (2010). 'Understanding Project Survival in an ES Environment: A Sociomaterial Practice Perspective', *Journal of the Association for Information Systems* 11/5: 276–298.

Whitehead, A. N. (1978). *Process and Reality: An Essay in Cosmology*, Corrected Ed., D. R. Griffin and D. W. Sherburne. Free Press, 7, 99–104.

Womack, J. P., and Jones, D. T. (1994). 'From Lean Production to the Lean Enterprise', *Harvard Business Review* 72/2: 93–103.

# 4

# Algorithmic Automation of Knowledge Work

## A Sketch for Exploring the Becoming of Knowledge Work

*Dubravka Cecez-Kecmanovic*

## 4.1 Introduction: Automation of Knowledge Work

The automation of knowledge work is fast growing and is predicted to be the most significant disruptive technology in the current decade (Steiner 2012; Webb 2019; Willcocks, 2020). Due to the increasing capabilities of Artificial Intelligence (AI) and especially of the algorithms that use big data to learn, predict, and make human-like decisions, the AI-powered automation of work is expanding to the domains in which human beings were previously considered irreplaceable (Holford 2019; Benbya et al. 2021). Algorithms are already displacing knowledge workers in jobs ranging from customer services, to transportation and logistics, to radiology and legal services (Khandani et al. 2010; Chalfin et al. 2016; Faraj et al. 2018). The promise that knowledge work automation will deliver unprecedented levels of efficiency and cost savings, when professionals and knowledge workers are replaced by intelligent machines, seems irresistible (Hasselberger 2019). This promise, however, is sold together with a more socially appealing one: by using powerful learning algorithms, the automation of knowledge work will result in better outcomes—more objective, fairer, and ethical judgements and decisions that overall are superior to human performance (Holford 2019, 2020). The spread and expansion of the automation of knowledge work are predicted to accelerate, limited only by the power of AI systems and the ability of organizations to acquire and appropriate them (Faraj et al. 2018; Hancock et al. 2020).

The deployment of algorithms to automate knowledge work, however, has been problematized since it began. Serious problems, to name a few,

Dubravka Cecez-Kecmanovic, *Algorithmic Automation of Knowledge Work*. In: *Organizing in the Digital Age*. Edited by: Michael Barrett, Emmanuelle Vaast, Ann Langley, and Haridimos Tsoukas, Oxford University Press.
 DOI: 10.1093/oso/9780198899457.003.0004

include inappropriate sources of data and the dubious quality of data used by algorithms to make decisions, including datafication effects (Galliers et al. 2017; Marjanovic and Cecez-Kecmanovic 2017); uncritical delegation of power to algorithms to make decisions without human oversight, transparency, and clear responsibility (Kitchin 2017); reproduction of biases and discrimination in algorithmic decision-making (Baer and Kamalnath 2017; Ferguson 2019); and privacy breaches (Clarke 2019). Furthermore, with the uncritical delegation of decision-making power to algorithms, numerous concerns have been raised about the lack of transparency, fairness, and accountability (Pasquale 2015; Edwards and Veale 2017; Kitchin 2017). Broader social consequences include the loss of jobs on a global scale (Frey and Osborne 2017; Cheatham et al. 2019); the changing demand for skills (Willcocks 2021); increasing poverty and inequalities (Eubanks 2018); and diminishing public trust (Steiner 2012). Scholars in management and organization studies and in information systems (IS) have only just begun to address these concerns, revealing unintended and intended harmful social effects of the algorithmic automation of knowledge work (Hadjimichael and Tsoukas 2019; Holford 2020; Marjanovic et al. 2021). Most importantly, the depth and scale of the transformation of work and organizing and its worrying human and social consequences are not well understood and require urgent scholarly attention (Faraj et al. 2018; von Krogh 2018; Benbya et al. 2021).

The purpose of this chapter is to better understand what knowledge work becomes when automated by AI-powered algorithmic systems and how harmful social consequences are performed. Drawing from examples of the algorithmic automation of knowledge work in the literature (in Section 4.2), I aim to: (i) reveal and problematize the fundamental assumptions about the nature of knowledge and knowledge work that underly the algorithmic automation of work; and (ii) demonstrate how the algorithmic automation of knowledge work (based on such assumptions) enacts a 'blob' world of knowledge work that is self-contained and disinterested in the harmful social consequences that occur (Sections 4.3 and 4.4). This investigation will enable a critical reflection on the very concept and purpose of knowledge work automation and its fundamental problems.

The prevailing view of the automation of knowledge work, certainly, is not the only way to use AI and algorithms to innovate and advance work and benefit mankind. In contrast to the blob world of work enacted by the AI automation of knowledge work, I imagine, thinking with Ingold (2015, 2017), a different world of knowledge work in which human knowledge workers and AI technologies *co-respond* to each other, bounded in sympathy as they cooperatively attend to and examine problems, investigate possible solutions and their implications, make proposals or decisions, and, in the process, learn (Section 4.5). By imagining and learning how knowledge workers and AI technologies can co-respond and work in harmony, we may hope to 'restore to life' a world of knowledge work that is in danger of being frozen and cut off from the flows of life.

## 4.2 Background

The widespread and increasing use of AI, algorithms, and big data in all domains of human endeavour marks the latest era of digitization, characterized by the transformation of work processes and the ways in which work is conceived and performed, in pursuit of the ceaseless increase of efficiency and productivity and the maximization of profitability. Due to the exponentially increasing power of information technologies (IT), and especially of AI and the 'intelligence' of algorithms and robots, the automation of human work and replacement of workers have disrupted labour markets, increased unemployment (especially in the medium skill range), and profoundly affected workplaces and the nature of work (Autor 2015; Davenport and Kirby 2016: Faraj et al. 2018).

The literature on the use of AI and robots that automate repetitive jobs has reported massive cost savings, increased efficiency and productivity, and improvements in performance (Autor 2015). Conversely, the important drawbacks reported include the major one of the loss of jobs among low-skilled workers on a global scale (Bughin et al. 2018). Furthermore, those workers still required in repetitive jobs often act as additions to machines, as illustrated in the well-publicized case of Amazon warehouses' automation (Lecher 2019). Acting and decision-making powers are shifting to automated machines and algorithms, making the remaining workers' jobs more precarious and subordinated. In the near future, most occupations are predicted to face either partial or full automation (Bughin et al. 2018). While it is expectated that new jobs related to digital transformation will be created (Willcocks 2020), serious concerns are being raised regarding the implications for workers and workplaces, such as job losses and increasing unemployment (Kim et al. 2017).

These trends are continuing and are extending to include knowledge workers and top-end professionals (Holford 2019, 2020). Algorithms are programmed to automate a variety of complex cognitive tasks, including reasoning, analysis, assessment, pattern recognition, prediction, classification, and diagnostics, and other cognitive and non-routine activities. Automated algorithmic decision-making systems are increasingly deployed to perform the work of highly skilled professionals in a range of technical, administrative, and managerial occupations in various industries. The literature on the algorithmic automation of knowledge work and decision-making provides numerous examples of how the replacement of knowledge workers—accountants, auditors, human resources (HR) professionals, judges, police officers, administrators, managers, etc.—changes the nature of knowledge work (e.g. O'Neil 2016; Eubanks 2018; Dickey et al. 2019; Ferguson 2019; Leicht-Deobald et al. 2019; Benbya et al. 2021). While the resulting loss of jobs and the impact on knowledge workers present a serious concern, even more worrying are the social implications of the outcomes of automated knowledge work (assessments, decisions) on those affected by these outcomes (individuals and whole communities).

One domain where the adoption of AI technologies is highly visible is recruitment and hiring. Companies are increasingly deploying AI technologies to automate sourcing and screening of job applications, conducting and assessing job interviews, and predicting applicants' fit with the job and company culture, all of which ultimately lead to the selection of candidates (Raghavan et al. 2020). The use of AI automation is radically transforming recruitment and hiring processes, the role of hiring managers, and the assessment and selection of job applicants which, in turn, is changing the way that applicants apply for jobs and present themselves (Harwell 2019; Ajunwa 2020). In their rationale for automating job recruitment and hiring processes, companies often argue that their prime motive is time savings and efficiency in identifying and selecting appropriate candidates among hundreds, sometimes thousands, of applicants. More importantly, AI hiring technology companies and hiring managers claim that the use of AI in hiring processes eliminates bias and leads to increased gender and racial equality, as well as diversity in educational backgrounds, ultimately contributing to better business performance (Leicht-Deobald et al. 2019; Aspan 2020). However, ample evidence from practice shows that these biases are often replicated, even amplified, when past decisions are used to train algorithms (Ajunwa 2020; Raghavan et al. 2020). In the case of use of facial recognition and algorithmic analysis of pre-recorded job interviews, other types of biases are reported, for example, misinterpretation of facial expressions, especially those of non-white women and people from foreign cultures (non-Americans) (Ajunwa 2020; Benjamin 2019). While AI hiring software companies cannot argue that software is bias-free, they still claim that the automation of recruitment and hiring processes is superior to those processes when conducted by humans (Bornstein 2018; Ajunwa 2020). Some of the leading AI technologies deployed by companies for recruitment and hiring have been criticized by AI scientists for using 'pseudoscience' (Harwell 2019). Ajunwa (2020) further emphasizes that the current use of AI technologies in the HR domain is unregulated and contradicts the fundamental principle of equal opportunity in employment.

In the auditing profession, algorithmic systems based on machine learning have been used by major consulting and auditing companies (Kokina and Davenport 2017; Vasarhelyi and Rozario 2018; Dickey et al. 2019). As documented in the report by Dickey et al. (2019), KPMG, PricewaterhouseCoopers, Ernst & Young, and other companies are using machine learning technologies and robotic process automation technology with significant impact on auditing processes and the work of auditors (Vasarhelyi and Rozario 2018). While these technologies initially automated repetitive and mechanical tasks, the new intelligent technologies with machine learning capabilities are gradually replacing human auditors in more complex tasks. The use of intelligent accounting and auditing technologies is significantly changing auditors' skill sets and is predicted to reduce the demand for auditors (Vasarhelyi and Rozario 2018; Dickey et al. 2019). Other important concerns are also arising regarding the kind of support provided by technologies. Sutton et al. (2018) warn that continued reliance on technology and the 'subservient position' of knowledge workers results in the attrition of existing skills and the lack of development of new skills that would otherwise be an inherent part of practice. The automation of work tasks and deferral of decision-making authority to the technology, they claim, ultimately lead to deskilling and loss of knowledge. The way in which intelligent technologies perform tasks and support auditors' work is very restrictive and limits auditors in their professional exploration and judgement, ultimately affecting the quality of auditing (Dowling and Leech 2014). Along a similar line to Dowling and Leech (2014), Sutton et al. (2018: 16) suggest that, in these new working configurations, the 'auditors are guided not much differently than factory workers on an assembly line'.

In the domain of criminal justice, courts, the police, and correctional departments are increasingly deploying the AI automation of knowledge work in the investigation, prosecution, and sentencing of offenders (Cino 2018; Sheehey 2018; Ferguson 2019). The deployment of technologies, such as facial recognition systems, probabilistic DNA genotyping, crime prediction software, assessment of recidivism risks, and systems that make bail and sentencing decisions, is often justified by increased fairness and objectivity. Automated decisions are claimed 'to be more objective than, for example, [those made by] a judge, jury, or law enforcement official'

(Cino 2018: 1078–1079). These technologies often include machine learning trained on the historical data of convicted offenders or arrested people that perpetuate historical biases and injustices. For instance, due to algorithmic sentencing, black and Hispanic offenders are found to receive longer sentences than white offenders for comparable offences (Data & Civil Rights 2015). Another type of algorithmic technique, so-called predictive policing, has been used to 'forecast and prevent' future crimes before they occur (Sheehey 2018; Ferguson 2019). This new 'proactive' style of policing is criticized for violating civil liberties through 'heightened surveillance, racial profiling, and bias' (Sheehey 2018: 49).

Sentas and Pandolfini (2017) report an illustrative case of predictive policing, the Suspect Targeting Management Plan (STMP) developed and implemented by the New South Wales Police Force, Australia (NSW Police). This risk assessment intelligence tool is used to identify individuals who are likely to commit future crime. Suspected individuals are included on the STMP and subjected to a 'targeted programme' by NSW Police officers (e.g. regular attendance at their houses, use of police powers of stop and search, and 'move on' directions). Developed in-house with the aim of supporting crime prevention, the STMP uses particular risk assessment algorithms to calculate a person's risk of offending or re-offending. Neither the STMP policy nor the risk assessment tools are publicly accessible; thus, they are not available for scrutiny. The study warns that the

> STMP presents great risks to accountable policing, procedural fairness and legality. ... The details of the risk assessment that is carried out, including the risk factors taken into account and how those factors are weighted and measured, are not available to the person placed on the STMP.
>
> (Sentas and Pandolfini 2017: 8)

Based on NSW Police data about STMP use during the 2014 and 2015 financial years, the study found: (i) disproportionate targeting of young people and Aboriginal peoples; (ii) patterns of oppressive policing that are damaging relationships between police and young people; (iii) no observable impact on crime prevention after STMP adoption; and (iv) lack of transparency and absence of oversight, scrutiny, or evaluation. Information is not publicly available about factors (variables) used for risk assessment, how the relevant data are obtained, and how the STMP algorithms learn and make predictions.

The key issues in the deployment of AI technologies that replace human judgement and deliberation in courts and police practices are: (a) the use of disparate and unreliable data sources, including historical crime data, to predict possible future crimes or to make sentencing decisions; (b) the belief that the past (criminal and other data) predicts the future (crimes); and (c) the view that expert knowledge and the 'logic' guiding human assessments, judgements, and decisions (e.g. sentencing) by humans (police officers, judges, managers, etc.) can be 'captured' and automated.

Another domain where AI technologies are increasingly used to automate knowledge work and decision-making previously conducted by knowledge workers (case managers) is welfare systems. Governments around the world are adopting Digital Welfare Systems (DWSs) that use AI, data analytics, and machine learning to perform risk scoring and needs classification; verify citizens' eligibility; automate calculation of benefit payments; detect and prevent fraud; and automate interaction between welfare agencies and citizens (Alston 2019). Professional staff and case managers are replaced by algorithmic decision-making that uses various data sets (not necessarily reliable or transparent) and apply rules to perform the tasks (e.g. verifying eligibility assessment or calculating benefit payments). While introduced to improve social protection and provide better services to citizens, DWSs have often been driven by efficiency, cost-saving measures, and welfare budget cuts (Alston 2019). It is claimed that DWSs use algorithms with accurate models and reliable data sets to automate assessments and make decisions and thus replace the work of professional staff and case managers. However, growing evidence shows systemic errors, biases and discrimination, unjustified and unfair decisions, and human rights' violations and illegality, often affecting citizens who are the most vulnerable (O'Neil 2016; Carney 2018; Eubanks 2018; Alston 2019; Gilman 2020). As Alston (2019) reports, DWSs operate 'in an almost human rights free-zone'.

One DWS case in Australia, the Online Compliance Intervention (OCI), known as Robodebt, is an illustrative example. Robodebt is an automated algorithmic decision-making system introduced in 2015 to enable efficient recovery of welfare overpayments given to welfare recipients (Carney 2018; Alston 2019; Zalnieriute et al. 2019). It replaced the traditional manual review previously conducted by Centrelink staff (from the Australian Department of Human Services). Based on data cross-matching algorithms between the Australian Taxation Office and Centrelink, Robodebt identified any declared income discrepancy in previous years, which was claimed as an overpayment in a debt letter to welfare recipients. The onus was on recipients to disprove the debt claim (e.g. by providing documents, such as payslips, for a specific time period). Private debt collectors were hired to pursue recipients who did not pay their alleged debt. After the first two years of implementation, the Australian government admitted that Robodebt had a 20% error rate (incorrect debt amounts, personal details, employment information, etc.). More serious problems were revealed during two Senate Inquiries (conducted in 2016 and 2019/20). Errors arose not only due to inaccurate data: the logic of the algorithm was clearly shown to be fundamentally flawed. The devastating impact on some individuals (especially people with disabilities or mental health issues) was exacerbated by the lack of direct contact with Centrelink staff and their inability to seek explanation and advice. Many welfare recipients did not understand the debt claims, could not find the required documents to disprove them, or were frightened and distressed by the debt letter. However, they were denied direct interaction with Centrelink staff and were instructed to interact instead with the MyGov online portal. Following the Senate Inquiries and a class action launched in 2019, growing public criticism forced the government to scrap the Robodebt system on 29 May 2020 (Hayne and Doran 2020) and to repay the full amount of 470,000 unlawful debts (estimated to be close to A$1.5bn) to 373,000 past and present welfare recipients (Henriques-Gomes 2020).

The literature reviewed above addresses the deployment of AI algorithms to replace the work of professionals and knowledge workers and to automate judgements and decision-making in a wide range of jobs in both private and public sector organizations. Work automation is justified by increased efficiency and speed of execution (such as selecting job applicants or conducting auditing) as well as increased accuracy or quality of work or decisions (e.g. in administering social security payments or selecting job applicants). Managers typically are the ones who make and justify decisions to use AI systems to automate the work of knowledge workers. However, managers themselves have not been spared from automation (Holford 2020). Kellogg et al. (2020), for instance, discuss the 'disintermediation of managers' in their roles of directing, evaluating, and disciplining workers. Their examples show how AI technologies are used to reconfigure the control of work that cannot (as yet) be automated. By automating managers' roles and eliminating human oversight of work allocation and assessment of outcomes, companies are enacting a novel form of algorithmic control of work and workers that is even more efficient, inhumane, and insidious than the traditional form of bureaucratic control (Weber 1947). As explained by Kellogg et al. (2020: 387):

> [t]echnical and bureaucratic regimes of control also included human decisions that could be made with varying degrees of discretion. The ability for workers

> to appeal to a human decision-maker means that bureaucratic systems, in many ways, allowed for more leeway than algorithmic systems that may remove human decision making altogether from control structures.

The replacement of managers by algorithms is happening via micro labour or on-demand labour platforms, such as Amazon Mechanical Turk (AMT), that provide infrastructure for employers to crowdsource work that cannot be automated. This can include, for instance, web content inspection and classification; training algorithms in pattern recognition; testing software; labelling images; translating; transcribing audio files; and other 'human intelligence tasks' (HITs) (Irani 2015). These HITs are typically atomized and offered as micro tasks on a platform, together with instructions on how to complete them and the associated payment rate (on average, a micro task on AMT is paid US$1–2). Completion of a single HIT can engage thousands of workers. This new phenomenon of 'human computation' hidden in the shadows of AI automation is called 'ghost work' by Gray and Suri (2019). Thousands of invisible, expendable, and unprotected ghost workers are momentarily contracted in digital assembly lines operating in the background of websites and AI systems.

The emergence of a new world of work through different forms and modes of the algorithmic automation of knowledge work is evident in all industry sectors and all types of organization. The dominant public discourse and literature across different disciplines largely celebrate the AI-powered automation of knowledge work and the global benefits of increasing efficiency, speed, and profitability. However, a growing number of studies questions these benefits and provides evidence of significant harmful social consequences, both unintended and intended (e.g. Pasquale 2015; O'Neil 2016; Eubanks 2018; Alston 2019; Ferguson 2019; Ajunwa 2020; Kellogg et al. 2020). The current discourse in the literature about the algorithmic automation of knowledge work suggests that it is now critical to understand the discrepancy between the claims of unquestioned benefits and superiority of the algorithmic automation of knowledge work and the emerging evidence of their harmful social consequences. To contribute to this understanding, I argue that it is necessary to engage with some fundamental questions regarding the nature of knowledge work and its algorithmic incarnation in AI automated systems. In the following sections, I therefore attempt to examine a few intriguing questions: What are the fundamental assumptions about knowledge work in AI-powered automated knowledge work systems? Why do these assumptions matter for making claims about the superiority (objectivity, accuracy, fairness, ethicality) of knowledge work automation?

Why are these assumptions problematic? What kind of world (of knowledge work) do the AI-powered automated systems enact?

These assumptions, however, are not inevitable and, by implication, neither are the consequences of AI-based systems. The nature of AI automation systems (i.e. their underlying assumptions) and their role in knowledge work could be otherwise. After examining the above questions, inspired by Ingold (2015, 2017), I will imagine another world of knowledge work in which AI-enabled systems 'co-respond' with human workers in the flows of work and life.

## 4.3 Assumptions about Knowledge Work in AI-powered Automated Systems

Examples of the AI automation of knowledge work and algorithmic decision-making—previously performed by professionals and knowledge workers, such as HR professionals, managers, auditors, social security case managers, judges, and police officers, as discussed above—share some important characteristics. Knowledge work in these contexts is conceived as a set of distinct, self-contained work and decision-making tasks, such as assessments, predictions or decisions, each describable by generic rules that apply to various 'objects of work', such as job applicants, recipients of social security, or police suspects.

To be precise, the generic rules are not applied to individuals as *objects of work*, but to the data sets 'representing' them, that is, to *datafied* individuals (Galliers et al. 2017; Marjanovic and Cecez-Kecmanovic 2017). The data sets are chosen to sufficiently accurately represent properties of the objects of work so that algorithmic execution of the work task—the production of assessments, predictions, or decisions—is objective, correct, and fair. The use of these data sets to execute a work task is a critical aspect of the algorithmic automation of knowledge work. While some data sets are collected directly from individuals (e.g. from job applicants or social security claimants), most are acquired from various external sources (e.g. health records, social media, and retail and browsing history). In situations in which accurate data cannot be obtained, the designers use so-called proxy data (e.g. an individual's postcode is used as a proxy for their socioeconomic status). While generic rules are applied to such data sets (datafied individuals), often unchecked and of questionable quality, the automated execution of a work task produces important outcomes (decisions/assessments/predictions) for *actual* individuals. For instance, an individual is allocated social security payments or is rejected, or a citizen is assigned a high-risk score by a risk assessment system and thus put on the list of suspects for predictive policing. Furthermore, these outcomes then become 'properties' of these individuals and are recorded in the data sets, which may then be used by other algorithmic automation systems as part of the ongoing datafication of individuals (Marjanovic and Cecez-Kecmanovic 2017). In such a way, data about individuals are propagated, become combined with other data and processed, and thus are amplified in unknowable ways (Pasquale 2015; Kitchin 2017). This suggests that problems with the use of data sets to 'objectively' and 'correctly' represent the objects of work in the algorithmic automation of knowledge work are largely hidden and much more complex than is admitted by the companies designing or applying them.

Furthermore, the generic rules that purportedly describe a work task are either explicitly defined in advance or learned by algorithms from past data sets. In the former case, known as the traditional analytical approaches to AI, algorithms include explicit rules, hard coded in the form of analytic models, which compute outputs based on input data sets (Chollet 2018; Reese 2018). This approach, also known as symbolic AI, is considered appropriate for well-defined knowledge work tasks, in which it is possible to define a set of relevant variables (and related data sets) and formal rules (e.g. analytics models) to execute a work task and compute the outcome.

However, for ill-defined, complex knowledge work tasks, such as those including judgement, experiential knowledge, and moral reasoning, analytical models cannot be developed. Instead, *learning algorithms* are used that draw from past data sets to infer the connection (i.e. correlations) between data points (Baer and Kamalnath 2017; Kitchin 2017). *Supervised learning algorithms*, for instance, learn from the training data sets that contain problem situations (parameters) and correct answers. Sometimes, they can also receive real-time feedback. Although these algorithms may use different techniques, they generally seek to 'uncover' patterns in the data and find the best parameter configurations to match known and/or correct answers (Buchanan and Miller 2017). *Unsupervised learning algorithms*, on the other hand, draw from large quantities of unstructured data and seek to identify patterns or clusters with some common characteristics. *Reinforcement learning algorithms* use a machine learning agent that observes an environment (such as a game) and learns how to connect conditions and decisions (moves). Different to these three types, *deep learning algorithms* are based on a distinct architecture while using any of these three types for specific learning tasks. Deep learning algorithms use neural networks (imitating the neurons in the brain) with input, output, and multiple hidden middle layers that are structured to 'optimize' learning (Buchanan and Miller 2017). They typically use large amounts of real-world sensory data (texts, images, sounds) to 'learn' how to recognize and classify patterns in input data linked to outputs (e.g. to connect past behaviour patterns to decisions), that is, to learn 'input–output mappings' (Chollet 2018). Outputs can be words, categories, places on a chess board, decisions, or any outcome to which the given input data can be mapped. In other words, a deep learning algorithm approximates 'an unknown function f(x)=y between any input x and output y ... often referred to as "the universal approximator", whereby it assumes that they are related either by correlation or causation' (Holford 2020: 61).

The rules learned by learning algorithms and, in particular, by deep learning algorithms are not known and typically remain opaque in the production of outputs. Most often not even the designers of these algorithms can explain how outputs are calculated. Given the rising concerns about the opacity and inscrutability of algorithmic decision-making, attempts are being made to regulate the 'right to explanation' and to design algorithms that include some forms of 'explanability' (Edwards and Veale 2017). With an inceasing sense of urgency there are calls for developments of 'explainable AI' and 'interpretable machine learning' (Murdoch et al. 2019).

From this short analysis, we can see that the algorithmic execution of knowledge work is premised on the existence of work tasks that are conceived as self-contained entities consisting of: (i) data sets that represent the objects of work sufficiently, accurately, and comprehensively; and (ii) generic rules (explicitly defined or learned from data) that apply to the data sets (representing objects of work) to produce correct and fair outcomes (assessments, predictions, decisions). Furthermore, algorithmic work automation systems themselves are considered 'technical, self-contained objects' (Beer 2017), existing separately from the social processes from which they acquire data as well as from those to which they provide outcomes, purportedly in an accurate, objective, and fair manner.

This suggests that the world of knowledge work executed by AI-powered automated systems is a paradigmatic case of the *entitative* or *substantialist* ontology which, following Descartes, assumes that reality consists of self-contained, bounded entities or substances that exist independently of other substances (Mesle 2008; Cecez-Kecmanovic 2016). Objects of work (applicants, citizens) are seen as substances that exist in reality as self-contained, bounded entities described by their properties. The properties of objects of work are 'represented' by various data sets, assumed to contain factual knowledge relevant and sufficient for the execution of work tasks (e.g. to assess and select job applicants, calculate risk scores, determine fraudulent welfare recipients), as discussed above. Furthermore, it is assumed that the generic rules encoded in algorithms (explicitly defined or learned) 'represent' the knowledge necessary to execute these work tasks. In other words, the rules represent the logic of work tasks, irrespective of a specific context. These epistemological assumptions are characteristic of *representationalism* (Healy 2005; Barad 2007).

In summary, the automation of knowledge work tasks by AI-powered systems is based on the following fundamental assumptions:

1. The **ontological assumption** about the *existence of knowledge work tasks* as independent, self-contained entities, each of which consists of

    a. *objects of work.* and
    b. *generic rules* that apply to objects of work.

    A knowledge work task is executed by applying rules to the objects of work to produce outcomes (decisions, assessments, predictions).

2. The **epistemological assumptions** that:

    a. data sets *represent* the objects of work objectively, accurately, and comprehensivel, and
    b. generic rules (explicitly defined or learned) *represent* the logic or reasoning involved in a knowledge work task, objectively, accurately, and comprehensively.

    Conseqently, when rules (encoded in algorithms) are applied to the given data sets, the work task is executed, producing or calculating accurate, objective, and fair outcomes.

The substantialist ontology and representational epistemology that underpin AI-powered automated knowledge work systems are of critical importance in understanding the claims made about their superior performance. These claims state that algorithmic systems that execute knowledge work are not only highly efficient but are also, and importantly, accurate and objective (neutral), fair, and ethical (not biased or discriminatory), and thus superior to the performance of the knowledge workers they replace (e.g. Kitchin 2017; Markus 2017; Caplan et al. 2018; Holford 2019, 2020). It is largely taken for granted that 'algorithms signify objectivity, consistency, impartiality, legitimacy and authority in the production' of outcomes (Sheehey 2018: 51). These claims cannot be made without implying the fundamental ontological and epistemological assumptions stated above. When evidence is provided to the contrary, the typical response by designers of AI systems, IT companies selling them, and those using them, is that any bias, unfairness, or inaccuracy is an unintended and temporary error that can and will be fixed. The solution is often seen as a question of correcting some data sets or improving the rules (e.g. the learning of the algorithms) (e.g. Bellamy et al. 2018). The underlying assumptions are not questioned.

## 4.4 The AI-powered Automation of Knowledge Work: Questioning the Assumptions

The world of work encoded in and enacted by the AI-powered automated knowledge work systems—underpinned by the substantialist ontology and representationalist epistemology as discussed above—is the world of *blobs*. As Tim Ingold reminds us, in sociology and other disciplines, it is

> usual to think of persons or organisms as *blobs* of one sort or another. Blobs have insides and outsides, divided at their surfaces. . . . They may bump into one another, aggregate together, even meld into larger blobs rather like drops of oil spilled on the surface of water.
>
> **(2015: 3, emphasis added)**

In the information systems (IS) literature, it is not uncommon to see reality composed of blobs: people, work processes, organizations, and technologies, are considered given and self-contained entities, described by properties and relationships with other entities (see the explicit elaboration by Weber [2012]). More specifically, in AI-powered automated knowledge work systems, individuals as objects of work are blobs (represented as data points), while rules that represent the logic of work tasks are another kind of blob. A work task automated by an AI system is also a blob consisting of two blobs—the objects of work blob and the rules blob—that interact to perform the task. The nature and boundary of each of these blobs are determined by the purpose of the automated system.

The promoted ideal of AI automated knowledge work—grounded in the fundamental assumptions of entitative ontology and representational epistemology (stated above)—is a pure world of blobs, involving the interaction of nothing but blobs. Thus, I call these assumptions 'blob world assumptions'. Why are these assumptions problematic?

First, as noted before, in AI-powered automated work systems, objects of work as blobs are not individuals but instead *datafied individuals* (data sets)—compiled from social media posts, health records, purchasing transactions, search history, crime records, social security evidence, tax records, and other sources. Rules (often learned from past data and opaque) are applied to these datafied individuals to calculate the outcomes (e.g. applicants are selected or rejected for a job; individuals are assigned risk scores that predict their likelihood of offending; citizens are eligible or not eligible for social security payments) that typically have material effects on the *actual* individuals. However, these effects on individuals are not of interest in the world of AI-powered automated knowledge work. This is the consequence of the ontological and epistemological assumptions stated above: work task blobs executed by algorithms include neither actual individuals nor the effects on these individuals. The only effect considered is the update of relevant data sets (e.g. the risk scores for individuals are updated in the police suspect data set) that may then be used by other algorithms. In the blob world of AI-powered automated knowledge work, no concerns exist for impacts on actual individuals or communities.

Second, in the blob world of AI-powered automated knowledge work, 'knowledge' for executing work tasks that is generic, value-free, and independent of contexts, implying a 'view from nowhere' (Adam 2006). The view from nowhere is Descartes' legacy that, as Nagel (1986) argues, perpetuates the objectivist belief that true knowledge is disembodied, value-free, and universal, expressing context-free reason and logic. Claimed to be capable of learning and reasoning in a manner that is independent of social context and the related biases of social actors (Kitchin 2017; Caplan et al. 2018; Sheehey 2018; Ferguson 2019; Holford 2019, 2020), AI-powered automated knowledge work systems espouse the view from nowhere. This view persists despite growing evidence that shows precisely the opposite: that AI-powered automated knowledge work systems imply a very distinct view from a position of power and privilege. Recall, for instance, as discussed above, the case of DWSs adopted by governments worldwide to improve social protection and provide better services to citizens (Alston 2019). Claimed to be objective, value-free, and fair, DWSs espouse the view from nowhere when they verify citizens' eligibility for various benefits, automate the calculation of benefit payments, or detect fraud and enact actions. As revealed in Alston's United Nations (UN) report (2019) about DWS deployment around the world, DWSs negatively affect the most vulnerable and often punish the 'intended beneficiaries' (having, in many cases, an undeclared objective of cutting social security budgets). Rather than the view from nowhere, DWSs clearly exemplify the view from the position of power, the view that often disregards human rights.

Third, the view from nowhere is grounded in representationalist thinking which is deeply entrenched in Western culture. Representationalism, Barad writes, 'is the belief in the ontological distinction between representations and that which they purport to represent; [and] in particular, that which is represented is held to be *independent of all practices of representing*' (2007: 46, my emphasis). Similarly, Healy argues that the key problem is that

> Representational thinking results from the erasure of the processes and practices enabling, generating and reproducing cognitive representations. This erasure legitimates representationalism because with it these representations then simply mirror the world. 'Facts' speak for themselves for precisely this reason. They are granted autonomy—*status as things in themselves*—by denying the human effort and artifice involved in their manufacture.
>
> (2005: 242, emphasis in the original)

Such representational thinking is reflected in the epistemological assumptions behind the AI automation of knowledge work articulated in Section 4.3. The data sets processed by algorithms in AI work automation systems are treated as facts that *represent* the relevant properties of targeted individuals or other entities accurately, objectively, and comprehensively, irrespective of data collection processes. In other words, data mirror the real world, while being ontologically separate.

Even when data are purposively collected, they reflect the commercial and power interests and agendas (Beer 2017) and are far from being objective and value-free. More often, as we have seen, data sets are acquired from a range of sources (social media, retail companies, health records) disregarding the processes of their creation, and the inherent issues in their re-use, re-combination, and re-interpretation that typically result in the distortion or loss of meaning (Marjanovic and Cecez-Kecmanovic 2017). Worryingly, these datafication practices and the resulting distortion of meaning of data sets used in AI work automation systems are opaque and not easily scrutinized (Caplan et al. 2018; Benjamin 2019). This reveals inherent flaws in such a representational view of the data in the AI work automation systems and the problems (and dangers) hidden behind the epistemological assumption about objective, non-biased, and fair representation of objects of work.

Furthermore, the epistemological assumption that the rules *represent* the logic of knowledge work tasks in the AI automation of knowledge work systems objectively, accurately, and comprehensively—ensuring that the outcomes (decisions/predictions) are accurate, objective, and fair—is yet another assumption requiring critical examination. Such a representation of the logic of knowledge work in automated systems is achieved by encoding rules in either explicit or implicit ways, as discussed above. In the case of encoding the explicit rules or models, it is assumed that the rules are correct, sufficient, and reasonably complete to accurately and fairly calculate outcomes based on input data sets. This analytic approach to the algorithmic automation of knowledge work reduces all human knowledge engaged in knowledge work—such as sensemaking, comprehension, assessment, judgement, learning, and moral reasoning—to explicit formal rules, ignoring the nature of human knowledge (Mackenzie and Vurdubakis 2011; Sanzogni et al. 2017; Hadjimichael and Tsoukas 2019; Holford 2019). Particularly striking is the disregard for knowledge as it is situated in practice (Suchman 2007; Gherardi 2019) and the notion of tacit knowledge that underlays all knowledge (Polanyi 1958, Polanyi 1966a; Polanyi 1966b; Tsoukas 2011). This reductionist view of knowledge work abstracts the key features of knowledge—how it is embedded in practice, how it is created and how it grows, always undergoing construction and transformation in use (Gherardi 2018, 2019). Furthermore, this view ignores the importance and contextual sensitivity of tacit knowledge and the ways in which it is embedded and embodied in work practices and co-constituted with explicit knowledge in skilled performance (Polanyi 1966a; Polanyi 1966b; Dreyfus and Dreyfus 2005; Tsoukas 2011).

This criticism has arguably been addressed by machine learning algorithms. As 'an atheoretical brute force technique' (Autor 2015: 25), machine learning only needs large training databases and sophisticated algorithms to identify patterns and purportedly capture the *actual* knowledge that governs specific knowledge work tasks, including whatever tacit knowledge is involved (Holford 2019, 2020). So, how do AI automated knowledge work systems based on machine learning address the criticism regarding the reductionist nature of knowledge in automated knowledge work? The answer is: with a peculiar representationalist claim that *unknown knowledge used in an actual work task that is discovered through machine learning is represented objectively (as it actually is) by implicit, opaque rules that nobody can know or scrutinize.* Despite the criticism of the 'black box' nature of 'knowledge' and of the inexplicability of their outcomes, AI automation of knowledge work systems is adopted and justified by perpetuating the myth that these systems 'learn' from past experience to imitate human reasoning, judgement, and decision-making.

Furthermore, this representationalist understanding of knowledge work—increasingly promoted by developers and adopters of AI-powered automated knowledge work systems—implies that the knowledge captured through machine learning maps the causal relationships between inputs and outputs. As Leetaru (2019) writes, there is a 'flawed tendency to interpret or describe the patterns captured in [machine learning] models as causative rather than correlations of unknown veracity, accuracy or impact'. While remaining unquestioned, representationalist assumptions effectively preclude wider understanding of the flaws and myths of AI automation of knowledge work and justify the disregarding of calls for accountability.

While machine learning technologies have advanced remarkably in recent years, especially in domains such as computer vision and face recognition, speech recognition and synthesis, and natural language translation, their adoption in the automation of knowledge work is problematic, to say the least, precisely owing to the reductionist nature of knowledge and the failure to address that well-argued criticism. This indicates why the 'translation' of machine learning technologies (such as Watson or DeepMind) from the complex but bounded and mechanical problem domains of games (such as chess and Go) to the social domain of knowledge work practices has not resulted in the transfer of success, despite claims to the contrary (Beer 2017; Buchanan and Miller 2017; Holford 2020). Neither analytic approaches to modelling knowledge tasks (in the form of formal rules and models) nor machine learning technologies can 'capture' or 'discover' the holistic nature of human knowledge—including its central tacit dimension—that is indispensable to knowledge work. While this topic deserves broader elaboration, for the purpose of this chapter, a brief discussion will suffice.

Knowledge work in everyday practices is not experienced as a set of self-contained work tasks performed by following rules. Knowledge work is instead perceived as skilful performance, situated in practice, implying 'knowledgeable practice' and 'knowing in practice' (Orlikowski 2002; Gherardi 2019). Drawing from the well-established stream of literature that builds from Ryle (1949) and Polanyi (1958, 1966a, 1966b), we can obtain a deeper understanding of human knowledge and knowing in practice. Polanyi's oft-quoted statement that '*we can know more than we can tell*' (1966a: 4, emphasis in the original), refers to knowledge that we cannot express in words, that is, tacit knowledge. Human knowledge, Polanyi writes, in agreement with Ryle, involves both the 'knowing how' (or tacit knowledge) and the 'knowing that' (or explicit knowledge) or, in other words, the practical and the theoretical knowledge which 'have a similar structure and neither is ever present without the other' (Polanyi 1966a: 7). Polanyi emphasizes that tacit knowledge or, more precisely,

> tacit knowing is not a static body of knowledge, but a perceptual process that relies on the integration of 'focal' and 'subsidiary' awareness. One must attend from aspects that are subsidiary to one's attention to be focally aware of something else about the action ... The integration of subsidiary and focal awareness is referred to as indwelling.
>
> **(Hadjimichael and Tsoukas 2019: 675)**

It is not only that we recall all relevant aspects of the action at hand (focal awareness), but we also intuitively engage particulars of which we are only subsidiarily aware. As these particulars are tacitly drawn from the inarticulate background and become integrated with our focal awareness, we cannot control or separate them. If we attempt to do so, we disrupt the process and disable our performance. For example, while playing, a pianist is focused on the music of which he/she is focally aware. If he/she suddenly draws attention to the movement of his/her fingers, he/she cannot play any more. Furthermore, any new situation and focal action invoke distinct particulars, leading to a novel integration of subsidiary and focal awareness. Through such indwelling, our skilled performance, in turn, becomes absorbed into the inarticulate background. Polanyi (1966b: 7) convincingly concludes that 'all knowledge is either tacit or rooted in tacit knowledge. A wholly explicit knowledge is unthinkable.'

In knowledge work in practice, becoming a knowledge worker and a skilled practitioner—as practice scholars emphasize—involves socialization into a sociomaterial practice (Brown and Duguid 2001). Through socialization, knowledge workers become culturally and socially embedded, and learn social norms and rules, professional language, routines, and vocabulary. By socializing in the way of life, knowledge workers 'learn to attend from certain subsidiary particulars to become focally aware of an object of perception ... [hence] the individual is seen to always dwell in social knowledge' (Hadjimichael and Tsoukas 2019: 690–691). It is important to understand that there is no contradiction here: by being human, knowledge is inherently social, and vice versa. 'Although practice scholars maintain that knowledge is inherently social, they emphatically underscore the personal nature of knowing' (Hadjimichael and Tsoukas 2019: 689).

While performing in practice, knowledge workers also encounter ethical and moral concerns. Knowing in practice, human knowledge and action also involve moral reasoning and judgement. 'Unlike the games at which AI has excelled, human morality is not a closed, well-defined domain with a finite list of identifiable features whose importance and relationships can be precisely analyzed in advance' (Hasselberger 2019: 988). In the practice of knowledge workers (HR professionals, auditors, managers, judges, police officers), every concrete work and decision-making situation potentially involves a new moral aspect that cannot be predicted in advance or inferred from past decisions. Therefore, the moral relevance of the features of particular situations are not generally predictable nor are they 'generically' specifiable.

The above, very brief elaboration on the nature of human knowledge and knowledge work in practice exposes some key arguments for problematizing the assumption that the generic rules (explicit or implicit) in the AI automation of knowledge work *represent* the essence of the work task and that, thereby, the task is performed accurately, objectively, and ethically. By mapping the categories of input into an output, drawing from past data (about work tasks such as sentencing), an algorithm can 'capture' post factum some logic (implicit rules) of decision-making in the past. However, in each new work task (a new court case, a new situation for welfare eligibility), human knowledge is not simply a replica from past judgements/decisions; rather, a novel integration of subsidiary and focal awareness is invoked, of which knowledge workers are not aware. Their insight into a case or a situation is holistic, involving particular and context-specific aspects, both 'know how' and 'know that', as well as empathetic understanding and moral judgement, that are always new and always specific.

The substantialist ontology and representationalist epistemology are not only assumed by the AI knowledge work automation systems, their continued execution present particular 'ways of worldmaking' (Goodman, 1995) and enacting the world in their image. Objects of work are performed in the image derived from datafied individuals by applying the flawed, often opaque and inscrutable logic encoded in algorithms. Citizens become crime suspects before committing any crime; welfare recipients become fraudsters without a due process; job applicants are made unfit for jobs, based on the algorithmic assessment of interviews. In the blob world enacted by AI automation, knowledge work is reduced to a bounded, self-contained mechanism, a blob detached from practice, that runs based on impoverished knowledge—rules applied to data sets, often unchecked and unreliable. Despite the overwhelming evidence of harmful social implications, the concept of AI-based knowledge work automation grounded on blob world assumptions persists and continues to be promoted as the bright future of highly efficient knowledge work. The dominant discourses, in response to the harmful social implications, focus, on the one hand, on demands for improving and regulating the use of big data and open data sets to eliminate biases, discrimination, and injustices. On the other hand, the focus is on advancing the algorithms, especially machine learning, that should make them more accurate, fair, and ethical. These discourses, however, have a somewhat paradoxical consequence: they legitimate and normalize the current approach to applying AI technologies to *automate* knowledge work. What is rarely questioned is the very concept of AI-based knowledge work automation and the blob world it assumes and reinforces. The blob world assumptions and their critical role in maintaining the myth of the objectivity and supremacy of the AI automation of knowledge work are neither revealed nor debated.

Deeper insight into the fundamental assumptions reveals that the 'perfect' blob world of AI automated knowledge work systems is far from perfect. As warned by Ingold (2015: 4): 'in the world of blobs there could be no social life'. Evidence from the literature reveals the cracks in the perfect blob world of AI automated knowledge work systems (Steiner 2012; O'Neil 2016; Wachter-Boettcher 2017; Eubanks 2018). As the 'lines' emerge from the cracks, we see the life beyond blobs. We see people 'identified' as high-risk citizens and subjected to surveillance and police checking (Sheehey 2018). We learn about gender and racial discrimination in algorithmic recruitment (Ajunwa 2020). The Australian government abandoned Robodebt and was forced to compensate citizens that it had unlawfully accused of fraud and accordingly charged (Hayne and Doran 2020). These 'lines of life' escape from the blob world of automated knowledge work systems, suggesting that the image of perfect blobs is a myth. The blob world, in Ingold's words, 'is profoundly out of touch with life' (2015: 16).

## 4.5 Reimagining Knowledge Work: Workers and AI Working in Sympathy

Thinking with Ingold's (2015), I invite you to imagine a different world of knowledge work, a world in which knowledge workers and AI-based algorithmic systems *co-respond* to each other and work in *sympathy* to innovate and enhance knowledge work beyond the capacity of each. Central to this imagining is our liberation from the ideal of (or obsession with) the *automation* of knowledge work and the ultimate *replacement* of knowledge workers by AI systems. Our imagining requires us to see the world of knowledge work as open and continually coming into being, offering innumerable and untapped possibilities for embracing the powers of AI technologies to enrich work and enhance human creative capacities. The ontology of becoming and Ingold's (2015, 2017) theory of correspondence help us to illuminate the vision of knowledge work. This vision is open to the dynamic potential of discovery and innovation when knowledge workers and AI systems are 'bound in sympathy' and 'joined inside' rather than interacting as blobs on the outside. Mutually related in sympathy while co-working, knowledge workers and AI systems would become affiliated, 'joined-with', while answering to one another, that is, working in correspondence with each other.

In order to continue imagining with Ingold (2015, 2017), let us briefly introduce his distinct vocabulary (or remind those already 'in the know'). Ingold talks of 'clinging' or 'holding on to each other' or 'joining-with' as the essence of sociality. Importantly, sociality is not 'limited to the human but extends across the entire panoply of clingers and those to whom, or that to which, they cling. But what happens when people or things cling to one another? There is an entwining of lines' (Ingold 2015: 3). For Ingold, every being or thing is a line or, more precisely, a 'bundle of lines'. So, when people and things cling to each other or join-with each other, their lifelines become entangled. To describe the entangling of lines in the mesh of social life, Ingold suggests:

> think[ing] in terms of knots. ... A knot is formed when a strand such as of string or yarn is interlaced with itself or another strand and tightened. I suggest that in a world where things are continually coming into being through processes of growth and movement—that is, in a world of life—knotting is the fundamental principle of coherence.... [A knot's] topology is such that one can never determine what is on the inside or on the outside. Knots don't have insides and outsides; they have interstices. Their surfaces, rather than enveloping their material mass, lie between the lines that make them up.
>
> **(2017: 10)**

In continuing to follow Ingold (2015, 2017), what if we were to think of knowledge work, knowledge workers, and AI systems not as bounded, self-contained blobs but as bundles of lines, perpetually in the process of entangling and untangling, while they co-work and grow knowledge? We might imagine knowledge work in which human workers and AI systems are 'joined-with' in complex problem-solving and decision-making processes, in such a way that their lines are creatively knotting within an unbounded nexus of relationships. Their knotting would involve the mutual drawing on each other's capacities for investigating, questioning, searching, processing, interpreting, analysing, and reasoning, to mention a few. They would build on each other's distinct strengths, in the ongoing process of engaging and growing knowledge. Such a vision of knowledge work assumes that knowledge workers and AI technologies attend to each other and respond with heed. For instance, humans would draw from the processing and analytical power of AI and machine learning capabilities, while AI systems would rely on human knowledge, experience, interpretation, intuition, creativity, heuristics, moral understanding and judgement, empathy with others, and a holistic assessment of a problem/situation. In such 'joining-with', knowledge workers and AI systems would co-create and grow human knowledge while, at the same time, advancing the processing and learning capability of AI systems.

Unlike the blob world, in which knowledge is formalized and packaged, applied as fixed in the automation of knowledge work, in the world of knots, in the meshwork of knowledge work,

> knowledge grows from the crucible of lives lived with others, in the in-between. This knowledge consists not in propositions about the world but in the skills of perception and capacities of judgement that develop in the course of direct, practical and sensuous engagements with the beings and things with whom, and with which, we share our lives.
>
> **(Ingold 2015: 157)**

In knowledge work, the crucible of lives lived with others cannot be limited to knowledge workers and AI technologies. In the open and fluid notion of knowledge work as flows of ongoing knotting and re-knotting of lines, problems and situations emerge (e.g. citizens lose jobs; police observe increased crime rates in a region; organizations search for talent) and the people concerned or affected become a focus of knowledge workers (e.g. as applicants for welfare benefits; as potential suspects; as applicants for jobs). Those about whom decisions are made and who thus become affected by the outcomes of knowledge work (assessments, predictions, decisions) cannot be assumed to be external, datafied entities (blobs), disconnected from work processes, as we see in the examples of automated work discussed earlier. The lifelines of actual people—citizens, clients, applicants, communities—are knotted in the flow of knowledge work, entangled with that of knowledge workers and AI systems. They are 'joining-with' and, at certain points, disentangling from the ongoing flow of knowledge work.

Furthermore, the meshwork of knowledge work involves lines 'joining-with' broader sociomaterial environments, such as organizational policies, values, norms, and laws, as well as professional knowledge, standards, and ethics. Socialization into the sociomaterial environment immanent to knowledge work practices can be imagined as the lines flowing from meshwork and knotting and unknotting with other lines. These are the lines along which attending to social norms, values, and rules, professional ethics and knowledge, and organizational processes and routines are enacted. Thus, these are the lines of socialization and learning, critical to the becoming of the knowledge workers and AI technologies relational complex.

As this discussion suggests, the meshwork of knowledge work continuously comes into being through the knotting of the whole panoply of lines that emerge in each concrete situation. While knowledge workers engage with people (subjects of work) they grow their skills of perception and their abilities to attend to and assess their specific circumstances. In this process, knowledge workers also co-respond with AI systems as they co-explore relevant histories, events, and additional evidence bearing on specific cases (court decisions, job applications). This mutually triggering process involves much knotting and unknotting of lines—drawing from workers' knowledge, including moral and ethical reasoning, while relying on AI processing and learning capacity (occurring in unpredictable cycles)—which, in turn, grow knowledge and enhance capacity for attending to people and their situations. As their knowledge about and attentiveness to subjects grow, knowledge workers' capacities for ethical and moral judgement and decision-making also grow. When knowledge workers ultimately arrive at an assessment or decision (outcome) about the subjects, their lines are re-knotted, affecting not only the subjects but also themselves as knowledge workers and AI systems in the process. This illustrates how practical and mutually attentive engagements in the meshwork of work is generative of the ongoing processes of becoming: knowledge workers are co-constituted as knowledgeable and competent professionals; AI systems are enacted as effective and reliable 'collaborators;' while individuals (subjects of work) are co-constructed as guilty/innocent offenders, un/successful job applicants, or un/deserving welfare recipients. They are all becoming who they are through a multiplicity of heterogeneous flows of lines in the meshwork of work. In other words, the meshwork of knowledge work is constitutive of their ongoing becoming.

Compared to the blob world of AI-enabled automation of knowledge work, the vision of knowledge work as meshwork offers a radically different view of the world of work that poses some new questions regarding ethics and responsibility. In the meshwork of knowledge work where lines of knowledge workers, subjects of work, and AI systems (as well as social, professional, and normative environments) co-respond, and where knotting enfolds, decisions or assessments (outcomes) are co-produced. That is, the outcomes that shape the conditions of possibilities for individuals and who or what they become—such as being imprisoned, getting a job, being a social welfare recipient—are co-produced. How can we conceive of ethics and responsibility for the outcomes thus co-produced?

First, the question is one of responsibility for outcomes and, ultimately, for the performing of the subjects of work. Responsibility lies in the attentional quality of the meshwork, that is, in responsiveness to the unfolding flow of lines (knowledge workers, AI systems, subjects of work, social, professional, and normative environments, etc.) and their knotting and unknotting that create new possibilities, while closing others down. In other words, being attentive and responsive to these ever-changing conditions of co-production is what enables responsibility. In Ingold's words, 'responsibility rests on responsiveness' (2017: 24). As responsive beings, knowledge workers are conditioned by the prior enfolding of possibilities for decisions in the meshwork but are, nevertheless, responsible for the choices made in any specific situation.

Second, in relation to the choices made, that is, the decisions regarding the subjects of work, knowledge workers have the 'responsibility of care'. Importantly, as Ingold reminds us, 'the responsibility of care is something that falls to us.... To care for others, we must allow them into our presence so that we, in turn, can be present to them. In an important sense, we must let them be, so that they can speak to us' (2017: 20). This might be a guiding principle of care that could take many different forms in concrete knowledge work practices. It may entail responsiveness to the multiple co-responding lines that have been knotting in the past, related to targeted individuals and their specific conditions. What are the appropriate and reliable sources of data? How are they acquired, checked, recorded, and processed by AI systems? Are the data collected and processed according to relevant values, norms, laws, and rules? Responsiveness to actual individuals (their current and future needs) is also entailed: what are the appropriate modes of communication with such individuals within the normative and ethical concerns and practical constraints of any given situation?

In the meshwork of knowledge work, the responsibility of care implies the extending of lines towards subjects of work in a way that is continually and skilfully responsive to their emerging co-construction and the creation/limitations of their possibilities to be. When responsiveness grows and becomes immanent in practice, knowledge workers' 'joining-with' AI technology develop their moral and practical knowledge about how to responsibly care for subjects of work. As part of the co-production of contextually sensitive and morally justified outcomes (assessments, judgements, decisions) about the subjects of work, knowledge workers are co-constructed as moral actors and knowledge work is regarded as a worthwhile and morally justified engagement. Compared to the blob world of AI-powered automated knowledge work, we can see—paraphrasing Hasselberger (2019)—the fundamental moral difference between knowledge work outcomes that result mechanically from an automated execution without any sense of value, purpose, or justification and the outcomes co-produced in the meshwork of knowledge work judged as good, worthwhile, and morally justified.

## 4.6 Conclusion

This chapter contributes to the discourse on the automation of knowledge work by AI-enabled systems and the emerging discrepancy between the harmful social consequences and the dominant claims that the AI-automated knowledge work systems are objective, fair, and ethical, and therefore superior to human knowledge workers. This discrepancy is intriguing. It seems to increase with the increasing sophistication of AI systems and the growing replacement of knowledge workers. Moreover, it is claimed that any unintended bias or discrimination can be eliminated by improving algorithms and the data sets.

The key argument provided in the chapter is that these claims are (and could only be) justified based on the fundamental ontological and epistemological assumptions about the nature of knowledge and knowledge work that underlie these systems. Based on the critical analysis of these assumptions, I show how the AI-enabled automation of knowledge work assumes and enacts the *blob world* of work. In this world, knowledge work is reduced to a bounded, self-contained mechanism, detached from practice, and based on a truncated and impoverished notion of knowledge that is often opaque and unable to be scrutinized. I also show why the blob world of automated knowledge work is fundamentally flawed and why building better algorithms and/or improving the data sets could not redress the harmful social consequences.

The ideal of the automation of knowledge work is certainly not the only way we can productively deploy AI to enhance and enrich knowledge work.

In this chapter, inspired by Ingold's (2015, 2017) theory of correspondence, I imagined another world of knowledge work in which AI-enabled systems 'co-respond' with human workers in the flows of work and life. The imagining of knowledge workers and AI systems working in sympathy, as presented here, is not as quixotic as it might seem. Proposals can already be found in the literature to abandon the idea of the *automation* of knowledge work, seeing it as a threat to performance and sustained competitive advantage (e.g. Davenport and Kirby 2016; Davenport and Bean 2017; Daugherty and Wilson 2018). Instead, it is the *augmentation* of human capabilities, based on 'human–machine symbiosis' and 'synergistic partnership' between AI and human decision makers, that promises significant gains in performance (e.g. Davenport and Kirby 2016; Hoffman 2016; Davenport and Bean 2017; Daugherty and Wilson 2018; Jarrahi 2018). As proposed by Jarrahi (2018), human–machine collaboration should be based on their comparative advantages. While machines are typically superior in dealing with complexity and processing huge quantities of data, humans are superior in dealing with the uncertainty and equivocality that characterize organizational decision-making. These proposals, and especially empirical studies on human–machine cooperative working in practice (Davenport and Kirby 2016; Davenport and Bean 2017; Shestakofsky 2017), emphasize significant organizational and work benefits, such as increasing flexibility and innovation, dealing better with complex and uncertain environments, and enrichment of managers' roles. It is important to note that the arguments put forward for abandoning the automation of knowledge work and for embracing the augmentation of knowledge workers, as presented in the literature, are primarily business- and performance-based, while largely disregarding the harmful social implications. Nevertheless, these arguments are important as they draw attention to the mindless pursuit of efficiency through the AI automation of knowledge work and contribute to wider discourses in society. It is yet to be seen whether such discourses would extend to include the harmful social consequences for organizations, individuals, and society, and whether they would encourage a broader critical attitude toward these consequences, as well as imagining and creating the new world of knowledge work, in which work is continually enhanced and enriched.

As AI developers, companies deploying AI systems, professionals, and scholars—entangled with AI technologies—we all play a part in the becoming of the new world of knowledge work. If we can convincingly imagine and explore in any concrete context how knowledge workers and AI technologies can work together 'in sympathy' and 'joined-with' in co-creating and re-inventing knowledge work as well as themselves, we might catch a glimpse of hope that it would be possible to 'restore to life' a world of knowledge work that has been cut off from the flows of life.

## References


Adam, A. (2006). *Artificial Knowing: Gender and the Thinking Machine.* Routledge.

Ajunwa, I. (2020). 'The Paradox of Automation as Anti-Bias Intervention', *Cardozo Law Review* 41/5: 1671–1742.

Alston, P. (2019). *Report of the Special Rapporteur on Extreme Poverty and Human Rights* (Advance unedited version). UN General Assembly. Report id A/74/48037 https://www.ohchr.org/Documents/Issues/Poverty/A_74_48037_AdvanceUneditedVersion.docx (accessed 24 March 2020).

Aspan, M. (2020). 'A.I. is Transforming the Job Interview—And Everything After; Some of the World's Biggest Companies are Relying on A.I. to Build a Better Workforce', *Fortune*, 20 January.

https://fortune.com/longform/hr-technology-ai-hiring-recruitment/?utm_source=email&utm_medium=newsletter&utm_campaign=eye-on-ai&utm_content=2020012116pm.

Autor, D. H. (2015). 'Why Are There Still So Many Jobs? The History and Future of Workplace Automation', *The Journal of Economic Perspectives* 2/3: 3–30.

Baer, T. and Kamalnath, V. (2017). 'Controlling Machine-Learning Algorithms and Their Biases'. McKinsey&Company. https://www.mckinsey.com/business-functions/risk/our-insights/controlling-machine-learning-algorithms-and-their-biases.

Barad, K. (2007). *Meeting the Universe Halfway: Quantum Physics and the Entanglement of Matter and Meaning.* Duke University Press.

Beer, D. (2017). 'The Social Power of Algorithms', *Information, Communication & Society* 20/1: 1–13.

Bellamy, R., Deym K., Hind, M., Hoffman, S.C., Houde, S., et al. (2018). 'AI Fairness 360: An Extensible Toolkit for Detecting, Understanding, and Mitigating Unwanted Algorithmic Bias', *IBM Research*, arXiv:1810.01943.

Benbya, H., Pachidi, S., and Jarvenpaa, S. (2021). 'Special Issue Editorial: Artificial Intelligence in Organizations: Implications for Information Systems Research', *Journal of the Association for Information Systems* 22/2: 281–303.

Benjamin, B. (2019). *Race after Technology.* Polity Press.

Bornstein, S. (2018). 'Antidiscriminatory Algorithms', *Alabama Law Review* 70/2: 519–570.

Brown, J. S., and Duguid, P. (2001). 'Knowledge and Organization: A Social-Practice Perspective', *Organization Science* 12/2: 198–213.

Buchanan, B., and Miller, T. (2017). *Machine Learning for Policymakers: What It Is and Why It Matters.* The Cyber Security Project. Belfer Center for Science and International Affairs, Harvard Kennedy School.

Bughin, J., Hazan, E., Lund, S., Dahlstrom, P., Wiesinger, A., and Subramaniam, A. (2018). *Skill Shift Automation and the Future of the Workforce.* McKinsey Global Institute (May 2018). https://www.mckinsey.com/featured-insights/future-of-work/skill-shift-automation-and-the-future-of-the-workforce.

Caplan, R., Donovan J., Hanson, L., and Matthews, J. (2018). *Algorithmic Accountability: A Primer.* The Congressional Progressive Caucus. 18 April. Data & Society, Washington, DC. USA.

https://datasociety.net/wpcontent/uploads/2018/04/Data_Society_Algorithmic_Accountability_Primer_FINAL-4.pdf (accessed 2 January 2020).

Carney, T. (2018). 'The New Digital Future for Welfare: Debts Without Legal Proofs or Moral Authority?', *UNSW Law Journal*, the Forum 1: 1–16.

Cecez-Kecmanovic, D. (2016). 'From Substantialist to Process Metaphysics—Exploring Shifts in IS Research', in Introna, L., Kavanagh, D., Kelly, S., Orlikowski, W., and Scott, S. (eds), *Beyond Interpretivism? New Encounters with Technology and Organisation.* IFIP, Springer, 35–57.

Cino, J.G. (2018). 'Deploying the Secret Police: The Use of Algorithms in the Criminal Justice System', *Georgia State University Law Review* 34/4: 1073–1102.

Chalfin, A., Danieli, O., Hillis, A., Jelveh, Z., Luca, M., Ludwig, J., and Mullainathan, S. (2016). 'Productivity and Selection of Human Capital with Machine Learning', *American Economic Review* 106/5: 124–127.

Cheatham, B., Javanmardian, K., and Samandar, H. (2019). 'Confronting the Risks of Artificial Intelligence', *McKinsey Quarterly* (April). https://www.mckinsey.com/business-functions/mckinsey-analytics/our-insights/confronting-the-risks-of-artificial-intelligence.

Chollet, F. (2018). *Deep Learning with R.* Manning Publications.

Clarke R. (2019). 'Risks Inherent in the Digital Surveillance Economy: A Research Agenda', *Data & Civil Rights* (2015). *Criminal Justice and Civil Rights Primer*, https://datasociety.net/wpcontent/uploads/2015/10/Criminal_Justice_and_Civil_Rights_Primer.pdf (accessed 2 February 2020).

Daugherty, P., and Wilson, H. J. (2018). *Human + Machine: Reimagining Work in the Age of AI.* Harvard Business Review Press.

Davenport, T. H., and Bean, R. (2017). 'How P&G and American Express Are Approaching AI', *Harvard Business Review.* 31 March, https://hbr.org/2017/03/how-pg-andamerican-express-are-approaching-ai.

Davenport, T. H., and Kirby, J. (2016). *Only Humans Need Apply: Winners and Losers in The Age of Smart Machines.* HarperCollins.

Dickey, G., Blanke, S., and Seaton, L. (2019). 'Machine Learning in Auditing: Current and Future Applications', *The CPA Journal*, June, https://www.cpajournal.com/?s=Dickey.

Dowling, C., and Leech, S. (2014) 'A Big 4 Firm's Use of Information Technology to Control the Audit Process: How an Audit Support System is Changing Auditor Behaviour', *Contemporary Accounting Research* 31/1: 230–252.

Dreyfus, H. L., and Dreyfus, S. E. (2005). 'Peripheral Vision Expertise in Real World Contexts', *Organization Studies* 26/5: 779–792.

Edwards, L., and Veale, M. (2017) 'Slave to the Algorithm? Why a "Right to an Explanation" Is Probably Not the Remedy You Are Looking For', *Duke Law & Technology* 16/1: 18–84.

Eubanks V. (2018). *Automating Inequality: How High-Tech Tools Profile, Police, and Punish the Poor.* St Martin's Press.

Faraj, S., Pachidi, S., and Sayegh, K. (2018). 'Working and Organizing in the Age of the Learning Algorithm', *Information and Organization* 28/1: 62–70.

Ferguson, A. G. (2019). *The Rise of Big Data Policing: Surveillance, Race, and the Future of Law Enforcement*, NYU Press.

Frey, C. B., and Osborne, M. A. (2017). 'The Future of Employment: How Susceptible are Jobs to Computerisation?', *Technological Forecasting and Social Change* 114: 254–280. https://doi.org/10.1016/J.TECHFORE.2016.08.019.

Galliers, R. D., Newell, S., Shanks, G., and Topi, H. (2017). 'Datafication and Its Human, Organizational and Societal Effects: The Strategic Opportunities and Challenges of Algorithmic Decision-Making', *Journal of Strategic Information Systems* 26/3: 185–190.

Gherardi, S. (2018). 'Practices and Knowledges', *Teoria e Prática em Administração* 8/2: 33–59.

Gherardi, S. (2019). 'Practice as a Collective and Knowledgeable Doing'. *Working Paper Series*, Collaborative Research Center 1187 Media of Cooperation. Universitat Siegen. Available at: http://wp-series.mediacoop.uni-siegen.de (accessed 15 October 2019).

Gilman, M. (2020). 'AI Algorithms Intended to Root Out Welfare Fraud Often End Up Punishing the Poor Instead', *The Conversation*, 14 February 2020, https://theconversation.com/ai-algorithms-intended-to-root-out-welfare-fraud-often-end-up-punishing-the-poor-instead-131625.

Goodman, N. (1995). *Ways of Worldmaking.* Hackett.

Gray, M. L., and Suri, S. (2019). *Ghost Work: How to Stop Silicon Valley from Building a new Global Underclass.* HMH Books.

Hadjimichael, D., and Tsoukas, H. (2019). 'Toward a Better Understanding of Tacit Knowledge in Organizations: Taking Stock and Moving Forward', *Academy of Management Annals* 13/2: 672–703.

Hancock, B., Lazaroff-Puck, K., and Rutherford, S. (2020). 'Getting Practical about the Future of Work', *McKinsey Quarterly* (Jan). https://www.mckinsey.com/business-functions/organization/our-insights/getting-practical-about-the-future-of-work.

Harwell, D. (2019). 'A Face-Scanning Algorithm Increasingly Decides Whether You Deserve the Job', *The Washington Post*,
https://www.washingtonpost.com/technology/2019/10/22/ai-hiring-face-scanning-algorithm-increasingly-decides-whether-you-deserve-job/.

Hasselberger, W. (2019). 'Ethics beyond Computation: Why We Can't (and Shouldn't) Replace Human Moral Judgment with Algorithms', *Social Research: An International Quarterly* 86/4: 977–999.

Hayne, J. and Doran, M. (2020). 'Government to Pay Back $721m as it Scraps Robodebt for Centrelink Welfare Recipients'. *ABC News*, 29/05/2020.
https://www.abc.net.au/news/2020-05-29/federal-government-refund-robodebt-scheme-repay-debts/12299410.

Healy, S. (2005). 'Toward a Vocabulary for Speaking of the Engagement of Things into Discourse', *Journal of Environmental Policy & Planning* 7/3: 239–256.

Henriques-Gomes, L. (2020). 'Robodebt: Total Value of Unlawful Debts Issued under Centrelink Scheme to Exceed $1bn'. *The Guardian*, 10 June 2020, https://www.theguardian.com/australia-news/2020/jun/10/robodebt-total-value-of-debts-issued-under-unlawful-centrelink-scheme-to-exceed-1bn-refund.

Hoffman, R. (2016). 'Using Artificial Intelligence to Set Information Free', *MIT Sloan Frontiers*, 14 June. https://sloanreview.mit.edu/article/using-artificial-intelligence-tohumanize-management-and-set-information-free/.

Holford, W. D. (2019). 'The Future of Human Creative Knowledge Work within the Digital Economy', *Futures*, 105: 143–154.

Holford, W. D. (2020). *Managing Knowledge in Organizations: A Critical Pragmatic Perspective*. Palgrave Macmillan.

Ingold, T. (2015), *The Life of Lines*. Routledge.

Ingold, T. (2017). 'On Human Correspondence', *Journal of the Royal Anthropological Institute* 23/1: 9–27.

Irani, L. (2015). 'Difference and Dependence Among Digital Workers: The Case of Amazon Mechanical Turk', *South Atlantic Quarterly* 114/1: 225–234.

Jarrahi, M. H. (2018). 'Artificial Intelligence and the Future of Work: Human-AI Symbiosis in Organizational Decision Making', *Business Horizons* 61/4: 577–586.

Kellogg, K.C., Valentine, M.A., and Christin, A. (2020). 'Algorithms at Work: The New Contested Terrain of Control', *Academy of Management Annals* 14/1: 366–410. https://doi.org/10.5465/annals.2018.0174.

Khandani, A.E., Kim, A.J., and Lo, A.W. (2010). 'Consumer Credit Risk Models via Machine-Learning Algorithms', *Journal of Banking and Finance* 34: 2767–2787.

Kim, Y. J., Kim, K., and Lee, S. (2017). 'The Rise of Technological Unemployment and Its Implications on the Future Macroeconomic Landscape', *Futures* 87: 1–9. https://doi.org/10.1016/j.futures.2017.01.003

Kitchin, R. (2017). 'Thinking Critically about and Researching Algorithms', *Information, Communication & Society*, 20/1: 14–29.

Kokina, J. and. Davenport, T.H. (2017). 'The Emergence of Artificial Intelligence: How Automation is Changing Auditing', *Journal of Emerging Technologies in Accounting* 14/1: 115–122.

Lecher, C. (2019). 'How Amazon Automatically Tracks and Fires Warehouse Workers for "Productivity"—Documents Show How the Company Tracks and Terminates Workers', *The Verge*, 25 April, https://www.theverge.com/2019/4/25/18516004/amazon-warehouse-fulfillment-centers-productivity-firing-terminations.

Leetaru, K. (2019). 'A Reminder that Machine Learning Is about Correlations Not Causation'. https://www.forbes.com/sites/kalevleetaru/2019/01/15/a-reminder-that-machine-learning-is-about-correlations-not-causation/#2080eeee6161 (accessed 15 Jan 2020).

Leicht-Deobald, U., Busch, T., Schank, C., et al. (2019). 'The Challenges of Algorithm-Based HR Decision-Making for Personal Integrity', *Journal of Business Ethics*, 160: 377–392.

Mackenzie, A., and Vurdubakis, T. (2011). 'Codes and Codings in Crisis—Signification, Performativity and Excess', *Theory, Culture & Society* 28/6: 3–23.

Marjanovic, O., and Cecez-Kecmanovic, D. (2017). 'Exploring the Tension between Transparency and Datafication Effects of Open Government IS through the Lens of Complex Adaptive Systems', *Journal of Strategic Information Systems* 26/3: 210–232.

Marjanovic, O., Cecez-Kecmanovic, D., and Vidgen, R. (2021). 'Algorithmic Pollution: Making the Invisible visible', *Journal of Information Technology*, 1–18. DOI: 10.1177/02683962211010356.

Markus, L. (2017). 'Datafication, Organizational Strategy, and IS Research: What's the Score?', *Journal of Strategic Information Systems* 26/3: 233–241.

Mesle, C. R. (2008). *Process-Relational Philosophy: An Introduction to Alfred North Whitehead*. Templeton Press.

Murdoch, W. J., Chandan Singh, C., Kumbiera, K., et al. (2019). 'Definitions, Methods, and Applications in Interpretable Machine Learning', *Proceedings of National Academy of Science (PNAS) USA*, 116/44: 22071–22080. doi: 10.1073/pnas.1900654116.

Nagel, T. (1986). *The View from Nowhere*. Oxford University Press.

O'Neil, C. (2016). *Weapons of Math Destruction: How Big Data Increases Inequality and Threatens Democracy*. Penguin Random House.

Orlikowski, W. J. (2002). 'Knowing in Practice: Enacting a Collective Capability in Distributed Organizing', *Organization Science* 13/3: 249–273.

Pasquale, F. (2015). *The Black Box Society: The Secret Algorithms that Control Money and Information*. Harvard University Press.

Polanyi, M. (1958). *Personal Knowledge: Towards a Postcritical Philosophy*. University of Chicago Press.

Polanyi, M. (1966a). *The Tacit Dimension*. The University of Chicago Press.

Polanyi, M. (1966b). 'The Logic of Tacit Inference', *Philosophy: The Journal of the Royal Institute of Philosophy* 41/155: 1–18.

Raghavan, M., Barocas, S., Kleinberg, J., and Levy, K. (2020). 'Mitigating Bias in Algorithmic Hiring: Evaluating Claims and Practices', in *Proceedings of the Conference on Fairness, Accountability, and Transparency*, ACM.

Reese, B. (2018). *The Fourth Age: Smart Robots, Conscious Computers, and the Future of Humanity*. Atria Books.

Ryle, G. (1949). *The Concept of Mind*, Hutchinson; Penguin Books.

Sanzogni, L., Guzman, G., and Busch, P. (2017). 'Artificial Intelligence and Knowledge Management: Questioning the Tacit Dimension', *Prometheus* 35/1: 37–56.

Sentas, V., and Pandolfini, C. (2017). *Policing Young People in NSW: A Study of the Suspect Targeting Management Plan*. A Report of the Youth Justice Coalition NSW (Sydney: Youth Justice Coalition NSW). http://www.yjc.org.au/resources/YJC-STMP-Report.pdf (accessed 1 February 2020).

Sheehey, B. (2018). 'Algorithmic Paranoia: The Temporal Governmentality of Predictive Policing', *Ethics and Information Technology* 21: 49–58.

Shestakofsky, B. (2017). 'Working Algorithms: Software Automation and the Future of Work', *Work and Occupations* 44/4: 376–423.

Steiner C (2012). *Automate This: How Algorithms Came to Rule Our World*. Penguin.

Suchman, L. A. (2007). *Human-Machine Reconfigurations: Plans and Situated Actions*. Cambridge University Press.

Sutton, S. G., Arnold, V., and Holt, M. (2018). 'How Much Automation Is Too Much? Keeping the Human Relevant in Knowledge Work', *Journal of Emerging Technologies in Accounting* 15/2: 15–25.

Tsoukas, H. (2011). 'How Should we Understand Tacit Knowledge? A Phenomenological View', in M. Easterby-Smith and M. Lyles (eds), *Handbook of Organizational Learning and Knowledge Management* (2nd ed.). Wiley, 453–476.

von Krogh, G. (2018). 'Artificial Intelligence in Organizations: New Opportunities for Phenomenon-Based Theorizing', *Academy of Management Discoveries* 4/4: 404–409, https://doi.org/10.5465/amd.2018.0084.

Vasarhelyi, V. and Rozario, A. (2018). 'How Robotic Process Automation Is Transforming Accounting and Auditing', *CPA Journal*, http://bit.ly/2F7t5aE.

Wachter-Boettcher, S. (2017). *Technically Wrong: Sexist Apps, Biased Algorithms and Other Threats of Toxic Tech*. W.W. Northon & Company.

Webb, M. (2019). 'The Impact of Artificial Intelligence on the Labor Market'. SSRN: https://ssrn.com/abstract=3482150 or http://dx.doi.org/10.2139/ssrn.3482150.

Weber, R. (2012). 'Evaluating and Developing Theories in the Information Systems Discipline, *Journal of Association of Information Systems* 13/1, Article 2.

Weber, M. (1947). *The Theory of Social and Ecŏnomic Organization* (Trans. by A.M. Henderson and T. Parsons). Free Press Falcon's Wing Press.

Willcocks, L. (2020) 'Robo-Apocalypse cancelled? Reframing the Automation and Future of Work Debate', *Journal of Information Technology* 35/4: 286–302.

Zalnieriute, M., Moses, L. B., and Williams, G. (2019). 'The Rule of Law and Automation of Government Decision-Making', *The Modern Law Review* 82: 425–455.

# 5

# Utopias as Borderlands: Reconceptualizing Post-pandemic Future(s)

## An Image: Post-pandemic *Gnosislíve*

*Dirk S. Hovorka*

Gnosislíve, or 'knowledge life' is the fastest growing lifestyle movement for the disenchanted knowledge worker. Visible in the rapid relocation of professional work from the office to exotic locales is a new paradigm in which no *workplace authority is physically alongside* the knowledge worker. Nor is *there any Taylorist implementation of workplace surveillance, planning, or rigid regimentation.* Indeed, this mobility paradigm is a promised escape from the *surveillance apparatus* in which *you've got to be seen, you've got to be here* (in the office). Management has made strides towards a way of working that treats *people like adults, rewarding them for the work that they do as opposed to the amount of time they sit at the office.* The *'rat race' of corporate, employed, and location-bound work* has been left behind for *location-independence and travelling the world for lifestyle, experience, and global arbitrage (earning a high income while living in low-cost countries). Productivity and retention are enhanced* so that *five-hour workdays produce results at least equal to eight-hour workdays and that four-day workweeks may be more effective than five-day workweeks for knowledge workers.* In this ideal future, *professional and work time is merged and interwoven with their leisure, travel, and personal time. Both spatially and temporally, work and life cannot be distinguished in any meaningful way.*[1]

Dirk S. Hovorka, *Utopias as Borderlands: Reconceptualizing Post-pandemic Future(s).* In: *Organizing in the Digital Age.* Edited by: Michael Barrett, Emmanuelle Vaast, Ann Langley, and Haridimos Tsoukas, Oxford University Press.
 DOI: 10.1093/oso/9780198899457.003.0005

## 5.1 Introduction: Challenging the Present from the Future

In a pandemic-induced disruption of everyday life in 2020, millions of people reconfigured a large proportion of their normal activities into digital environments almost overnight. The everyday operational practices of living were upended as work, teaching, professional, and social gatherings, learning, health check-ups, and most routine activities suddenly were relegated to online environments. A McKinsey report states, 'We are witnessing what will surely be remembered as a historic deployment of remote work and digital access to services across every domain ... we have vaulted five years forward in consumer and business digital adoption in a matter of around eight weeks' (Baig et al. 2020).

During the Covid-19 pandemic, we were all participants in a natural experiment involving millions of people, thousands of organizations, a vast suite of digital technologies and global involvement. New configurations and practices of managerial relations, spatial allocations of work and other-than-work, suites of technologies, and processes of organizing were not the result of careful planning and design. Instead, wayfaring as a form of movement in the world through which we 'know as we go, not before we go' (Ingold 2000: 239) became a common mode of responding to unprecedented circumstances. The immediate need to relocate from communal places of work and learning to places of isolation bypassed traditional implementation processes and created a borderland between the accepted understanding of work in the past and the non-stabilized practices which may become our futures.

Organizational white papers, consultancies, and academics rushed to understand these new digital practices and organizing processes devised to maintain organizations, education, and services. Now, many of these socio-technical configurations and practices are becoming normalized and managed (Leclercq-Vandelannoitte and Aroles 2020; Marabelli et al. 2021. However, the immediate post-Covid-19 moment also provides an opportunity for a fundamental rethinking of the research apparatus (e.g. the concepts, logics, relationships, and power structures) through which we seek to understand the unprecedented digitalization of organizational practices and configurations of technology in our lives. Rather than settling into a 'new normal' defined by past socio-technical conceptualizations, it is incumbent on researchers to challenge their conceptual apparatus if we are to come to understand how these phenomena came to be, how they are different from the past and what implications they have for our futures.

Scrutinizing the status quo conceptual apparatus reveals two related but irreducible challenges. First is the challenge of recognizing that unprecedented phenomenon exists when our tendency is to interpret the world 'through the lenses of familiar categories thereby rendering invisible precisely that which is unprecedented' (Zuboff 2019: 12). Have new concepts or power structures been disclosed in the diverse socio-technical-political-economic configurations created during the pandemic wayfaring? Or have we, as researchers, embedded the concepts, logics, and relationships of past research into our analysis of new practices and, by doing so, constrained how we can envision the future? Second, we now have an opportunity to recognize *what has been done* and consider *what ought to be done* (Jasanoff 2016) and explore the implications of doing so. For example, new enactments of remote work may be emancipatory or may have perpetuated inequalities and new forms of control (Leclercq-Vandelannoitte and Aroles 2020). Digital workers may experience newly created freedoms or be subject to the 'utopia of cows'[2] with gamification, surveillance, and algorithmic decision-making optimizing higher worker productivity at the expense of other values. Addressing these challenges requires that we develop conceptual apparatus with which to scrutinize the unprecedented.

To address these two challenges, this chapter employs *utopia* as a speculative engagement (Hovorka and Peter 2021b) to use images of futures that unsettle our research in the present. The utopia approach envisions futures as a digital geography; a class of research methods which present internally consistent, coherent, richly described, technoculture that is cognitively plausible but estranging (Hovorka and Peter 2021a). Future geographies create a site of inquiry from which to disclose new concepts, relationships, and values in the present practices and operational configurations of organizing created during the Covid-19 pandemic. The technique of *thinking with* utopias adds richness and layers to the people, technologies, relationships, and spatial connections we assume in our research rather than reducing multi-faceted phenomenon to fit within current categories (de la Bellacasa 2012). This 'method of simultaneously critiquing the present, exploring alternatives, imagining ourselves otherwise and experimenting with prefigurative practices' (Levitas 2013: 16) allows us as researchers to challenge and dissent from the dominant conceptualizations of the world. In doing so researchers can recognize and reconceptualize futures before unprecedented changes become reified into concepts from the past.

The narrative fragment with which this chapter begins is a fictionalized account of a post-Covid-19 workplace which was inspired by research that describes a set of paradigmatic ideal types for researching 'potential futures of knowledge work' (Wang et al. 2020: abstract). The utopian image of a future was created by drawing upon specific idealized aspects of that research and are presented without the dialect context of their original presentation. This image does, however, envision an ideal endmember of the spectrum of concepts proposed as a paradigm for research on the future of work. In this chapter, the utopian paradigmatic workplace image is subjected to multiple readings to disclose perspectives from which to critique our present-day research apparatus regarding work/life balance, organizing, and power relations. The viewing of utopia as a hermeneutic in this way shifts our thinking towards the construction of research apparatus itself as a question of the production and reproduction of scientific practices in moments of crisis (Kuhn 1964).

### 5.1.1 Responses and Opportunities

During the unfolding Covid-19 crisis, researchers in organizational and management studies and in Information Systems recognized the magnitude of the changes underway. Research on readily visible phenomenon such as contact tracing (Riemer et al. 2020; Rowe et al. 2020; Urbaczewski and Lee 2020) and combating misinformation (Kharod and Simmons 2020; Zarocostas 2020) was published. While essential and timely, these immediate research responses largely abide within the concerns, concepts and relationalities understood as salient from the perspective of our current research apparatus.

By accounting for the unprecedented change enacted during this natural experiment without interrogating our current research apparatus we risk overlooking fundamental changes in the processes and configurations of organizing. Further reifying this conceptual apparatus as the dominant approach for *research in the future* assumes the future to be fundamentally similar to the past. Our apparatus and expectations condition what we are capable of conceptualizing and observing by providing *the world with which we think* as we engage with changes brought forth in the crisis wayfaring. This status quo orientation leaves unaddressed the questions of whether new phenomena that lie outside the gaze of our current conceptual apparatus are present and if our assumed conceptualizations remain suitable. An alternative orientation would be open to more speculative phenomena that may, yet, not have strong empirical support. For example, new constructs such as *digital scars* have been proposed to capture 'ethically problematic socio-technical innovations that outlast their emergency rollouts, when broader effects of these technologies could not be carefully examined' (Marabelli et al. 2021, and issues of surveillance and privacy as mechanisms of societal control have been deconstructed (Leclercq-Vandelannoitte and Aroles 2020).

In this chapter, a hermeneutic style reading of a *utopian digital geography* aids navigation of a crisis by providing tools with which to think. The Covid-19 pandemic has elicited a vast variety of responses regarding organizational structure and behaviour, workforce attitudes and demands, educational environments, and social interactions. The range of organizational and educational responses to the crisis invites researchers to assess the values and relationalities which have been enacted within these new organizational and digital worlds (Haraway 1991). This requires us to question newly developed digital practices not as *what they are* but rather for *what cultural norms they enact, what vocabulary and conceptualization create them and what research problems and practices are disclosed and carry on into our futures.*

## 5.2 Utopia: History and Method

The concept of Utopia, commencing with Thomas More (1516/1965), has received extensive treatment in numerous academic fields and the broader society (Sargent 1994; Gordin et al. 2010; Vieira 2010; Claeys 2011). Literally meaning *no place*, the scholarship of utopias and utopianism presents imaginary but desirable societies and critiques of the limitations of planning a perfect future society. In modern times, utopias are often considered to be the result of 'the desire for a better life, caused by a feeling of discontentment towards the society one lives in' (Vieira 2010: 6). Utopias reflect the concerns of the time and thus are framed in the concepts and relationships of the society in which they are imagined. In this regard, utopias are viewed as a *principle of hope* (Bloch et al. 1986) for the future, worlds of *not yet* where everything is in a process of constant formation. These two concepts: that utopias present the concepts and principles through which society views itself and that the world is a process of *constant becoming* shifts attention to relationality and recognition that what we can know and how we think 'are inconceivable without a multitude of relations that also make possible *the worlds we think with*' (de la Bellacasa 2012: 198). In this regard utopias provide worlds which make visible the values, concerns, and aspirations of the present society for the future.

Using utopias *as method* (Levitas 2013; Jasanoff and Kim 2015) reveals that radical shifts in culture and the organization of society (e.g. office-less organizations; rapid digitalization of work) requires that certain values, commitments, and power structures be reconceptualized and enacted. By creating a speculative world (Hovorka and Peter 2021b) to act as a mirror 'at a (temporal or spatial) distance ... utopian creators defamiliarize the world they know and inhabit; in the process they enable taken-for-granted aspects to be questioned and rethought' (Cooper 2014: 5) thus identifying what concepts, relationships, and configurations of power must be discarded or reformulated to achieve a better society.

Utopias do not claim to provide empirical knowledge. Instead, they reveal the culturally, and in the case of research, scientifically enforced concepts with which we understand the world. Utopias, in presenting *no place* worlds, reveal the real-world social-political-economic-technological configurations of the present day which would necessarily be dismantled or reconfigured to achieve the perfect imagined state. In this way geographies of utopia become an analytical tool to encourage fundamental conceptual reform during crisis situations (Kuhn 1964). In experiencing and then rereading the utopian world we can produce new understandings not of the empirical world but rather of the conceptual apparatus with which researchers co-construct the world (Kuhn 1977).

Utopian geographies reveal the commitments and values which underlay how peoples and organizations wayfared into new organizing practices, and which become durable and precede us into futures through our own research. To disclose and rethink the values and conceptual boundaries enacted in socio-technical practices created during the crisis, utopian digital geographies provide a foray into the lived experience of people who inhabit that world and who understand the values, relationships, and configurations of power as normal everyday life.

Utopias, in narrative form, are navigable, enabling researchers to overcome the common image of futures as uninhabited, the temporal version of *terrus nullius*.[3] In the dominant future-studies approaches, our images of futures are as an outsider, a visitor unaware of the everyday customs, culture, and practices of that (future) world. As an alternative, the world envisioned in a utopia enables researchers to make visible the local practices and understanding which would go unremarked to local inhabitants but that provide a sense of estrangement and dislocation to readers in the present day (Hovorka and Peter 2021a). As inhabited and embodied worlds, utopias are familiar and integrate with existing and fundamental societal discourses. Folding this critical view back into our present provides new pragmatic perspectives of the organizational practices which we now seek to normalize or to discard. In creating estrangement from what we expect of our future, multiple readings of utopias assist in the critical reformulation of existing concepts and concurrently provides clarity regarding those concepts prior to reformulation.

## 5.3 The Gnosislíve Utopia: Reading the Present from the Future

The opening paragraph of this chapter is derived from research which presents a Hegelian dialectic contrasting ideal types and which envisions and bounds the spectrum of digital futures of knowledge work (Wang et al. 2020). By envisioning digital futures, the authors provide researchers with research concepts to address 'organizing work, working with technology, delineating work/life boundaries, and provisioning the social safety net' (ibid.: abstract) in a future composed of an increasingly mobile and entrepreneurial workforce. The idealized paradigms of a post-Covid world identify specific practices, orientations to technologies and power relations which are offered as central to research on digital futures in both utopian and less desirable forms. The authors thus articulate a conceptual apparatus suitable for analysing the future world as it is anticipated to become.

The ideal types presented are derived from the dominant characterization of work in the twentieth century which arose during the industrial revolution. A question arises regarding the suitability of research apparatus created to describe an industrial conception of *work* for describing and analysing digital futures. Does the conceptual language, the distinctions between 'life' and 'work' and enactments of scientific management practices (Taylorism) remain the same (albeit in digital form) and capture the experiences of inhabitants of the anticipated digital futures? To address this question, the estrangement of utopian geography is used to critique our current research apparatus because 'any attempt to think outside the sphere of given experience ... ironically recapitulates the existing structure of power/knowledge' (Gardiner 1992: 24). Scrutinizing the utopian fragment allows us to highlight assumptions and speculatively reconstruct the text's meaning to the inhabitants of that future world. This requires interpreting the text at two levels: (1) illuminating the concepts, relationships and power structures which are frequently presented as the inevitable (and desirable) outcomes of social-technical change; and (2) illustrating how the presuppositions of the historical contexts of our current research apparatus can be revitalized with new concepts, values, and relationality to account for the unprecedented reconfigurations which have occurred.

### 5.3.1 First Reading: Work, Life, and Time

In the first reading, the text emphasizes new spatial, technological, and social configurations in which *work* is performed independent of a prescribed location. As observed during the Covid-19 pandemic, this was frequently *work from home* (WFH), when work was forced into a digital environment and the non-work activities of life were experienced from the same physical location as work activities. Personal computing devices supported both personal and professional activities, bedrooms and kitchen tables became workplaces, leisure wear became *defacto* office attire. In alignment with common conceptual apparatus, the utopian fragment is suggestive that research into digital futures centres on work: its organizing ontology, use of technology, boundaries, and configuration of power (Wang et al. 2020). The utopia explicitly reflects the dominant conceptual distinction between *life* and *work* (something not-life) and the subsequent need to create 'balance' between two opposing concepts. Indeed, a utopian reading indicates that, for the lucky few in the idealized mobility paradigm, there is no such distinction. For these few people, the utopian state of affairs is conceptualized as 'work' being indistinguishable from personal interests, social life becomes doing business with friends and every day is casual day. Thus, a central concept of the utopia remains work—even as it is subsumed and disappears into lifestyle. Does the concept of work, as distinct from life, still provide any analytic traction when describing people who experience no distinction? Perhaps new concepts and new distinctions (e.g. between activities for which compensation is paid/not paid; transactional tasks, activities of joy vs activities of obligation) are required. If work-life is no longer a distinction, what then becomes of the concept of life as a contrast-class to work? In addition, such perfect utopian outcomes are not considered widely available in futures and dystopic shadows appear with the recognition that, for most people, future research 'would also need to resolve tensions between approaches to work/life balance' (Wang et al. 2020: 1387). What new concepts are needed to account for the existence of people with no work-life to balance and those who continue to experience such bifurcation?

Work in this utopian future remains framed as a clock-time relation between the corporation and the worker. Improved efficiencies from the newfound flexibility of clock-time (e.g '*5-hour workdays produce results at least equal to 8-hour workdays*') are celebrated as achieving the goal of improved productivity and increased worker retention, reflecting the values of the corporation, not of the individual. Work itself is composed of discrete and bounded tasks, which can be completed by skilled gig-workers depending on their availability and price. The perceived emancipation from authority and spatial workplace concentration is gained only in relation to greater productivities and efficiencies thus increasing worker 'free-time'. The radical new future of knowledge work remains strangely resistant to actual changes in power relations or the objectives of corporate ideology.

This conceptualization of time as objective places it external to 'social relations and governed by laws of mechanical functioning that have no regard for human feeling. It is, of course, the time of the clock.... This is what is colloquially called "free time" ... time associated with what we call "leisure" when this is defined by its contrast to work' (Ingold 1995: 328). The inhabitants of this utopian future experience this increased free time as the ability to engage in leisure travel, 'sitting on a tropical beach or in a trendy coworking space, working on a laptop, producing work for clients while admiring the tropical scenery' (Wang et al. 2020: 1380). Free or personal time remains a relation to productivity and work.

### 5.3.2 Second Reading: Privacy, Surveillance, and Power

A second reading surfaces the future of work as an emancipation from both surveillance and workplace authority. While maintaining the implied power relationship carried by the designation as 'workers', people are 'treated as independent, responsible professionals, in charge of which technology they want to use for which purposes' (Wang et al. 2020: 1391). Technology use is envisioned as solely for support of human goals and creativity and not for surveillance or control. The complete autonomy of workers from structure, and a persistent state of fluidity, frees them to establish their own social networks, collaborations, and to secure their own financial futures.

The rapid shift to work-from-home or worksites outside the office environment highlights the increased formation of distributed work cultures. The focus on surveillance in this second reading foregrounds increasing collection, analysis and visibility of private information as a necessary trade-off for tele-presence and organizational connectivity (Hafermalz 2020). Yet surveillance and privacy are well-used concepts whose meanings have become a carry-all for an expansive set of psychological, political, social, and technical constructs. These are frequently used to illustrate the emancipatory character of new work configurations as an escape from surveillance anxieties and a release from the spatio-temporal requirements to be present *in the office.*

But conceptually, workers are not emancipated as the spectre of surveillance still lurks in the technology. To prevent the misuse of new work practices and technologies to control and manipulate workers, political interventions are needed. The power imbalance between workers and employers remains conceptually intact and political effort is needed to protect workers from the very technologies underlying the utopian imaginary (Susskind 2018). The power dynamic between workers and organizations is unstable with workers required to strive against the collapse of the utopian imaginary into dystopian worlds of Digital Taylorism, a concept which continues to maintain a grip on social beliefs and values (Ingold 1995; Holford 2019). The stark contrast between these visions, of unfettered freedom and creative engagement with technology versus scientific management and concerns across a much wider range of jobs including service and knowledge workers and managers themselves (Holford 2019), is indicative of the hold these concepts have on researchers' understanding of the world.

Taken together, these two readings indicate the attraction of conceptualizing the future with the same relationships, concepts, and power arrangements deployed in the past, despite the variety of digital configurations for organizing developed during the Covid-19 crisis. This commitment to stable research apparatus is necessary for research fields in that such apparatus defines the problems available and the nature of solutions acceptable to the field. The commitments are also constructive in providing researchers 'with an immensely sensitive detector of the trouble spots from which significant innovations of fact and theory are almost inevitably educed' (Kuhn 1963: 302). By creating a no-place utopia which extends beyond the innovation dialectic of Wang et al., we can recognize new relations and make visible shifts in underlying values concealed withing the conceptions, relations and understanding of organizational politics (Susskind 2018) of our current research apparatus. We can open the doors to speculative engagement and unsettle the research apparatus through which we engage phenomena and practices which may become our futures (Hovorka and Peter 2021b).

## 5.4 Where to From Here?

The goal of this chapter is not to suggest that the concepts underlying past research be abandoned or discarded. In the immediate term, the apparatus of our research serves to comprehend the world from a specific and valuable perspective. The function of a utopian geography is to highlight the concepts and relationships *with which we think* as we move forward in researching and stabilizing the new organizing practices we are observing. These readings of utopian geography argue that in our research 'discourse not only creates its objects, but also constructs (or reconstructs) the identities of it users' (Czarniawska 2013: 15). In deploying research apparatus previously used to describe industrialization and corporate management practices, we risk reifying these same concepts to theorize entirely new configurations of technology, people, and life. Revitalizing our research apparatus to recognize new configurational stabilities and values enacted by people and organizations as they navigated unforeseen new situations is necessary. More speculative research approaches may better prepare researchers to understand the worlds which people encounter as the *new normal* and to discard practices which have dystopian leanings.

We see in our two readings of the utopia of location-independent work, a continuation of the dominant emphasis on an industrial-era concept of work as a contrast between *life* vs *work* (something not-life) and clock-time efficiency for work completion. Technology is presented as a means of escaping the institutionalized Taylorist or Fordist industrial configuration of work developed during the Industrial Revolution. The utopian geography maintains this distinction (life vs work) as normal and perhaps even desirable for inhabitants of the future. Concurrently we see that, except for the few who can be emancipated, the digital revolution maintains the industrial conceptualizations of work as the place you went when you left home: 'Setting off to work in the morning, a man not only leaves his dwelling but also, in a much stronger sense, ceases to dwell. He is not himself: as his activity no longer belongs to him, so too he is a stranger to the world whose forms and meanings are created through this activity' (Ingold 2000: 331).

In addition, our reading highlights the tradition of autonomy as freedom from institutional constraint, which has become influential in organizational thinking and underlies utopian images of the post-Covid workplace. In its utopian sense it is freedom of a person from 'the intrusion into evenings and weekends ... by emails and KPIs ... empowered by professional autonomy, [and] responsible for organizing his or her own work schedule ... There is no micromanagement or leadership via surveillance and control' (Wang et al. 2020: 1391). Such a conception of autonomy has long been part of the analysis of work in terms of control vs autonomy (Knights and Willmott 2002).

Maintaining these conceptualizations is resonant with past spatio-temporal forms of work. But they expose a space within which to ask, 'what's an office for? Is it a place for newbies to learn from experienced colleagues? A way for bosses to oversee shirkers? A platform for collaboration? A source of friends and social life? A reason to leave the house?' (Seabrook 2021). These questions reveal a paucity of vocabulary and analytic tools with which to address the increasing intertwining and flux of space, time, technologies, and attitudes among the activities for which we are compensated and those we do for pleasure or commitment. Initial evidence of digital isolation in remote working configurations suggests scepticism regarding autonomy and the abandonment or partial inhabitation of offices which may (further) 'isolate us from those who could be a source of collective strength in resisting what we have been made to become' (Knights and Willmott 2002: 61). There is a need for organizational processes regarding who and what can be accomplished remotely, supporting new patterns of team cohesion, and for understanding new sources of physical, technological, and psychological stress and the need for personal recognition and compensation. This will require a more holistic understanding of new organizing practices and their underlying values and space–time enactments. This requires research that goes beyond current categories of work vs life, because maintaining this categorical distinction when 'work and life cannot be distinguished in any meaningful way' seems contradictory.

We may also need to question the dominant assumption that work can be broken into discrete tasks that are socially isolated and thus can be completed by anyone or any machine with the functional capability. This decomposition provides the logics underlying predictions of both the freeing of humans from mundane repetition and substantive job losses through automation. The visibility of these assumptions invites an alternative view of tasks as socially embedded activities with an intrinsic component of experienced time, not clock time (Ingold 1995). This exposes the dangerous dichotomy of work vs life in which work is distinct from social relations and in contrast, life is socially embedded. New conceptualizations of categories of activity, skills, tasks, and identity requires more careful analysis of the overlaps and tensions among professional identities and tasks and individual identities and the persistent forward movement of living (Ingold 1995). A long-standing goal has been to use technology to build skill into machines through algorithms. However, new human skills form around the new machines highlighting the 'law of the irreducibility of skills' (Ingold (2000) citing Sigaut (1994)), thus enabling a reformulation of what machines cannot do and repositioning humans in the discourse of AI, cyborgs, and labour. Reformulating tasks as the heart of human lived experience then draws from a richer palette of concepts, which would recognize the flux and variability in the socio-technical configurations of all forms of remote activity. This recognition reinvigorates the role of professional identity, and the importance of expertise and knowledge based on historical organizational decisions rather than reducing professional effort to merely a matter of efficiency and optimized completion of non-interacting tasks.

The desire to escape an emerging panopticon-like surveillance and a breakdown in privacy has come to infuse modern organizational narratives (Leclercq-Vandelannoitte et al. 2014), reflecting the present-day concerns with power enacted through technology. But within this narrative lies the opportunity to reformulate our conceptions of the phenomenon and an invitation to engage the concerns of the inhabitants of the futures our research addresses. With increased mobility and the loss of office-based organizational inclusion, people who work remotely may be less concerned with surveillance than with invisibility and exile (Hafermalz 2020). New meanings, relations, and symbols of power are exerted in digital work configurations, which are themselves subject to the patterns of activity enabled/prevented by multiple overlapping and competing technology platforms. Alternative conceptualizations move away from the grab-bag of concepts labelled as privacy and recognize the tensions between public and personal, the implications of persistence of data across both time and space, and the desire for personal and professional connections. Our colloquial term 'privacy' is outdated, particularly given that we live a world where our every keystroke, login, website, or location can be/is monitored and as we desire some companies, medical clinics, employers, and even friends to *know us*. Thus the concept of *being known* (Igo 2018) and the desire for 'competitive exposure and existential recognition ... the non-abstract concerns of people regarding who, knows what and what they can do' (Hafermalz 2020: abstract) becomes more salient than preserving an ambiguous concept of privacy best described as 'the creepy factor'. A shift to an alternative understanding of what is known and what is acted upon in organizational practices would cast light on how probabilistic identities (Cheney-Lippold 2018), algorithmic capitalism (Zuboff 2019), and the freedom to be left alone (Susskind 2018) become meaningful in these new digital configurations.

## 5.5 Seeing the World through *Other* Eyes

Researchers have pointed out that the futures our descendants will inhabit do not happen on their own (Jasanoff 2016; Hovorka and Peter 2021b). The apparatus of our research commits us to images of futures. In many instances our 'theorization implicitly conceptualize *the future* as a teleologically driven extension/extrapolation of a familiar present to a mostly-as-familiar future state' (Hovorka and Peter 2021b) and constrain how the world is experienced. In the post-pandemic borderlands where old organizational practices are in flux and new practices are not yet stabilized, expanding our research apparatus opens pathways for what we can comprehend as we consider what configurations we desire to carry into the future.

Utopian fragments, images, and research narratives have ebbed and flowed throughout recent history. They have provided visions inspiring progress and recalcitrant fear, have identified what futures to seek and which to avoid and each has conditioned social and technological critique. Their appearance in management and Information Systems literatures reveals an underlying optimistic instrumentalism which itself has become part of the normalizations of novel organizational and technological configurations in a post-Covid world by conditioning and moulding people's perceptions of what is desireable and true (Leclercq-Vandelannoitte and Aroles 2020).

In this chapter, a utopian digital geography provides tools with which to think. Utopian fragments derived from published research provide friction with our existing conceptualizations and encourage us to resist interpreting unprecedented phenomenon solely through extant theory, language, and concepts. Although utopias are an imaginary place, this form of speculative engagement provokes researchers to focus attention on the changes which are occurring not as an extrapolation from past research but as a speculative engagement through the eyes and experiences of the inhabitants of such a perfect future.

In examining a fragment of a utopian work-future, an idealized social imaginary of democratic and humane decision-making is foregrounded precisely in contrast to the bleak alternatives of industrial wage slavery or digitally enforced Taylorism. This is where the Utopian vision serves to highlight the dystopian human condition of those who cannot inhabit the idealized *no-place* inherent within this future vision. The role of organizing with technology is exposed as enforcing an increasing divide in which some people flourish by perfecting technological practices while the majority are subject to greater control and exploitation with the same technologies. This utopia reveals that the common technological and institutional vision of progress carries within itself 'the other side of the tracks' and unequal distribution of benefits and burdens of the new socio-technical configurations. As a critical tool, 'utopian visions often serve important roles in giving people a positive sense of direction, they can mislead when their architects exaggerate the likelihood of easy and desirable social changes' (Kling 1996: 52).

Every idealization obscures the messiness and variability in how people experience the world. We can easily lose sight of the differences among people who integrate, segment, or blur professional and personal tasks (Ciolfi and Lockley 2018), how identities are enacted (Petriglieri and Petriglieri 2010) and the different needs for personal connections (Hafermalz and Riemer 2020). As we navigate the borderland between organizational practices of the past and some new and unknown stability of future practices, utopian geographies reveal the need for conceptual adjustment and reformulations surrounding organizing in regard to coordinating in-office and remote teams, establishing visibility and opportunity for remote employees, the design of spaces, technologies and information, and the rebalancing of tasks for which compensation is expected. To study the implications of the wide range of organizational practices created during this wayfaring, we need to reconsider such taken-for-granted concepts as the home office, professional norms on platforms which are also used socially, and performance measures.

The utopian images that appear in management and IS research, in white papers, and in the press can be understood as a critique of the present and as hopes for the future. Speculative engagements with utopias create openness to recognizing different values, logics, and conceptualizations enacted in the wide variety of solutions created during an unprecedented period of pandemic responses. But as management practices and new configurations are becoming woven into our lives, understanding how future people will conceptualize these practices will help ensure that organizational configurations created during a crisis are understood in their own terms, rather than through the lenses created to understand the transformations of the past.

## Notes

1. Fictionalized from (Wang et al. 2020). Direct quotes are italicized (p. 1385).
2. Cows are provided VR headsets of pastoral scenes to enhance their productivity; https://www.bbc.com/news/world-europe-50571010.
3. Terra nullius ('nobodies land') was the European term for Australia which conceptualized the continent as uninhabited, thus denying the existential status of Indigenous peoples.

## References

Baig, A., Hall, B., Lamarre, E., and McCarthy, B. (2020). *The Covid-19 Recovery Will Be Digital: A Plan for the First 90 Days*. McKinsey.

Bloch, E., Plaice, N., Plaice, S., and Knight, P. (1986). *The Principle of Hope*. MIT Press.

Cheney-Lippold, J. (2018). *We Are Data: Algorithms and the Making of Our Digital Selves*. NYU Press.

Ciolfi, L., and Lockley, E. (2018). 'From Work to Life and Back Again: Examining the Digitally-Mediated Work/Life Practices of a Group of Knowledge Workers', *Computer Supported Cooperative Work (CSCW)* 27/3: 803–839.

Claeys, G. (2011). *Searching for Utopia: The History of an Idea*. Thames and Hudson.

Cooper, D. (2014). *Everyday Utopias: The Conceptual Life of Promising Spaces*. Duke University Press.

Czarniawska, B. (2013). 'Organizations as Obstacles to Organizing', *Organization and Organizing: Materiality, Agency, and Discourse*, pp. 3–22.

de la Bellacasa, M. P. (2012). '"Nothing Comes without Its World": Thinking with Care', *The Sociological Review* 60/2: 197–216.

Gardiner, M. (1992). 'Bakhtin's Carnival: Utopia as Critique', *Utopian Studies* 3/2: 21–49.

Gordin, M. D., Tilley, H., and Prakash, G. (2010). *Utopia/Dystopia: Conditions of Historical Possibility*. Princeton University Press.

Hafermalz, E. (2020). 'Out of the Panopticon and into Exile: Visibility and Control in Distributed New Culture Organizations', *Organization Studies*: Special Issue on Organizational Control and Surveillance of New Work Practices, 5: 1–21.

Hafermalz, E., and Riemer, K. (2020). 'Interpersonal Connectivity Work: Being There with and for Geographically Distant Others', *Organization Studies* 41/12: 1627–1648.

Haraway, D. (1991). 'The Actors Are Cyborg, Nature Is Coyote, and the Geography Is Elsewhere: Postscript to "Cyborgs at Large"', *Technoculture* 3: 183–202.

Holford, W. D. (2019). 'The Future of Human Creative Knowledge Work within the Digital Economy', *Futures* 105: 143–154.

Hovorka, D. S., and Peter, S. (2021a). 'From Other Worlds: Speculatively Engagement through Digital Geographies', *Journal of the Association of Information Systems* 22/6: 1736–1752

Hovorka, D. S., and Peter, S. (2021b). 'Speculatively Engaging Future(s): Four Theses', *Management Information Systems Quarterly* 45/1: 461–466.

Igo, S. E. (2018). *The Known Citizen: A History of Privacy in Modern America*. Harvard University Press.

Ingold, T. (1995). 'Work, Time and Industry', *Time & Society* 4/1: 5–28.

Ingold, T. (2000). *The Perception of the Environment: Essays on Livelihood, Dwelling and Skill*. Psychology Press.

Jasanoff, S. (2016). *The Ethics of Invention: Technology and the Human Future*. WW Norton & Company.

Jasanoff, S., and Kim, S. H. (2015). *Dreamscapes of Modernity: Sociotechnical Imaginaries and the Fabrication of Power*. University of Chicago Press.

Kharod, H., and Simmons, I. (2020). 'How to Fight an Infodemic: The Four Pillars of Infodemic Management', *Journal of Medical Internet Research* 22/6: e21820.

Kling, R. 1996. 'Hopes and Horrors: Technological Utopianism and Anti-Utopianism in Narratives of Compuertization', *Computerization and Controversy: Value Conflicts and Social Choices* 40.

Knights, D., and Willmott, H. (2002). 'Autonomy as Utopia or Dystopia', *The Sociological Review* 50/1 (suppl): 59–81.

Kuhn, T. (1977). 'A Function for Thought Experiments', in T. Kuhn, *The Essential Tension*. Univ. of Chicago Press, 240–265

Kuhn, T. S. (1963). 'The Function of Dogma in Scientific Research', in A.C. Crombie (ed.), *Scientific Change Historical Studies in the Intellectual, Social and Technical Conditions for Scientific Discovery and Technical Invention, from Antiquity to the Present: Symposium on the History of Science, University of Oxford, 9–15 July 1961*. Heineman Educational Books, 301–313

Leclercq-Vandelannoitte, A., and Aroles, J. (2020). 'Does the End Justify the Means? Information Systems and Control Society in the Age of Pandemics', *European Journal of Information Systems* 6 1–16.

Leclercq-Vandelannoitte, A., Isaac, H., and Kalika, M. (2014). 'Mobile Information Systems and Organisational Control: Beyond the Panopticon Metaphor?', *European Journal of Information Systems* 23/5: 543–557.

Levitas, R. (2013). *Utopia as Method: The Imaginary Reconstitution of Society*. Springer.

Marabelli, M., Vaast, E., and Li, L. (2021). 'Preventing the digital scars of COVID-19', *European Journal of Information Systems* 30/2: 176–192.

More, T. (1516/1965). *Utopia*. Penguin Classics.

Petriglieri, G., and Petriglieri, J. L. (2010). 'Identity Workspaces: The Case of Business Schools', *Academy of Management Learning & Education* 9/1: 44–60.

Riemer, K., Ciriello, R., Peter, S., and Schlagwein, D. (2020). 'Digital Contact-Tracing Adoption in the Covid-19 Pandemic: It Governance for Collective Action at the Societal Level', *European Journal of Information Systems* 29/6: 731–745.

Rowe, F., Ngwenyama, O., and Richet, J.-L. (2020). 'Contact-Tracing Apps and Alienation in the Age of Covid-19', *European Journal of Information Systems* 29/5: 545–562.

Sargent, L. T. (1994). 'The Three Faces of Utopianism Revisited', *Utopian Studies* 5/1: 1–37.

Seabrook, J. (2021). 'Has the Pandemic Transformed the Office Forever?', *The New Yorker*.

Sigaut, F. (1994). 'Technology', in T. Ingold (ed.), *Companion Encyclopedia of Anthropology: Humanity, Culture and Social Life*. Routledge, 420–459.

Susskind, J. (2018). *Future Politics: Living Together in a World Transformed by Tech.* Oxford University Press.

Urbaczewski, A., and Lee, Y. J. (2020). 'Information Technology and the Pandemic: A Preliminary Multinational Analysis of the Impact of Mobile Tracking Technology on the Covid-19 Contagion Control', *European Journal of Information Systems* 29/4: 405–414.

Vieira, F. (2010). 'The Concept of Utopia', *The Cambridge Companion to Utopian Literature*, Cambridge University Press, 3–27.

Wang, B., Schlagwein, D., Cecez-Kecmanovic, D., and Cahalane, M. C. (2020). 'Beyond the Factory Paradigm: Digital Nomadism and the Digital Future(s) of Knowledge Work Post-Covid-19', *Journal of the Association for Information Systems* 10: 1379–1401.

Zarocostas, J. (2020). 'How to Fight an Infodemic', *The Lancet* 395(10225): 676.

Zuboff, S. (2019). *The Age of Surveillance Capitalism: The Fight for a Human Future at the New Frontier of Power*. Profile Books.

# 6

# Physics or Archaeology?

## Process Organization Studies in the Age of Data Abundance

*Matthew Jones*

## 6.1 Introduction

It would be hard to dispute that the volume of data on organizational processes that is made available by digital technologies is unprecedented. With so much of contemporary work involving computers, elements of more and more organizational activities are textualized (or, as Zuboff (1988) would put it, informated), leaving traces that create a rich, and, importantly, potentially much more accessible and searchable, representation of activities that were previously only, at best, partially visible.

It is not just the digitalization of established organizational processes that has contributed to the growth in data. Information technologies have also given rise to many new activities and digital products, such as websites and social media, that have expanded the number and variety of organizational data sources. Online services also don't simply supplement, or possibly supplant, established processes, they necessarily create a digital record of each step, including those that do not lead to completion of the activity, enabling insight on where, and possibly why, organizational processes fail.

Even if it is not universally recognized that these data offer significant opportunities for organizational research (perhaps, in part, because their nature and scope is not always appreciated—even in fields such as Information Systems that might be expected to be more alert to the proliferation of digital data (Hedman et al. 2013)), there is nevertheless considerable support for such claims. This is often framed in terms of debates around 'big data'. George et al. (2016: 1496) propose, for example, that 'the continuous, ubiquitous nature of the data means that for the first time scholars can focus on the microfoundations of organizational strategies or behaviors;

Matthew Jones, *Physics or Archaeology?*. In: *Organizing in the Digital Age*. Edited by: Michael Barrett, Emmanuelle Vaast, Ann Langley, and Haridimos Tsoukas, Oxford University Press. © Oxford University Press (2024).
DOI: 10.1093/oso/9780198899457.003.0006

for instance, we can examine the dynamics of how business processes and opportunities evolve on a minute-to-minute, day-to-day basis, rather than being constrained to assess snapshots such as quarterly inputs and outcomes, or sales cycle trends'. Wenzel and Van Quaquebeke (2018) argue similarly that big data yield more unobtrusive, faithful and honest signals (relating to significant organizational phenomena) than those that have hitherto been available for organizational research, while Braun et al. (2018: 634) specifically identify the potential of digital data to provide 'more comprehensive understanding and finer-grained insights into individual, team, and organizational processes'.

In the wider social sciences this new capacity to collect and analyse massive amounts of (predominantly digital) data has been heralded by some as presaging the emergence of a 'computational social science' that will 'transform our understanding of our lives, organizations, and societies' (Lazer et al. 2009: 721). This is sometimes equated with the emergence of a new mind-set in research that Breiman (2001) describes in terms of a shift from a data modelling culture (in which data are collected according to some prior model and validated in terms of their goodness-of-fit) to an algorithmic culture (where the search is for a function that best describes the response process and validity is assessed by predictive accuracy). Whether this marks the demise of theory, as Anderson (2008) argued, continues to be contested, but it is generally agreed in this literature that a new era of interdisciplinary research is emerging in which 'social and behavioural scientists, cognitive scientists, agent theorists, computer scientists, mathematicians and physicists' will collaborate to 'uncover the laws of society' through 'the analysis of huge datasets' (Conte et al. 2012: 327).

Big data may thus be seen as finally realizing the vision, advanced nearly two hundred years ago by Auguste Comte (in what is often identified as the foundational text of sociology as an academic discipline) of a 'social physics' (Comte, 1835: 22) comparable, and complementary, to other branches of the natural sciences (that he referred to as inorganic and organic physics). Central to this project was the idea of a unity of the sciences, and the establishment of universal laws of society, based on the observation of facts. Indeed, this heritage is explicitly acknowledged in the title given by Alex 'Sandy' Pentland, one of the leading lights of computational social science, to his book exploring how the 'digital breadcrumbs' we leave behind in our daily lives can provide 'revolutionary insights' into how social networks spread ideas and shape human behaviour (Pentland 2014). Pentland earlier described his research as 'reality mining' (Pentland 2009: 80) and as providing a 'God's Eye view of ourselves'.

A comparable paradigm shift in management and organizational research is foreseen by a number of authors. Thus, Chang et al. argue (2014: 77) that big data 'capture information that represents the fundamental elements of human actions and interactions ... directly from the real world as digital traces of human behaviour' and are leading to 'fundamental changes' (Chang et al. 2014: 67) in the research questions that can be asked and the methods that can be applied. Similarly, George et al. (2016: 1494), see management research as on the verge of 'its next generational leap forward' as the vastly expanded scope and granularity of big data allows researchers to 'get more accurate estimations of effect sizes and their contingencies' and to 'establish clearer causal mechanisms'.

Other organizational researchers have also heralded the revolutionary potential of big data for 'quantitatively minded scientist-practitioners' (Tonidandel et al. 2018: 525) or have described them as a 'nascent paradigm' (Wenzel and Van Quaquebeke 2018: 549), but see them as complementing, rather than replacing, traditional methods. Nevertheless, despite evincing an appreciation of the risks, as well as opportunities, that big data may bring to organizational research, these authors mirror the computational social scientists in treating data as directly representing reality. Wenzel and Van Quaquabeke (2018: 575) argue, for example, that big data 'can reveal remarkable vistas about the means by which reality can be accessed and analysed'. Furthermore, the reference point for this 'advancement of organizational and management scholarship and practice' is explicitly identified as the 'real' sciences, not least physics. Big data, Wenzel and Van Quaquabeke (2018: 576) argue, can 'transform organizational *research* into organizational *science*' (emphasis in the original).

Adopting a process perspective on data, however, this chapter will seek to show that physics, as conventionally understood, may not be the most suitable model for organizational research in the age of data abundance. Data, perhaps especially of the big variety, it will be argued, are not naturally occurring givens that stand in a direct relationship with organizational reality. Rather, following Jones et al. (2019), they should be understood as the outcome of processes, the contingencies of which need to be recognized in their interpretation.

Archaeology, it will be proposed, may therefore be a more useful model than physics in understanding data in organizational research. The data we gather, for example, have always been constructed and are never a complete representation of the phenomena they are taken to be evidence of. However rigorous, systematic and reflective we may be, the full circumstances of the data's creation are likely to evade us and we necessarily reconstruct their meaning from our own presuppositions. The implications of such a reconceptualization of data in process organization studies will be explored.

## 6.2 Digital Data and Social Research

Discussion of big data in relation to social (and organizational) research typically proceeds from an enumeration of the volume, velocity, and variety, and sometimes several other 'Vs' (Uprichard 2013), of the digital data resources now available for the study of social phenomena. Notwithstanding the 'Everest' quality of some of these arguments (these data are important because they are there, in previously inconceivable abundance, not because they necessarily represent social phenomena better than other types), digital data are often also portrayed as an ineluctable force that will revolutionize social research. As Watts (2011: 266) puts it: 'just as the invention of the telescope revolutionized the study of the heavens, so too by rendering the unmeasurable measurable, the technological revolution in mobile, Web and Internet communications has the potential to revolutionize our understanding of ourselves and how we interact ... three hundred years after Alexander Pope argued that the proper study of mankind should lie not in the heavens, but in ourselves, we have finally found our telescope.' Taking a similar historical perspective, Shneiderman (2008: 1350) argued that 'Science 1.0 heroes such as Galileo, Newton, and Einstein produced key equations that describe the relationships among gravity, electricity, magnetism, and light. By contrast, Science 2.0 leaders are studying trust, empathy, responsibility, and privacy. The great adventure for the next 400 years will be to define, measure, and predict the interaction among these variables.'

Venturini and Latour (2015) foresee a similar revolutionary potential for digital data but propose that this lies not in refining and extending existing methods, but in providing an opportunity for the wholesale restructuring of social research. 'Endowed with a quantity of data comparable to the natural sciences', they argue, 'the social sciences can finally correct their lazy eyes and simultaneously maintain the focus and scope of their observations.' The old distinction in the social sciences between narrow and detailed (ethnographic) studies of specific interactions and broad, but superficial, studies of global structures thus becomes irrelevant. With every interaction passing through electronic media, they argue, it is now possible not just to track every social actor and their interactions with others, but to distinguish their individual contributions to the construction of social phenomena. Investigating these digital traces, however, will require new 'quali-quantitative' methods to be developed that will, they propose, 'reconnect micro and macro and show how global phenomena are built by the assemblage of local interactions' (Venturini and Latour 2015: 3).

While these studies typically pay little attention to specifically organizational phenomena, they are often cited in discussions of big data in management and organizational research and themes they promote, of revolutionary change, of greatly enhanced capabilities for measurement and prediction, and of micro–macro bridging inform some prominent discussions of big data in the organizational field.

## 6.3 Digital Data and Organizational Process Research

Despite recognition that digital data can provide highly granular, almost continuous and potentially real-time traces, that would, prima facie, seem to have potential to provide insight on the dynamics of organizational practices; however, these discussions in the social research literature do not appear, as yet, to have received much attention in organizational process research. In part this may be because, with its talk of clearer causal relationships and direct measurement of constructs, computational social science adopts, at best, a 'weak- process' perspective (Bakken and Hernes 2006) that seeks, as Langley and Tsoukas (2017: 3) put it, 'to provide the arrows that connect pre-existing, relatively stable boxes'. This may be considered a valued contribution in more formal process studies, such as sequence analysis (Poole et al. 2016), but would seem unlikely to hold much appeal for researchers adopting a 'strong-process' view that sees the world as process. Nor would the pursuit of a synoptic account of social interaction in the style of Venturini and Latour (2015) seem well matched to such a perspective, the focus of which tends to be on the situated enactment of specific practices.

Perhaps of more importance in the context of a discussion of the contribution of digital technologies to process research in organizations, however, is the way that data are viewed in the literature on big data/digital traces and organizational research. Consistent with their weak-process perspective, data in this literature are typically treated as a given, as entities that exist independently of the processes in which they may be used. Papers may therefore list the sorts of data that digital technologies make available, such as 'email communication, office entry and exit, radio-frequency identification tagging, wearable sociometric sensors, web browsers, and phone calls'

(George et al. 2016: 1494), but there is no analysis of how these data are produced or of their relationship to potential phenomena of interest.

Consider, for example, the claim of George et al. (2016: 1496), that 'once researchers can observe and analyze email communication or online search data, they can ask questions concerning the processes by which executives make decisions as opposed to studying the individual/top management team characteristics that affect managerial decisions'. While it would indeed seem reasonable that email and online search data may provide more insight on executive decision-making than the characteristics of individuals or the top management team, they do not necessarily provide access to decision-making processes. Rather this will depend on the way that data are recorded on executives' email and online searches, how executives use email and online search in their work practices, and what role email and online search play in their decision-making. If email logs record only the time, size, and recipients of messages, for example, then the insights will be more limited than if the message contents are also recorded (and accessible). Or, if executives use email only for certain tasks, and perhaps not at all for decision-making, then the data will be able to provide only partial insight on the process.

This does not mean that digital data can make no contribution to process research in organizations, rather it highlights the need for a more detailed and critical analysis of the particular types of data that might be drawn on in this research: how they are produced, how they are used, and how they contribute to the organizational phenomena being studied. This requires an understanding of data as a process (Jones 2019; Jones et al. 2019), that is as the product of sociomaterial practices that both shape and are shaped by the phenomena they are seen to represent.

Recognition of such an understanding is limited, however, not just in the organizational literature, but also in fields such as information systems that purport to have special insight on data. Indeed, it challenges a number of the central, if often tacit, assumptions of this literature in which data are typically defined as 'simple observations of states of the world' (Davenport and Prusak 1997: 9) and are seen as being 'out there', ready to be gathered by researchers. While some constraints on access to data may be acknowledged, these are rarely considered to affect their representation of the phenomena of interest, nor are data considered to be affected in the process of being gathered. In the context of process organization studies, especially those adopting a strong process perspective, however, it would seem important to recognize the processual character not just of the phenomena under investigation, but also of the data that are used to study them.

## 6.4 Data as Process

Jones (2019) identifies two stages in the process whereby data are constituted. The first comprises those activities that lead to particular aspects of a phenomenon of interest being recorded as data. Contrary to how they are generally presented in the big data literature, however, digital data are not, as Hedman et al. (2013: 6) would have it 'objective' or 'naturally occurring', even when they are nonreactive (Janetzko 2017), that is, collected without the awareness of the person(s) being studied. All digital data will at some point have been created, intentionally, or as byproduct of some other objective such as selling advertising, managing a building or caring for a patient. Digital traces, as Breiter and Hepp (2018: 391) argue, are therefore 'not "neutral phenomena"; rather, they rely on the technical procedures of governing institutions: the companies, administrations and agencies that produce this kind of data'. While this act of creation may be temporally distant from their designation as data, they are always a product of human-designed systems (including when they record natural phenomena and including when these systems malfunction and create spurious recordings). The capabilities of these systems, moreover, are always limited (Olteanu et al. 2017) so their representation of the phenomenon, while it may be sufficient for the functional purposes for which the systems were designed, will always be incomplete and potentially inaccurate. The Wayback Machine (https://web.archive.org/), for example, seeks to maintain an archive of the Internet as it evolves over time. To date it has archived 446 billion publicly accessible web pages since 2001, but the data it collects is limited by what website owners allow access to and by technical limitations of the crawler in extracting certain features of websites.

What is created, moreover, only becomes data through their being identified as such. Following Tuomi (1999), this may be seen as proceeding from a prior understanding within a thought collective (Fleck 1981) that identifies particular 'states of the world' as representing the phenomenon. This is the case even in physics, as Tuomi describes. The readings given by a thermometer (that has been designed according to established conventions) are taken as data reporting what temperature *is*.

It might be argued that there is a 'ground truth' to physics data, that they describe phenomena that exist independently of their representation, although this does not make the data any less dependent on the prior understanding of what they stand for. Furthermore, as Wenzel and Van Quaquebeke (2018) note, albeit in a defence of the potential of big data to make organizational research more scientific, physics also addresses phenomena, such as dark matter, the existence and properties of which can only be inferred from data taken as evidence of them. Few organizational phenomena (exceptions might include size, age, or presence or absence of certain roles or attributes) have an evidently independent existence, however, and most are inferred from particular understandings of their nature.

This relationship between data and phenomenon is further attenuated in the case of digital data, especially where these are traces collected for purposes other than the representation of organizational phenomena. Indeed, a key issue in much research using digital traces relates to deciding (and justifying) what the traces may be considered to be data about. Data do not exist independently of their designation, therefore, but are constituted, as data (representing a particular phenomenon), in this process (summarized in Figure 6.1). The complexities of the sociomaterial activities and transactions that contribute to the constitution of data in the case of a Clinical Information System are illustrated by Jones et al. (2019).

The outcome of the process described in Figure 6.1, however, are simply records, usually held in some sort of database. For the data held in these records to contribute to organizational practices such as product design or executive decision-making, there needs to be a second process in which data are retrieved and used. Only those data that have been created and made available in the first stage will be in a position to be retrieved and used, but only a proportion of these data may actually be retrieved and used in practice. Those data that are not retrieved and used are, Jones et al. (2019) argue, only 'data in principle' and can only indirectly affect social practice (for example if awareness of email data being collected influences executives' decision-making).

Olteanu et al. (2017), present one possible account of the activities comprising this second stage in terms of an 'idealized data processing pipeline', as shown in Figure 6.2. Thus, before data can play a role in organizational processes or contribute to research, sources of data need to be identified,

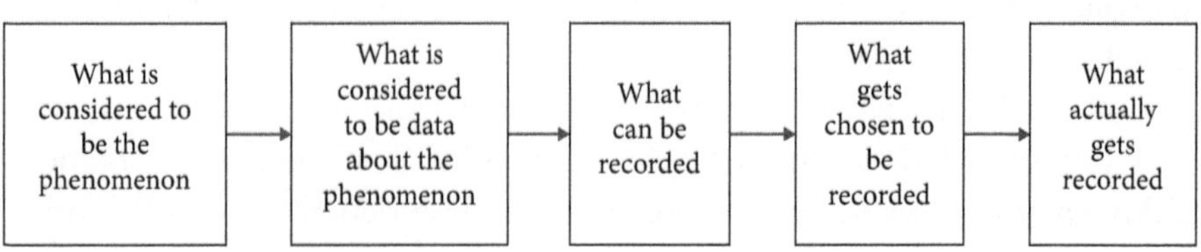


**Figure 6.1** The constitution of data

*Source:* after Jones et al. 2019.

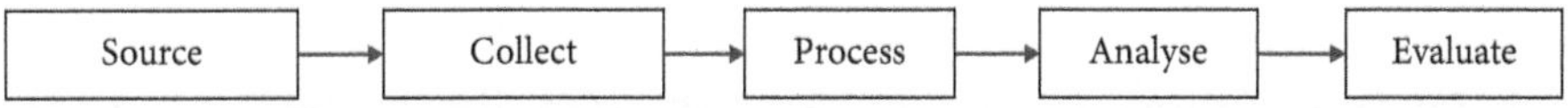


**Figure 6.2** Idealized data processing pipeline

*Source:* after Olteanu et al. 2017.

and data retrieved from them. They may also need to be processed (cleaned, reformatted), analysed (to characterize and make inferences about user populations and behaviours), and evaluated for reliability.

As Olteanu et al. recognize, in describing the data processing pipeline in Figure 6.2 as 'idealized', not all data are necessarily processed in the same way and in particular instances some steps may be reduced, omitted, or modified. The pipeline metaphor also suggests a linearity, seamlessness, and integrity to the 'flow' of data that may be misleading. Nevertheless, considering the process involved in retrieving and processing data, such that they may be used in organizational practices, as comprising a series of steps may be helpful in structuring an analysis of digital data from a process perspective.

The current focus will be on the first three steps, though, as these are the ones at which the effects of the volume and velocity of digital data are most noticeable. Choosing how to analyse and evaluate digital data would seem to involve similar issues (e.g. appropriate analyses, sensitivity, publication bias) to those encountered with more traditional data sources.

### 6.4.1 Not All (Digital) Data Are Equal

Before considering the implications of this process view of data for the contribution of digital data to organizational process research, however, it would seem important to recognize the heterogeneity of digital data, as claims in relation to particular types of data may not apply to all others. This has not always been adequately addressed in prior literature exploring the potential of digital data for organizational research, especially in papers that address the issue through the lens of 'big data', which tend to discuss data as an undifferentiated quantity.

Although not exhaustive, several different types of data potentially relevant to organizational process research may be identified. The first, and a particular focus of 'big data' social research (Bruns 2013), is social media entries, such as Twitter and Facebook posts. A second is organization websites (e.g. Gehman and Grimes 2017). A third is blog posts and contributions to online communities (Hookway and Snee 2017) and a fourth is organizational email and other messaging records (e.g. Akemu and Abdelnour 2018). A fifth type can be broadly described as digital traces (Breiter and Hepp 2018), which may be further subdivided between: those actively registered by individuals, for example through completion of online time-sheets or use of personal health monitors; those directly generated in the course of interactions between an individual and an organization, such as credit card transactions or use of an access card to gain entry to a building; and those gathered as a byproduct (sometimes without the individual's knowledge) of these interactions, such as by web trackers, or location tracking on mobile phones. These types vary widely on a number of dimensions including volume, accessibility, structure, and granularity and how they are created.

Social media entries, for example, are typically qualitative and unstructured, but of high volume (and rate) and high granularity, down to the level of individual posts and likes. Access to such data has varied over time, becoming increasingly restrictive in the face of privacy concerns, and is now largely controlled by the companies involved who grant, or sell, access to curated data sets. Organizations may also have their own social media presence that may be a source of data on company practices (or of the way in which they are presented to the public).

Organizational websites are similarly intended to be publicly accessible, although there may be sections that are kept private. Organizations may also adopt measures to restrict or block access to their sites by the web-scraping tools typically used to gather such data at volume. There is little standardization of website data structure or content and content may be highly dynamic. Blogs and online community posts are another source of generally publicly accessible, qualitative, and unstructured data, but generally created by individuals.

Access to emails is likely to require permission from the organization and may be restricted to highly structured log data, simply reporting the time of sending and recipients of messages, analogous to telephone Call Detail Records (CDRs). A rare exception is the Enron dataset comprising the full text of 200,000 messages exchanged between 151 senior managers that were released as part of the investigations of the company after its collapse (Klimt and Yang 2004).

Digital traces are also generally private and organizations are likely to be reluctant to allow access to them, as they are seen as potentially commercially confidential and may raise privacy concerns. Getting hold of these data is therefore likely to require lengthy negotiation. Digital traces will typically be highly structured and granular, as they are produced to support automated processes. Their content, format, and duration of storage will also be determined by the uses to which they are put in the organization, which may limit their suitability for secondary use in research.

Bearing these differences in mind, it would therefore seem important for studies of digital data in process organizational research to be specific about the data (cf. Monteiro and Hanseth 1996) and to pay attention to their particular characteristics rather than treating data as a uniform entity. While specific dimensions may be more or less significant in different contexts an awareness of the potential scope of variation can help to moderate generalizations about 'digital data' as a whole.

### 6.4.2 Digital Data in Organizational Process Research Revisited

With this qualification in mind, we can now begin to consider the processes by which digital data may come to used in organizational process research. This begins with their initial designation as data. Whether they are social media entries, emails, websites, or digital traces they are not a natural expression of a phenomenon, in the way that, in the natural sciences, radiation emitted by a pulsar might be. Rather they will necessarily have been created, whether knowingly or not, by the person(s) who designed and developed the digital technology that produced them. A researcher designating them as 'data about phenomenon X' is therefore engaged in an act of interpretation (unavoidably shaped by their interests in seeking data about the phenomenon), that may or may not correspond to what was understood by those original designers and developers. While in many instances the conventions for recording particular data items may be standardized, in the absence of any independent record of those phenomena it may be impossible to know whether this designation is correct.

Even if it is assumed that what is taken to be data about a phenomenon are a sufficient representation of it, digital data may face particular problems of data quality. This is not necessarily because digital data are of inherently lower quality than other types of data, but rather because the volume and velocity at which they are produced may make it difficult to detect problems. The discourse around big data also promotes attention to the findings that can be produced from data without interrogating their quality too closely. As Cukier and Mayer-Schonberger (2013: 29) put it, big data mean that we need to 'shed our preference for highly curated and pristine data and instead accept messiness: in an increasing number of situations, a bit of inaccuracy can be tolerated, because the benefits of using vastly more data of variable quality outweigh the costs of using smaller amounts of very exact data'.

Data quality may be measured along a number of dimensions (Rasmussen 2017), among which completeness, correctness, concordance, plausibility, and currency are commonly identified (Weiskopf and Weng 2013). Although, on each of these dimensions digital data may potentially be of higher quality than data that are manually recorded, this may not always be the case and the volume of digital data may impede the evaluation of quality.

When data collection is automated digital data also face the problem of unpredictable and potentially undetected errors due to equipment malfunction or miscalibration. Similarly, given the ease with which digital data are generated and the continuing evolution of technology there can also be problems of data sparsity and discontinuity as multiple, often inconsistent, data series are successively accumulated. Even without considering potential issues in the gathering and processing of data therefore, it would seem important for researchers to be more aware of the possible deficiencies of available data as a representation of a phenomenon of interest.

Too often in the literature, however, digital data are treated as a given and discussion proceeds from the assumption that they are a sufficient representation of the phenomenon. Sometimes this assumption is explicit. Hedman et al. (2013: 15) argue, for example, that 'Bluetooth communications, Facebook updates, Internet purchases, and Twitter interactions promise to reveal what contemporary life is all about', while Wenzel and Van Quaquebeke (2018) talk of reality being converted into data. Frequently, however, the representational fidelity of digital data is simply taken for granted.

This view is challenged by authors such as Olteanu et al. (2017) who review a wide range of biases and inaccuracies that social data (which they define as the product of social software such as social media and networking sites, recommendation and Q&A sites, collaborative sites and search platforms) may be subject to. Among the general challenges they discuss are population biases, behavioural biases, temporal variations, and redundancy.

Population biases relate to the differences in demographics or other user characteristics between a population of users represented in a dataset and those of the population they are seen as representing. The users of different social media platforms vary by age, gender, and ethnicity, for example, and users of social media are not necessarily representative of the population as a whole. There may also be cultural norms that influence how particular populations use social media and inferences drawn from social data about the demographics and personal traits of users may not be reliable.

Behavioural biases are concerned with differences in user behaviour across platforms or contexts. The way that people communicate varies on different social media, for example, or the traces left by users may vary with the tasks for which they use platforms such as search engines. Social data may also rely on some degree of, often unreliable, self-reporting and may be influenced by content consumption biases leading to 'filter bubbles'.

Olteanu et al.'s category of temporal variations refers to differences in populations and behaviours over time. These may reflect changes in the population using social software as well as temporal variations in interaction patterns, including in response to changes in the platforms themselves. Social software use may also exhibit seasonal and periodic patterns and may be significantly affected by sudden-onset events. Of potential significance for process studies, Olteanu et al. suggest that the time granularity of social data may not be well-matched to particular phenomena and emphasize that datasets decay and lose utility over time, for example as content gets deleted (by users, or the platform).

The final general challenge identified by Olteanu et al. relates to the redundancy of data due to the same entity posting from multiple accounts (i.e. spam), multiple entities posting from the same account (e.g. organizational accounts) and multiple accounts posting the same content (e.g. retweeting). It may therefore be problematic to interpret evidence based on the incidence of data.

Olteanu et al. (2017) also identify additional, more specific, challenges that may arise at each step of their data pipeline. At the source stage, for example, they identify functional biases that may arise from the particular configuration of platforms. These include the effects of platform design and algorithms on user behaviour. They also identify written or unwritten norms that may influence user behaviour and the potential contamination of findings by the activities of bots. At the data acquisition stage, platforms may only allow restricted access to parts of their data, applying opaque sampling strategies. Data querying may also be limited by the expressiveness of APIs, the operationalization of information needs and the consistency of metadata. Data processing involves cleaning, enrichment, and aggregation and may be done manually or automatically. This can introduce bias either by suppressing differences or by exacerbating them. The distinctive challenges of such 'data wrangling' in the context of big data are explored by Braun et al. (2018).

Although Olteanu et al.'s only discuss the biases and pitfalls of social data, many of the issues they identify may also apply to other forms of digital data. Thus, as Blank (2017) observes, digital traces are often transactional, because that reflects the purposes for which they are generated, and provide no access to attitudes, motivations, meanings. They are also recorded for the convenience of users, not researchers, and so generally lack nuance or context. Repurposing of traces for research purposes thus has to rely on assumptions that cannot be validated from the 'thin description' (Janetzko 2017) of phenomena that the traces themselves provide.

A further problem with digital traces is what Tufekci (2014) calls the missing denominator problem. That is, claims made from trace data should relate to the sub-population that might have been in a position to generate that trace, but some of these will have taken no action or will have taken action in ways that were not captured by the trace. Rarely, however, is it possible to estimate the potential size of this sub-population (precisely because they leave no trace), let alone to know how representative they are of any larger population about which it may be intended to make inferences.

The combination of these biases and methodological pitfalls means that claims that digital data provide a direct and transparent representation of organizational phenomena needs to be subject to multiple caveats. This does not necessarily invalidate findings based on such data, but it should invite greater caution in the claims that are made from them.

Questioning digital data in this way is not about denying their potential contribution but about encouraging organizational process researchers to treat them in ways that are more consistent with the principles on which their research is based.

A process perspective on digital data also needs to go beyond a simple balance sheet of 'opportunities and risks' of digital data of the sort presented by Wenzel and Van Quaquebeke (2018) that treats big data as undifferentiated, to recognize the contingencies by which data are materialized in specific contexts. This will require, as Ruppert et al. (2013: 32) argue, attention to the specificity of digital technologies and the data they produce: 'where and how they happen, who and what they are attached to and the relations they forge, how they get assembled, where they travel, their multiple arrangements and mobilizations, and, of course, their instabilities, durabilities'. This would seem an agenda that organizational process research would seem well positioned to pursue.

## 6.5 Discussion

The idea that digital data instrument reality, providing direct access to organizational phenomena in a way that would have been previously inconceivable, would seem to be highly seductive, especially, to those who would identify themselves as organizational scientists (e.g. Tonidandel et al. 2018, Wenzel and Van Quaquebeke 2018). It is also fed by what Elish and Boyd (2017) refer to as the 'magic of big data' that, we are told, has created an unprecedented cornucopia of information that can transform our understanding of organizations and the world. The question now, it is suggested, is no longer what data on the phenomena we study can we gather by arduous and inefficient traditional methods, but how can we use the ever-growing mountains of data that are being continuously churned out by digital technologies to understand these phenomena.

As this chapter has sought to argue, though, this is to put the cart before the horse. We need to understand what these data may be seen as saying about the phenomena we are studying before we start deciding what they tell us. Such critical analysis is too often lacking in discussion of digital data, yet, as has been shown, such data are neither uniform in their character, nor a natural, transparent, or complete representation of the phenomena they are taken to be a record of.

It is not just that there may be biases, technical problems, and errors in the data, but that their existence as data 'about' a phenomenon does not reflect a natural condition. It is an interpretation placed on them by particular social actors in whose practices they are used. Some designations may be strongly institutionalized, such that what counts as data about particular phenomena is taken for granted. With the proliferation of digital data, and especially of digital traces, whose meaning may be less fixed, however, it is often necessary for those using the data (including organizational researchers) to persuade others that particular data items may be reasonably considered to represent the phenomenon. Rarely, however, do such claims address the ways in which data come to be constituted, or even set out the reasoning behind the designation. While it may be a counsel of perfection to expect this to be done in every instance, the more frequent surfacing of these assumptions would seem important, especially in process research that may be expected to be sensitive to the activities and transactions that constitute data.

In considering the implications of the process perspective on data discussed in this chapter for organizational process research, four different ways in which digital data may figure in such research may be distinguished. The first comprises process studies of digital data themselves. While there has been work in the critical data studies field that has addressed digital data in general (Ruppert et al. 2013; Kitchin and Lauriault 2018) and work in science studies on data journeys in the sciences (Leonelli and Tempini 2020) little of this has a specifically organizational focus.

There would therefore seem to be a considerable opportunity for process studies of particular, organizationally significant, digital data. How, for example, do digital traces of the work of gig economy employees come to be constituted as resources for their management (and how do employees seek to respond to this)? The specific focus in such studies would be on tracing the biography of particular data objects.

The second way expands the focus to address the sociomaterial apparatus that is involved in the constitution of particular types of digital data. There are some existing organizational studies of this type, such as Dourish (2017) on spreadsheets, Kelly and Noonan (2017) on datafication in the Indian healthcare system, or Pollock and D'Adderio (2012) on the Gartner Magic Quadrant, although these do not always conceptualize this as a process. Such studies seem likely to emphasize the enactment of digital data in specific, situated practices, for example in the assessment of corporate board diversity. As more and more organizational processes are informated, the range of practices that could be the potential subject of such studies is rapidly expanding.

The third type studies organizational phenomena that make use of digital data, but where the focus is not on the constitution of the data themselves but on how the digital data contributed to new organizational practices. Vaast et al. (2017), for example, studied the use of Twitter in supporting new forms of collective engagement in response to the Gulf of Mexico oil spill, while Glozer et al. (2019) examined the use of corporate social media in legitimation processes. Despite digital data not being the main focus of such studies, a process perspective on data may nevertheless support critical reflection on the representation of the phenomenon and the significance of the findings.

The final type of study is those, such as Gehman and Grimes' study of category promotion among certified B Corporations (Gehman and Grimes 2017) or Riedl and Seidel (2018) on learning in an online innovation contest. The data in these studies are digital, but the focus is not on how this changes organizational practices. Rather the research is on a phenomenon (category promotion, learning) which it is possible, with digital data to study at a previously inconceivable scale. While the data are even more peripheral to the research than in the third type, the possible effects of biases and pitfalls of digital data, such as those discussed by Olteanu et al. (2017), would still seem to deserve consideration.

The process perspective on data can therefore contribute to each of these streams of research by unsettling the, often tacit, assumptions that data are naturally occurring and that they directly represent reality. Paying attention to the contingent construction of data and recognizing the biases and inaccuracies that they are subject to may also help to dispel the stupefaction that seems to overcome discussions of digital data at scale. Contrary to the claims of some big data proponents, the volume of data should not lead us to abandon critical scrutiny of them (even if it may make it harder to spot flaws).

This does not mean that scope and richness of digital data does not offer a potentially significant resource for process organizational research, but the challenge is to employ this resource skilfully, with an awareness of its limitations. Nor does it mean there are no circumstances in which the computational social science approach will be effective. Clearly there are many companies and researchers who have been very successful in gaining insights from big data. The issue is not that it is not possible to do worthwhile research or to increase company performance with big data, but whether doing so shows that their assumptions about data are valid. If the limitations of digital data as a representation of organizational phenomena are not significant to the questions they want to answer then the issues raised in this chapter need not be a concern.

From Facebook's point of view, for example, it is not necessary that the data they hold is representative of any population other than users of Facebook, or that the data accurately represent these users, so long as the data are good enough that advertisers believe they can reach an audience more effectively through Facebook than by other means. Similarly if researchers can gather large volumes of data, for example on personality (Kosinski et al. 2013), through Facebook and correlate this with other data from Facebook then these findings are valid for that, potentially very large, sample, whether or not they would hold for a wider population or other measures might provide more insight on the correlated data.

Opening up digital data to more critical scrutiny also highlights three significant issues that have implications for process research: fluidity, validity, and representativeness. With respect to the first of these, although the idea that digital data are not permanent, but come and go and mutate over time might seem particularly problematic for research that seeks to identify enduring causal relationships and places a strong emphasis on standardization and replication, it still raises issues for strong process research that views organizations as constantly in flux. The instability and unboundedness of digital artefacts (Ekbia 2009) renders the representations of organizational phenomena that they provide and the claims that may be made from them context-dependent and impermanent. Of itself, this is not necessarily anything completely new for process research but requires that the accounting for contingency now be extended beyond the researcher's own actions to include the data sources on which they draw. Ultimately, strong process research still rests on a claim that the data employed are an adequate representation of the relevant phenomenon, however reflexive we may be about the constructions of our accounts.

Concerns regarding the validity of digital data relate to the biases and omissions to which they may be subject. This is not to suggest that other data have no biases or omissions, but that the automation of many of the processes of data production and their inaccessibility in many commercial situations means that their significance is not easily evaluated. The arguments of big data proponents that data quantity makes concerns about their accuracy no longer relevant, however, seem highly debatable. The quality of inferences still relies on the accuracy of the data about a phenomenon however large the volume of data may be. If digital data misrepresent the phenomenon then any findings from their analysis will be suspect. Indeed, this problem is potentially exacerbated where the volume of data means that analysis is only possible using machine learning techniques that need to be 'trained' on data that may exhibit the same biases, producing analyses that simply entrench the original distortions (O'Neil 2016). Process research would seem well-placed to advance a more systematic and critical approach to digital data.

The question of the representativeness of digital data is perhaps less of an issue for strong process research that does not usually seek to make population level generalizations. It offers a direct challenge, however, to proponents of the view that big data enables organizational research to become more like physics, that 'ever more precise data and analyses' (Wenzel and van Quaquebeke 2018: 576) will transform organizational research.

Even researchers who accept that, as Kitchin puts it (2014: 4), 'all data provide oligoptic views of the world: views from certain vantage points, using particular tools, rather than an all-seeing, infallible God's eye view', may nevertheless see digital data as opening new research vistas. Venturini and Latour (2015: 7), for example, argue that digital data enable a continuity of vision 'from the tiniest micro-interaction to the largest macro-structure'. The conditions for achieving this continuous span of data, however, seem no more realistic than that of computational social scientists' panopticon, depending, as it does, on the digitization of the entire social research chain, from the identification of digital data sources to the online, open publication of results. Nor, the argument of this chapter suggests, will this digitization necessarily make the representation of the world provided by digital data complete in their coverage at any level or continuous in their spanning of these levels. Contrary to the claims of some proponents, big data (and digital data more generally) do not abolish the question of how well data represent a phenomenon being studied and this will continue to be a significant issue in process research.

In suggesting that digital data are not the methodological panacea that their proponents present them as, it is important recognize that, as Powell et al. (2016) observe, fluidity, opacity, context-dependence and the potential for misrepresentation and sampling bias are no less of an issue with traditional data sources. The passage of time may have blunted awareness, for example, that interview data are 'researcher-provoked', as Silverman (2009) argues, or that observational research tends to rely on informants who may be marginal in the social structures being investigated (Pettigrew 1973), but they are no less a challenge to claims that direct, face-to-face interaction with the individuals engaged in them should necessarily be privileged as a source of insight on organizational practices. A critical perspective needs to be applied to all data, therefore, not just those that are the product of digital technologies.

## 6.6 Towards an Archaeology of Digital Data

That the vision that digital technologies will provide abundant, objective, and detailed data that will finally enable an understanding of organizations equivalent to the understanding of the physical world provided by the natural sciences is a mirage, would seem unlikely to comes as surprise to many process research scholars. Big data brings us no closer to an organizational physics. Data are always a construction, carved, as Gitelman and Jackson (2013: 3) argue, out of the 'seamlessness of phenomena'. This is not a discovery of a natural resource, but an imagining into being that is shaped by a prior conception of the phenomenon that the data are considered as standing for.

Nor, however would there seem to be any necessary complementarity between digital and traditional data as authors such as Bornakke and Due (2018) and Wenzel and Van Quaquebeke (2018) suggest. As Blaikie (1991) argues in relation to methodological triangulation, it would seem no more likely that the combination of digital and traditional data will compensate for each other's weaknesses than that they will reinforce each other's limitations. If digital data, in themselves or in combination with traditional data, do not make possible an organizational physics of an objective reality subject to precisely understood forces, therefore, then how may we understand their contribution to organizational research?

This chapter has proposed archaeology as a more fitting model for understanding data from a process perspective. As with any analogy, it may disguise as much as it reveals, but would seem to offer a number of suggestive parallels. An archaeology of digital data, for example, would highlight the incompleteness of representation. What is found by an archaeologist is what has survived, that has not been displaced too far and that has been recognized as material remains. Correspondingly, digital data that are used in organizational process research need to have been both recordable and recorded as data, to have been identified as representing the phenomenon of interest and to have been successfully retrieved. At each of these stages the representation of the phenomenon may lose some resolution.

In organizational research, including the process variety, however, the existence of data is often treated as a black box and attention is focused exclusively on what the data show rather than how they come to be. Simply ignoring the problem in this way, though, as Sullivan (1978) argues in relation to archaeology, is to make strong assumptions 'about the processes responsible for producing the sample examined by the archaeologist to generate the requisite data'. Greater recognition of equivalent data generation processes and their possible effects on the understanding of organizational phenomena would therefore seem desirable (and consistent with a process orientation).

If we accept the incompleteness and contingency of the representation of phenomena that data can provide, then we need also to reconsider how we make sense of data. Data do not speak to us directly, offering us a clear picture of what they portray. Rather what we see in the data is shaped by our preconceptions. In archaeology this has led to a recognition that any reconstruction of what was there before will necessarily be based on conjecture, or what Schmidt (1999: 66) describes more forcefully as 'the fantasy of the archaeologist'.

Sullivan (1978) draws a distinction between deposits of material remains (which he describes, in terms that resonate with the argument of this chapter, as 'phenomena which archaeologists manipulate to generate data') and the evidence or data that they are seen to offer. In archaeology, he argues, the temporal distance between deposition and excavation, means that any account made of finds that goes beyond description of their properties must be inferential.

The same may be argued in relation to digital data. Though there may be little, if any, temporal distance between phenomena and the data generated from them, we may have no more access to the processes involved and can only infer how they may have operated. Thus, any model of organizational phenomena that we may build from data, whether causal or processual, potentially bears no more relation to the phenomenon than Evans' reconstruction of Knossos, described by German (2018) as 'as much evocative and picturesque as historically accurate', does to the original Minoan palace.

Even if we can show that the materials were found at the site, or that the data are plausibly indicative of the phenomenon, the original relationship of the materials to each other, or of the data to the phenomenon, cannot be definitively known and we must make assumptions about their relationship. More data, per se, will not improve the situation if these assumptions are incorrect, or necessarily get us nearer to the truth, since we don't know what we are missing or misreading. It is therefore necessary for us to be alert to the potential fallibility and contingency of our understanding and to try to surface the assumptions we make in doing so. It may also be helpful to consider what data might cause us to doubt our understanding and whether the data we have might sustain other interpretations. Promoting such analytical scepticism may not be a radical suggestion for process organization research, but does not always seem to be applied in relation to data, especially those designated as 'big'.

Another potential way that perspectives on data in process organization research may be informed by archaeology relates to the variable survival of particular types of materials, which may find an echo in the ability of digital data to record particular sorts of phenomena relative to others. We may be able to use sensors, or even mobile phones, for example, to record when individuals in an organization come into proximity with each other, but this does not provide any information on the form or content of any associated interaction. We therefore need to give consideration to what aspects of a phenomenon are highlighted in, and which omitted from, the digital record.

Even if archaeological materials survive, the relationship between deposits of remains and their original form and location and between different types of deposits is highly uncertain. Remains may have been displaced, intentionally or by physical or biological processes, for example, or have been altered over time. Archaeologists therefore pay particular attention to three related concepts—association, context and provenience—that seek to inform the interpretation of these relationships (Lyman 2012). Provenience (to be distinguished from the more familiar provenance which describes the place of origin of a find) refers to the precise location of a find in four-dimensional space (vertical, horizontal latitude and longitude and geological or stratigraphic), relative to some reference system. Provenience is empirical and absolute and may be more or less detailed. Association, on the other hand, refers to the mutual positioning of two or more finds. It is therefore relative and inferential. So too is the third concept, context, which refers to the broader physical and cultural environment within which particular remains are found.

While, for much digital data, there may no such absolute reference system, nor can all relationships between data necessarily be mapped on the same dimensions, the idea that researchers should analyse and report the context within which digital data have been created, their relationship with other data sources and the circumstances of their retrieval may be helpful in enabling other researchers to gain some insight on their suitability in representing the phenomenon. We see this, to some extent, with the dating of access to websites and with efforts to contextualize digital traces (Breiter and Hepp 2018) or online community posts (Vaast and Levina 2015), but this tends to be the exception rather than the rule. Greater attention to, and discussion of, the conditions of data production would seem needed.

## 6.7 Conclusion

The profusion of digital data related to organizational processes has led to claims that they will at last enable organizational research to become a proper science, that a physics of organizations is now possible. Although process organization researchers, especially those adopting a strong process ontology, would seem unlikely to share this objective, the way in which they talk about data often does not appear very different from that of computational social scientists. Data are treated as a given and discussion focuses on what analysis of them can tell us about organizational processes. This discussion may be more nuanced, and more cautious about the truth and universality of the claims that can be made, but the status of the data, on which these claims are based, as a representation of reality is rarely interrogated. Indeed, any questioning seems to become lost in the excitement at the burgeoning data resources that are now available. Even if they do not subscribe to the view that 'with enough data the numbers speak for themselves' (Anderson 2008) there is just too much that can be done with digital data to look this particular gift horse in the mouth.

This chapter has sought to suggest that, in this new era of data abundance, it would seem important for process organizational scholars to remain consistent with the logic of their own position and apply a process perspective to digital data. Building on the process conception of data introduced in Jones et al. (2019), the contingencies involved in the constitution of data as entities available to be 'gathered' and their shaping as they are subsequently retrieved for analysis are explored. On this view, data, even digital data, do not provide a natural, transparent, or complete representation of organizational phenomena. Similar arguments have been made in the fields of critical data studies and science studies, but do not seem to have been widely addressed in the organizational literature.

One way in which the implications of such a shift in perspective might be understood is in terms of the model of the process of knowledge acquisition that organizational research might aspire to. If, explicitly for advocates of a computational organizational science and implicitly for unreflective enthusiasts for the potential of big (digital) data in organizational research, the reference point is taken to be physics, then the alternative, for researchers adopting a processual approach to data, might be archaeology.

Features of an archaeology of digital data might include: attention to data generation processes; recognition of the necessarily inferential character of most accounts of organizational phenomena; acknowledgement of the assumptions contributing to these accounts; appreciation of the aspects of organizational phenomena that are more strongly or weakly registered by digital data; and a greater effort to disclose and reflect on the conditions of data production. A number of these may already be part of the research approach of process organization scholars, but, in providing a framework and rationale for such practices, the hope is to encourage a more considered response to the ever greater abundance of digital data that are available to organizational researchers.

## References

Akemu, O., and Abdelnour, S. (2018). 'Confronting the Digital: Doing Ethnography in Modern Organizational Settings', *Organizational Research Methods* 23/2: p. 1094428118791018.

Anderson, C. (2008). 'The End of Theory: The Data Deluge Makes the Scientific Method Obsolete', *Wired*, 23 June 2008.

Bakken, T., and Hernes, T. (2006). 'Organizing Is Both a Verb and a Noun: Weick Meets Whitehead', *Organization Studies* 27/11: 1599–1616.

Blaikie, N. W. H. (1991). 'A Critique of the Use of Triangulation in Social Research', *Quality and Quantity* 25/2:115–136.

Blank, G. (2017). 'Online Research Methods and Social Theory', in Fielding, N. G., Lee, R. M., and Blank, G. (eds), *The SAGE Handbook of Online Research Methods*. Sage, 537–550.

Bornakke, T., and Due, B. L. (2018). 'Big–Thick Blending: A Method for Mixing Analytical Insights from Big and Thick Data Sources', *Big Data & Society* 5/1: 1–16.

Braun, M. T., Kuljanin, G., and DeShon, R. P. (2018). 'Special Considerations for the Acquisition and Wrangling of Big Data', *Organizational Research Methods* 21/3: 633–659.

Breiman, L. (2001). 'Statistical Modeling: The Two Cultures', *Statistical Science* 16/3: 199–231.

Breiter, A., and Hepp, A. (2018). 'The Complexity of Datafication: Putting Digital Traces in Context', in Hepp, A., Breiter, A., and Hasebrink, U. (eds), *Communicative Figurations: Transforming Communications in Times of Deep Mediatization.* Springer International Publishing, 387–405.

Bruns, A. (2013). 'Faster than the Speed of Print: Reconciling "Big Data" Social Media Analysis and Academic Scholarship', *First Monday* 18(10).

Chang, R. M., Kauffman, R. J., and Kwon, Y. (2014). 'Understanding the Paradigm Shift to Computational Social Science in the Presence of Big Data', *Decision Support Systems* 63: 67–80.

Conte, R. et al. (2012). 'Manifesto of Computational Social Science', *The European Physical Journal Special Topics* 214/1:325–346.

Cukier, K., and Mayer-Schoenberger, V. (2013). 'The Rise of Big Data: How It's Changing the Way We Think about the World', *Foreign Affairs* 92: 28–40.

Davenport, T. H., and Prusak, L. (1997). *Information Ecology: Mastering the Information and Knowledge Environment.* Oxford University Press.

Dourish, P. (2017). *The Stuff of Bits: An Essay on the Materialities of Information.* MIT Press.

Ekbia, H. R. (2009). 'Digital Artifacts as Quasi-objects: Qualification, Mediation, and Materiality', *Journal of the American Society for Information Science and Technology* 60/12: 2554–2566.

Elish, M. C., and Boyd, D. (2018). 'Situating Methods in the Magic of Big Data and AI', *Communication Monographs* 85/1: 57–80.

Fleck, L. (1981). *Genesis and Development of a Scientific Fact.* University of Chicago Press.

Gehman, J., and Grimes, M. (2016). 'Hidden Badge of Honor: How Contextual Distinctiveness Affects Category Promotion among Certified B Corporations', *Academy of Management Journal* 60/6: 2294–2320.

George, G., Osinga, E. C., Lavie, D., and Scott, B. A. (2016). 'Big Data and Data Science Methods for Management Research', *Academy of Management Journal* 59/5: 1493–1507.

German, S. (2018). 'Conservation vs. Restoration: The Palace at Knossos (Crete)'. Available at https://smarthistory.org/conservation-knossos/.

Glozer, S., Caruana, R., and Hibbert, S. A. (2019). 'The Never-Ending Story: Discursive Legitimation in Social Media Dialogue', *Organization Studies* 40/5: 625–650.

Hedman, J., Srinivasan, N., and Lindgren, R. (2013). 'Digital Traces of Information Systems: Sociomateriality made Researchable', in Baskerville, R. and Chau, M. (eds), *Proceedings of the 34th International Conference on Information Systems, Milan, Italy*. Atlanta, GA: Association for Information Systems

Hookway, N., and Snee, H. (2017). 'The Blogosphere', in Fielding, N. G., Lee, R. M., and Blank, G. (eds), *The SAGE Handbook of Online Research Methods*. Sage, 380–398.

Janetzko, D. (2017). 'Nonreactive Data Collection Online', in Fielding, N. G., Lee, R. M., and Blank, G. (eds), *The SAGE Handbook of Online Research Methods*. Sage, 76–91.

Jones, M. (2019). 'What We Talk about When We Talk about (Big) Data', *The Journal of Strategic Information Systems* 28/1: 3–16.

Jones, M., Blackwell, A., Prince, K., Meakins, S., Simpson A., and Vuylsteke, A. (2019). 'Data as Process: From Objective Resource to Contingent Performance', in Reay, T., Zilber, T., Langley, A., and Tsoukas, H. (eds), *Institutions and Organizations: A Process View*. Oxford: Oxford University Press, 227–250.

Kelly, S., and Noonan, C. (2017). 'The Doing of Datafication (and What This Doing Does): Practices of Edification and the Enactment of New Forms of Sociality in the Indian Public Health Service', *Journal of the Association for Information Systems* 18/12: 872–899.

Kitchin, R. (2014) 'Big Data, New Epistemologies and Paradigm Shifts', *Big Data & Society* 1/1: 1–12.

Kitchin, R., and Lauriault, T. (2018). 'Towards Critical Data Studies: Charting and Unpacking Data Assemblages and Their Work', in J. Thatcher, A. Shears, and J. Eckert (eds), *Thinking Big Data in Geography: New Regimes, New Research*. University of Nebraska Press, 3–30.

Klimt, B., and Yang, Y. (2004). 'The Enron Corpus: A New Dataset for Email Classification Research', in Boulicaut, J.-F. et al. (eds), *Machine Learning: ECML 2004*. Springer Berlin Heidelberg, 217–226.

Kosinski, M., Stillwell, D., and Graepel, T. (2013). 'Private Traits and Attributes Are Predictable from Digital Records of Human Behavior', *Proceedings of the National Academy of Sciences* 110(15): 5802–5805.

Langley, A., and Tsoukas, H. (2017). 'Introduction: Process Thinking, Process Theorizing and Process Researching', in A. Langley and H. Tsoukas (eds), *The Sage Handbook of Process Organization Studies*. Sage, 1–24.

Lazer, D. *et al.* (2009). 'Computational Social Science', *Science* 323(5915): 721–723.

Leonelli, S., and Tempini, N. (2020). *Data Journeys in the Sciences*. Springer International Publishing.

Lyman, R. L. (2012). 'A Historical Sketch on the Concepts of Archaeological Association, Context, and Provenience', *Journal of Archaeological Method and Theory* 19(2): 207–240.

Monteiro, E., and Hanseth, O. (1996). 'Social Shaping of Information Infrastructure: On Being Specific about the Technology', in Orlikowski, W. J. et al. (eds), *Information Technology and Changes in Organizational Work*. Springer US, 325–343.

Olteanu, A., Castillo, C., Diaz, F., and Kiciman, E. (2017). *Social Data: Biases, Methodological Pitfalls, and Ethical Boundaries* Available at SSRN: https://ssrn.com/abstract=2886526.

O'Neil, C. (2016). *Weapons of Math Destruction: How Big Data Increases Inequality and Threatens Democracy*. Allen Lane.

Pentland, A. (2009). 'Reality Mining of Mobile Communications: Toward a New Deal on Data', in Dutta, S. and Mia, I. (eds), *The Global Information Technology Report 2008–2009*. World Economic Forum, 75–80.

Pentland, A. (2014). *Social Physics: How Good Ideas Spread—the Lessons from a New Science*. Scribe.

Pettigrew, A. M. (1973). *The Politics of Organizational Decision-making*. Tavistock.

Pollock, N., and D'Adderio, L. (2012). 'Give me A Two-by-Two Matrix and I Will Create the Market: Rankings, Graphic Visualisations and Sociomateriality', *Accounting, Organizations and Society* 37(8): 565–586.

Poole, M. S., Lambert, N, Murase, T. Ascensio, R., and McDonald J. (2016). 'Sequential Analysis of Processes', in Langley, A. and Tsoukas, H. (eds), *The SAGE Handbook of Process Organization Studies*. SAGE, 254–270.

Powell, W. W., Horvath, A., and Brandtner, C. (2016). 'Click and Mortar: Organizations on the Web', *Research in Organizational Behavior* 36: 101–120.

Rasmussen, K. B. (2017). 'Data Quality in Online Environments', in Fielding, N. G., Lee, R. M., and Blank, G. (eds), *The Sage Handbook of Online Research Methods*. Sage, 38–53.

Riedl, C., and Seidel, V. P. (2018). 'Learning from Mixed Signals in Online Innovation Communities', *Organization Science*, 29(6), pp. 1010–1032.

Ruppert, E., Law, J., and Savage, M. (2013). 'Reassembling Social Science Methods: The Challenge of Digital Devices', *Theory, Culture & Society* 30(4): 22–46.

Schmidt, H. (1999). 'The Impossibility of Resurrecting the Past: Reconstructions on Archaeological Excavation Sites', *Conservation and Management of Archaeological Sites* 3(1–2): 61–68.

Shneiderman, B. (2008). 'Science 2.0', *Science* 319(5868): 1349–1350.

Silverman, D. (2009). *Doing Qualitative Research*, 3rd ed. SAGE.

Sullivan, A. P. (1978). 'Inference and Evidence in Archaeology: A Discussion of the Conceptual Problems', in Schiffer, M. B. (ed.), *Advances in Archaeological Method and Theory*. Academic Press, 183–222.

Tonidandel, S., King, E. B., and Cortina, J. M. (2018). 'Big Data Methods: Leveraging Modern Data Analytic Techniques to Build Organizational Science', *Organizational Research Methods* 21(3): 525–547.

Tufekci, Z. (2014). 'Big Questions for Social Media Big Data: Representativeness, Validity and Other Methodological Pitfalls', *Proceedings of the Eighth International AAAI Conference on Weblogs and Social Media* 505–514.

Tuomi, I. (1999). 'Data Is More than Knowledge', *Journal of Management Information Systems* 16(3): 107–121.

Uprichard, E. (2013). 'Focus: Big Data, Little Questions?', *Discover Society*. Available at: https://discoversociety.org/2013/10/01/focus-big-data-little-questions/.

Vaast, E., and Levina, N. (2015). 'Speaking as One, but Not Speaking Up: Dealing with New Moral Taint in an Occupational Online Community', *Information and Organization* 25/2: 73–98.

Vaast, E., Safadi, H., Lapointe, L., and Negoita, B. (2017). 'Social Media Affordances for Connective Action: An Examination of Microblogging Use during the Gulf of Mexico Oil Spill', *MIS Quarterly* (41:4), pp. 1179–1205.

Venturini, T., Jensen, P. and Latour, B. (2015) 'Fill in the Gap: A New Alliance for Social and Natural Sciences', *Journal of Artificial Societies and Social Simulation*, 18(2).

Watts, D. J. (2011). *Everything Is Obvious: How Common Sense Fails Us*. Crown Business.

Weiskopf, N. G., and Weng, C. (2013). 'Methods and Dimensions of Electronic Health Record Data Quality Assessment: Enabling Reuse for Clinical Research', *Journal of the American Medical Informatics Association* 20/1: 144–151.

Wenzel, R., and Van Quaquebeke, N. (2018). 'The Double-Edged Sword of Big Data in Organizational and Management Research: A Review of Opportunities and Risks', *Organizational Research Methods* 21/3: 548–591.

Zuboff, S. (1988). *In the Age of the Smart Machine. The Future of Work and Power* Heinemann.

7

# Processual Shadows

## What Can We See with Digital Trace Data?

*Brian T. Pentland, Julie Ryan Wolf, Yunna Xie, Inkyu Kim, Kenneth Frank, and Alice Pentland*

### 7.1 Introduction

Digital trace data are getting a lot of attention as a resource for research (Berente et al. 2019).[1] Trace data seem particularly relevant for research on processes in general and routine dynamics in particular (Feldman et al. 2016). This is because archival trace data can be used to conduct diachronic analysis (Barley 1990) that helps us see how routines form and change over time. Trace data are attractive partly because they are generated systematically (literally by a computerized system), so they can embody a level of precision and uniformity that would be impossible to achieve by other means. Unlike an ethnographer, a computer system can be multiple places at once and it never needs to take bathroom breaks.

At the same time, there is growing recognition that digital trace data has limitations that need to be considered carefully (Howison, Wiggins, and Crowston 2011; Freelon 2014; Latzko-Toth, Bonneau, and Millette 2017). Trace data seems to provide an objective record, but it is not a mirror (Jungherr 2018). Computer systems create records from a particular point of view, with a particular level of granularity, using a particular lexicon. Like any kind of data, digital trace data needs to be interpreted carefully and there are limits on what it allows us to see.

In this chapter, we use two years of electronic medical record (EMR) data to examine how roles and actions change over time in dermatology clinics at the University of Rochester Medical Center. We find that while role patterns churn constantly from day to day, action patterns are quite stable unless there is an external event or a management policy change. The trace data reveal changes in action patterns that were invisible to the clinical staff until they saw our analysis of the data.

Brian T. Pentland et al., *Processual Shadows.* In: *Organizing in the Digital Age.* Edited by: Michael Barrett, Emmanuelle Vaast, Ann Langley, and Haridimos Tsoukas, Oxford University Press. © Oxford University Press (2024).
DOI: 10.1093/oso/9780198899457.003.0007

These findings provide an opportunity to reflect on a larger question: what can we see with digital trace data? Feldman (2016) has suggested that we need to have better ways to visualize patterns of action, but those visualizations must be based on some kind of evidence. Jarzabkowski et al. (2014) and Van Hulst et al. (2016) articulate the value of ethnographic methods for analysing process, but a full diachronic analysis can be time-consuming and challenging (Barley 1990). Digital trace data is becoming more available and would seem to provide a tremendous resource for process research (Berente et al. 2019). The question is, what can we expect from digital trace data? It can be used to visualize a process, but what does digital trace data really allow us to see? Is the visualization more like a direct image of the process or more like a shadow?

## 7.2 Motivation: Documenting Patterns of Action

When work is distributed in time and space it is difficult to document what is going on. Participant observation relies on 'being there' (Van Maanen 2011; Hannerz 2003). Co-presence can provide an unmatched view of a situation, but if a process extends to multiple times and places, it requires making a trade-off: in which part(s) of the process will we participate and/or observe? Which parts will we observe today and which parts will we observe next week, next month, or never? Unless the focal phenomenon occurs in a single, human-scale location, this trade-off is inevitable. Even a team of ethnographers (as in Jarzabkowski et al. 2015) has a limited point of view and has to think carefully about how to allocate time and attention (Hannerz 2003).

We can think of digital trace data as a way to relax this constraint on data collection. Researchers can supplement participant observation or interviews with additional sources of data, such as archival records, sensors, and video. All of which can generate digital traces of some sort (Freelon 2014). Each of these strategies has strengths and weaknesses, depending on the situation and the research question.

### 7.2.1 Archival Records

Nowadays, many of our computer-supported activities leave some kind of digital exhaust (Neef 2014) or a structured event log (Berente et al. 2019) that allows us to trace sequences of actions over time. This provides an archival record of the activity. Much of this data is produced as an unobtrusive by-product of the activity in question (e.g. making a purchase). In the case of business processes, the data are intended as an auditable record of what occurred, so they are ostensibly accurate. It may be difficult to retrieve the data, but it does not require any special effort to record the data. The EMR data that we analyse here falls into this category.

Of course, any kind of archival data is subject to the limitations identified by Garfinkel (1967): there are good organizational reasons for bad clinical records. Systems are designed to record and report some events and not others, for particular reasons, from a particular point of view (Drury 1995). Our inability to measure waiting time (discussed below) provides a classic example. So, while digital archival records can provide greater spatio-temporal coverage than traditional participant observation, they introduce other trade-offs and limitations.

### 7.2.2 Sensors

When archival records are insufficient or unavailable, one can add specialized sensors to track activity. For example, in research on animal behaviour, many aspects of animal behavior (such as migrations) are unobservable (Brown et al. 2013). For human interaction, sociometers and other kinds of wireless tracking devices offer a way of tracking movement and proximity (Fernández-Llatas et al. 2013). These tools can provide an accurate but narrow view of what is happening (Chaffin et al. 2017). They show the location of actors over time, but do not indicate what they are doing or saying.

### 7.2.3 Video

Video offers a richer picture but is extremely time consuming. LeBaron et al. (2016) offer a recent example of handoffs between shifts in a hospital. While video documentation may be especially convincing, it is limited to what can be seen, recognized, and coded in the images and sound. With advances in image recognition and machine learning, it is becoming possible to code video data automatically (Camastra and Vinciarelli 2015). This may eventually reduce the cost of video-based research. However, while CCTV has become nearly ubiquitous in some places, using video for research raises privacy concerns.

In short, in spite of our innovations and aspirations, it remains very difficult to 'capture reality in flight' (Pettigrew 1990: 270). There is no practical way to get a complete, unbiased view of processual phenomena. We must accept the limitations and trade-offs inherent in whatever data we can get. With that over-arching caveat in mind, we turn to an example of a large, detailed set of digital trace data to see what we can see.

## 7.3 Example: Electronic Medical Records (EMR)

To demonstrate the strengths and weaknesses of digital trace data, we will use data generated by EPIC, a widely used EMR software system. The data includes two full years of patient visits from four dermatology clinics (over 7.5 million time-stamped records that provide a trace of actions for 56,361 patient visits, from January 2016 through December 2017). The data we analyse here traces actions in the EMR record-keeping process, not the actual work in the clinic. For example, it records when the patient's blood pressure was entered into the system, but it does not record the conversation between the patient and nurse when the blood pressure was taken. Like the event log analysed by Pentland et al. (2010), it includes actions taken by the clinical staff as well as actions taken by the system itself. Actions in the EPIC audit trail are time-stamped to one second, so it provides an extremely detailed record, but from the narrow point of view of the computer system. The question is, what can we see from EPIC's point of view?

### 7.3.1 Example 1: Wait Time

Patients do not like to wait. The time that patients wait before seeing a doctor is an important determinant of patient satisfaction. With time-stamped data on 57,000 patient visits, it seems like it should be possible to get an accurate picture of wait time. There are two specific waiting periods in each visit to the clinic that we wanted to measure:

1. **Waiting to be taken to an exam room.** Patients wait in the reception area after checking in but before being taken to an examination room.
2. **Waiting to see a doctor.** Patients wait in the examination room before they see a doctor. Typically, a clinical technician or nurse brings patients to the exam room and gets some preliminary information. Then, the patient waits to see the doctor.

**Waiting to be taken to an exam room.** This is the time spent in the waiting room after checking in. In theory, the calculation is simple: find the time of an event that happens when the patient is in the exam room and subtract the check-in time. We knew from our co-PI who manages the clinics that vital signs (blood pressure and heart rate) are always taken when the patient enters the exam room. There are two different action codes for entering vital signs, but they both contain the word 'VITALS', so computing the wait time seemed simple and reliable.

In practice, however, we discovered some anomalous results. In one of the clinics, the initial wait time for nearly all patients was eight hours. This seemed impossible, until we realized what was going on. In that clinic, they printed arrival sheets at the beginning of the day for all of the scheduled patients. Then, at the end of the day, they entered all of the EMR data for each patient visit. Thus, clinic 'arrival' was roughly the same for all patients; it had nothing to do with when the patients actually arrived or if they showed up at all. We assume that vital signs were *measured* when the patient entered the exam room, but they were not *recorded* in the EMR until long after the patients had left the building.

**Waiting to see a doctor.** We were unable to get any reliable estimate for the second waiting time (to see a doctor) in any of the clinics. In retrospect, the reason is obvious: the EMR system does not record when people enter or exit the examination room. It only records when the staff access or edit the medical record. The system simply does not capture the necessary information.

With nearly eight million observations of clinical process, accurately time stamped at one-second intervals, we were unable to estimate two of the most salient and easily observed features of the patient experience. We can interpret this as a gap between clinical practice and clinical record-keeping: the electronic records do not necessarily reflect the timing of what happens in the clinics. This makes sense, because the exact timing of when caregivers enter and exit the exam room is not a salient part of the medical record. There is also a gap between our information needs, as researchers, and the information produced by the EMR system. In the case of the first waiting time, the gap has to do with system utilization. The medical staff were using the system in a way that met their needs but that made the archival data useless for our needs. In the case of the second gap, it has to do with system design. Because the system does not track actual movement of medical staff, the necessary data was simply not recorded. Either way, the EMR system cannot be used to track waiting time accurately.

### 7.3.2 Example 2: Diachronic Analysis of Actions and Roles

We were also interested in a central question for routine dynamics: does the clinical process change over time? To address this question, we represent the data as a series of narrative networks (Pentland and Feldman 2007). We used the algorithm developed by Pentland, Recker, and Wyner (2017) to transform digital threads into narrative networks. This algorithm is available in *ThreadNet,* an R package that is freely accessible at http://github.com. To apply this algorithm, we treat the digital trace of each patient visit as a 'thread' (a set of sequentially related events). To create the network, we follow along each thread from one event to the next. Nodes in the network represent the categories of events that are found in the data. Edges in the network represent the sequential relationships between events as found in the data. Once the series of networks is constructed, they can be visualized and analysed in many ways, such as network movies (Moody et al. 2005; Handcock et al. 2008), where each network represents one day in one clinic. More details on the methodology can be found in Pentland, Vaast, and Ryan Wolf 2021).

To provide some visual intuition about this approach, Figure 7.1 shows a series of three networks for one clinic. Each network represents one day (about 40 patient visits). The networks include only visits that occurred in that clinic on that day. Thus, there are changes from day to day. On each day, a different set of actions may be present, and there may be different sequential relations among them. From our data, we generate a series of 1767 such networks: one for each day in each of the four clinics. Note that there are 300 possible actions, not all of which occurred on every day in every clinic.

Using *ThreadNet*, we can produce a similar analysis based on the roles, rather than the actions, that appear in each row of the event log. Figure 7.2 shows a series of three networks from the same three days shown in

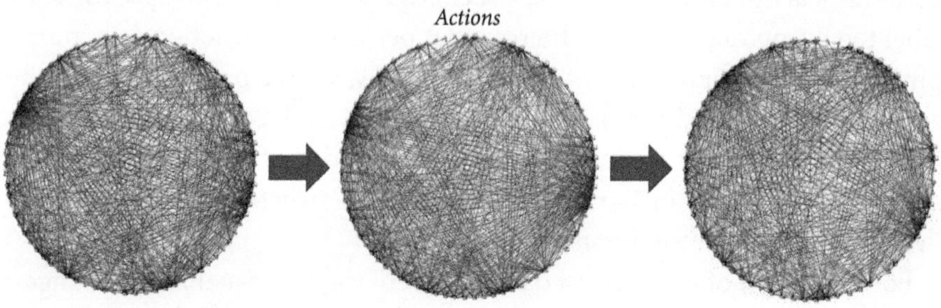


**Figure 7.1** Actions on three clinic-days

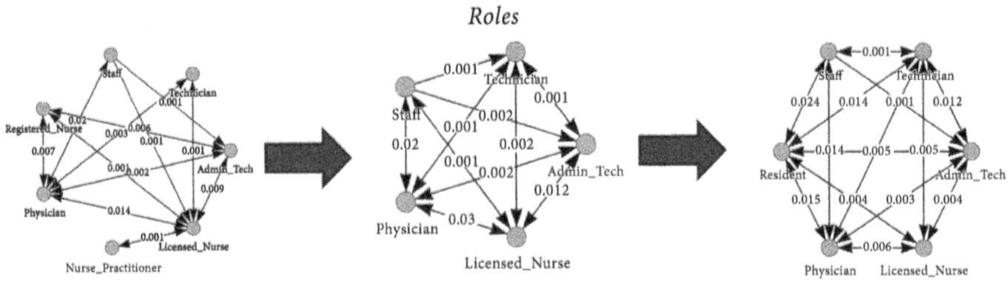


Figure 7.2 Roles on three clinic-days

Figure 7.1. However, instead of tracing relations between actions, we are tracing relations between roles. Each node in the network is a category of events defined by the role that performed the event (e.g. nurse, physician, resident, technician). These are not social networks; the nodes represent categories of action and the edges represent sequential relationships between those categories as observed in the data. The networks are much smaller because there are only seven roles in the data. Notice that not every role occurs every day, and they may be related differently, so these role-based event networks provide another point of view on routine dynamics within the clinics. These are weighted graphs, so they allow us to visualize differences in the extent to which different roles participate in the work process.

### 7.3.3 Visualizing Routine Dynamics

The sequence of networks allows us to show how the clinical routine has changed over time. In this section, we analyse two different points of view: actions and roles. To analyse actions, we label the events according to the action performed in that event. From this point of view, we see only actions (what happened and what happened next). Since routines are often defined as patterns of action, this point of view seems quite natural. To analyse roles, we label the events according to the role that performed the action (e.g. nurse, physician, technician). From this point of view, we see only the roles (who acted, and who acted next). Focusing on roles is less common in the literature on routines but is a central topic in sociology of organization. It was also the major focus of Barley's (1986) study of structuration in radiology departments, which we discuss below.

For each point of view, we used two different ways to visualize the changes: (1) by comparing each clinic-day to a common reference and (2) self-comparison. This technique allows us to visualize synchronic and diachronic comparisons on the same graph. We can see how the clinics compare to each other and how they change over time (Barley 1990). To do this, we compare the frequency of pairs of events taken in each clinic on each day. Pairs of events correspond to the edges in the graphs in Figure 7.1. We could undertake more extensive comparisons, but this is adequate for our purposes in this chapter.

### 7.3.4 Routine Dynamics from an Action Point of View

Figure 7.3 shows the results of this analysis of the four dermatology clinics. The horizontal axis represents time, from January 2016 through December 2017, measured in days, without gaps for weekend or holidays. The vertical axis is cosine similarity (1 = same, 0 = different). For the common reference, we picked the first day at one clinic of the clinics (HHPOB in Figure 7.3). If we picked a different reference, the graph would be qualitatively similar. For the self-comparison, we use a moving window of five days before and after a focal date (Maaradji et al. 2016). In other words, we are asking 'is this week like last week?' in each clinic, but we compute the comparison for each day. This allows us to accurately identify particular days when there were changes in the pattern of actions.

Figure 7.3(a) shows that initially the clinics were all quite similar to each other. Furthermore, over the first few months, there was very little change. Then, suddenly, in June 2016, there was a significant change in all four clinics. Throughout the rest of the two-year period, we see on-going changes.

Figure 7.3(b) shows the self-comparison. If the routines were stable and unchanging, the graph would remain close to the top (1.0). The intuitive interpretation would be that one week is the same as the next. When there are spikes in the graph, it indicates a sudden change, and deeper spikes mean

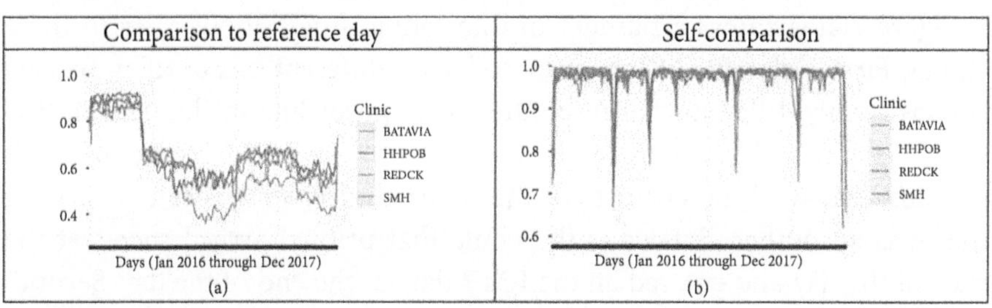


**Figure 7.3** Changes in action patterns over two years

bigger changes. Figure 7.3(b) shows that the largest changes can be pinned down to specific dates. Between these spikes, however, the pattern of action in the clinics are relatively stable.

After some investigation, we discovered that these changes in the action pattern correspond to two different kinds of events, both of which we interpret as exogenous. The first change (June 2016) resulted from a change in management policy concerning privacy. Visually, this is the first big drop in Figure 7.3(a), which corresponds to the first big spike in Figure 7.3(b). The rest of the changes were due to the flu season, which officially starts on 1 September and ends on 15 April each year. When the flu season started, there was a significant shift in the process. When the flu season ended, the process returned to normal.

These changes are interesting because the clinical staff and the IT staff could not explain them at first. When shown the graphical representation of process change in all four clinics on the same days, they could not think of an explanation. There were no system upgrades on those days and no changes in staffing that affected all the clinics. After considerable investigation, they realized that those dates corresponded to the flu season. The beginning and ending of the flu season are entirely unremarkable, since they happen every year, but they trigger a markedly different set of actions in the event log. Thus, the trace data revealed changes (admittedly minor ones) that were invisible to the people who worked in the clinics.

## 7.3.5 Routine Dynamics from the Role Point of View

When we look at handoffs between roles in the dermatology clinics, we see a very different picture. Figure 7.4 shows the same data as Figure 7.3, except the events have been labelled according to the roles instead of actions. Where Figure 7.3 is based on handoffs between actions, Figure 7.4 is based on handoffs between roles.

Figure 7.4(a) shows a number of interesting things about roles in these clinics. First, different clinics appear to have a different mix of roles. Batavia is consistently different than the others (the lower line in the figure). It is a smaller clinic that was recently brought into the URMC system, and it has different work practices than the other clinics, so it is not surprising that it is an outlier. Batavia is the clinic that printed arrival sheets at the start of the day and entered all the EMR data at the end of the day. Second, while the mix of roles in each clinic changes over time, there is not a readily discernable pattern. Unlike the action data, there are no clear shocks or

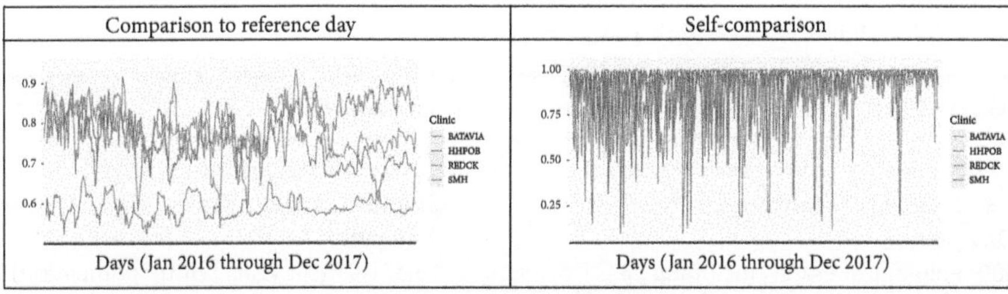


**Figure 7.4** Changes in role relationships over two years

persistent realignments. Also, there is no accumulation or sedimentation of change, as reported in Barley (1986). Rather, there is an appearance of constant small-scale churning. The self-comparison in Figure 7.4(b) reinforces this impression of on-going but unstructured changes in the roles.

## 7.4 Discussion

The analysis presented in Figure 7.3 and 7.4 represents a new state of the art in the diachronic analysis of action patterns and roles. We are using fine-grained process data (time-stamped to the second) to analyse and visualize two years of clinical work. The digital trace data provides a window onto patterns of action and relationships between roles that should be a valuable basis for theorizing. For example, the comparison of Figures 7.3 and 7.4 raises an interesting question that we could not begin to ask without this analysis: How can the action patterns undergo such clear, distinctive phases of stability and change while the roles appear to be churning constantly? The simple answer appears to be that the EPIC EMR system constrains the pattern of action to a considerable extent, regardless of who is performing the recordkeeping. However, we should be careful not to jump to conclusions, since the data are solely from the computer system perspective.

### 7.4.1 Comparison to Participant Observation

It is instructive to contrast the current study to Barley's (1986) comparison of the implementation of CT scanners in two different radiology departments, which provides an example of diachronic analysis using participant observation. By carefully observing and recording fieldnotes on the utilization of the CT scanners, Barley was able to document changes over time in

**Table 7.1** Qualitative and quantitative studies

| Barley (1986) | This study |
|---|---|
| Observations of actual clinical work | Traces of EMR record-keeping |
| Two radiology departments | Four dermatology clinics |
| One year | Two years |
| 400 radiological exams, including 96 CT Scans | 56,361 patient visits (entire population) |
| 14 codes | 300 codes |

how radiological exams were conducted in each hospital. He conceptualized clinical work in terms of scripts that showed the sequential interactions of technicians, radiologists, and other clinical staff. Table 7.1 compares Barley's ethnographic data to the trace data we use here.

Barley (1986) tracked the structuration process in two hospitals, called Urban and Suburban. The introduction of new CT scanner technology provided an exogenous shock to the work system in each radiology department. Radiologists and technologists who were experts with x-ray technology were novices with creating and interpreting CT scans. The new technology created an opportunity to reconfigure the roles in the radiology departments at the two hospitals. The key contribution of Barley's study was the demonstration that action patterns and roles in the two hospitals diverged over time. Given the same technology, for the same kind of work, the roles and action patterns that emerge over time were not the same.

In the dermatology clinics, there was not a similar technological intervention during the two-year period of our data collection. There was no exogenous shock to set off the kind of role-making behaviour observed by Barley. There were policy interventions, but these did not seem to result in structural changes. The visualizations in Figures 7.3 and 7.4 do not reveal the detailed patterns within the data; they only reveal changes to those patterns. The next step would be drill down into the data at various points in time (e.g. before and after one of the policy-related punctuations) to compare how specific action patterns changed. While the logic of this strategy makes sense, our earlier examples concerning patient waiting times provide a cautionary tale about the limits of drilling down into trace data.

As Jarzabkowski et al. (2014: 282) put it, ethnography 'is revelatory of processual dynamics'. That is certainly clear from Barley's (1986) study. He was able to clearly document how the roles of the technicians and the radiologists at Urban and Suburban changed over time. Yet there is no way that an ethnographer could have picked up on the process changes documented in Figure 7.3 because even the participants were unaware of them. They were aware of the flu season, of course, but not aware of its effect on record-keeping.

At the same time, there is no way to guarantee that our digital trace data would capture the introduction of new clinical technology (e.g. a new way to perform a biopsy). Each procedure does have a unique billing code, so a new procedure would get a new code. However, the billing codes go into the billing data, not the EMR audit trail, which is the source of our time-stamped digital trace. Unless trace data includes new event codes that reflect changes in technology, researchers who rely on trace data alone might miss those changes.

Finally, no amount of luck or care will allow us to analyse interactions among the patients and the medical staff because interactions are not recorded in the digital trace data. At best, different kinds of data reveal different aspects of processual dynamics, which is why we should view them as complementary, as suggested by Berente et al. (2019).

## 7.4.2 The Best of Both Worlds?

If trace data and traditional fieldwork are truly complementary, we ought to be able to integrate this data into a more comprehensive picture. Researchers often speak of 'triangulation' between qualitative and quantitative data (Jick 1979). In the past, archival resources such as memos, reports, and email would be regarded as qualitative. Here, the archival resource is the time-stamped digital trace data and it seems rather quantitative. As a practical matter, how can this fire-hose of fine-grained information be integrated into fieldwork?

In practice, it may be helpful to think of the computer system as another member on your ethnographic team. This new team member can only see shadows, speaks a different language and is very rigid about how it likes to communicate. At the same time, your digital team member has some advantages: it can be everywhere at once and it never sleeps. It misses events that would be obvious to any human observer, but it can record system-level events that are invisible to everyone else. This is because computerized systems are not just observers, they are *participant* observers; they are an essential part of the sociomaterial ensemble that actually gets the work done.

The question is how to make the best use of this new team member. For example, a human might observe the same work that is being traced by the computer in order to validate the trace data (or vice versa). We know in advance that human observations will not match the digital record, but comparing traces (digital and observational) would help to determine the strengths and weakness of each source of data. What does the computer see that people miss and vice versa?

In our project, we conducted over 100 interviews in the dermatology clinics to understand the workflow and help us interpret the trace data. However, for privacy reasons, we limited our fieldwork to interviews and did not attempt to match observations of specific cases to specific EMR trace data. Rather, we used the interview data to conduct a parallel inquiry into how different clinical roles perceive the work process.

Ultimately, some kind of fieldwork is needed to interpret trace data. When we see a particular set of codes in the trace data, what was happening? Without access to insider knowledge, we cannot know what a specific code or pattern of codes signifies. Thus, even in a project that is heavily reliant on trace data, some level of fieldwork is required to make sense of the data.

Likewise, whenever a process or routine is distributed in time and space, it is increasingly important to have a digital member on your team that can see what is happening from start to finish. To paraphrase Jarzabkowski et al. (2014: 282), ethnography is revelatory of the portion of processual dynamics that ethnographers can see. Realistically, digital trace data is the only resource that can provide a comprehensive view of what happens in our increasingly distributed, digital world. In recognition of this, new varieties of ethnography are emerging that include digital resources in various ways, such as computational ethnography (Zheng et al. 2015), digital ethnography (Varis 2016), trace ethnography (Geiger and Ribes 2011) and Netnography (Kozinets 2010). Going forward, digital resources will be an increasingly common part of ethnographic research.

### 7.4.3 Tracing the Effects of the Covid-19 Pandemic

The Covid-19 pandemic provided yet another opportunity to reflect on the strengths and weaknesses of trace data for analysing clinical routines. A detailed archival resource seems like an ideal way to understand changes in clinical routines imposed by this enormous event. In principle, one can 'observe' what happened without having to risk infection or intrude on the work of the clinical staff.

During the initial stages of the Covid-19 pandemic, the URMC dermatology clinics shut down nearly completely. Only patients with extremely urgent problems were seen in person, reducing in person patient visits by 80%. Naturally, this would show up vividly in the digital trace. To continue providing patient care, the URMC clinics quickly ramped up their capability to offer video- and telephone-based appointments. Patients could upload photographs to a secure web portal. It was a sudden, dramatic change in clinical routines.

The IT department added a new 'visit type' to keep track of these services, and the clinical staff started entering the new visit type, so the EPIC computer system could discern telemedicine visits as a distinct category. For billing purposes, this code was also quickly added, but many other aspects of this profound change in workflow would not be apparent in EPIC. For example, the clinics added a 'triage' stage to patient scheduling to decide which patients needed to be seen in person and which could be 'seen' via telemedicine. This part of the process was not recorded in EPIC because it is not part of the patient's medical record. This example underscores the basic limitation of digital trace data imposed by the design and use of the system. We could use the digital trace to conduct diachronic analyses that would be difficult or impossible with traditional fieldwork, but the EMR data would not reveal the reorganization of the roles and resources that was taking place in the clinics. To see that point of view, someone had to be there.

## 7.5 Conclusion

Our experience with the EMR audit trail data suggests that trace data are really just shadows of the actions and events that they purport to record. Shadows are not necessarily a bad thing. Consider, for example, that x-rays are shadows. They can provide precise and useful information that is not available any other way. However, shadows can also magnify, distort, and blur their subjects. It is important to understand how the shadows were produced and how to interpret them. And of course, like any image, they reflect a particular point of view. In the case of digital trace data, that point of view is limited by design and use of the computer system that is storing and retrieving the actions that make up the processes we want to study.

As these examples illustrate, trace data can provide an extremely detailed indication of process change, but it is not a universal panacea. It provides shadows of process that need to be carefully interpreted. For this reason, it needs to be supplemented by some other source of data that provides a resource for interpreting the shadows. Our experience with clinical trace data suggests that, at the very least, one needs to match the data to the research question. Trace data may be suitable for some kinds of questions but not others.

## Note

1. This material is based upon work supported by the National Science Foundation under Grant No. SES-1734237. Any opinions, findings, and conclusions or recommendations expressed in this material are those of the author(s) and do not necessarily reflect the views of the National Science Foundation. This research was also supported in part by University of Rochester (UL1 TR002001) from the National Center for Advancing Translational Sciences (NCATS) of the National Institutes of Health (NIH). The content is solely the responsibility of the authors and does not necessarily represent the official views of the National Institutes of Health.

## References

Barley, S. R. (1986). 'Technology as an Occasion for Structuring: Evidence from Observations of CT Scanners and the Social Order of Radiology Departments', *Administrative Science Quarterly* 31: 78–108.

Barley, S. R. (1990). 'Images of Imaging: Notes on Doing Longitudinal Field Work', *Organization Science* 1/3: 220–247.

Berente, N., Seidel, S., and Safadi, H. (2019). 'Research Commentary—Data-Driven Computationally Intensive Theory Development', *Information Systems Research* 30/1: 50–64.

Brown, D. D., Kays, R., Wikelski, M., Wilson, R., and Klimley, A. P. (2013). 'Observing the Unwatchable through Acceleration Logging of Animal Behavior', *Animal Biotelemetry* 1/1: 20.

Camastra, F., and Vinciarelli, A. (2015). *Machine Learning for Audio, Image and Video Analysis: Theory and Applications.* Springer.

Chaffin, D., Heidl, R., Hollenbeck, J. R., Howe, M., Yu, A., Voorhees, C., and Calantone, R. (2017). 'The Promise and Perils of Wearable Sensors in Organizational Research', *Organizational Research Methods* 20/1: 3–31.

Drury, C. G. (1995). 'The Use of Archival Data', in E. N. Corlett and J. R. Wilson (eds), *Evaluation of Human Work.* Taylor and Francis, 101–112.

Feldman, M. S., Pentland, B. T., D'Adderio, L., and Lazaric, N. (2016). 'Beyond Routines as Things: Introduction to the Special Issue on Routine Dynamics', *Organization Science* 27/3: 505–513.

Fernández-Llatas, C., Benedi, J. M., García-Gómez, J., and Traver, V. (2013). 'Process Mining for Individualized Behavior Modeling Using Wireless Tracking in Nursing Homes', *Sensors* 13/11: 15434–15451.

Freelon, D. (2014). 'On the Interpretation of Digital Trace Data in Communication and Social Computing Research', *Journal of Broadcasting & Electronic Media* 58/1: 59–75.

Garfinkel, H. (1967). Studies in Ethnomethodology. Englewood Cliffs. New Jersey: Prentice-Hall.

Geiger, R. S., and Ribes, D. (2011). 'Trace Ethnography: Following Coordination through Documentary Practices', in *2011 44th Hawaii International Conference on System Sciences*, Washington, DC: IEEE Computer Society, 1–10.

Handcock, M. S., Hunter, D. R., Butts, C. T., Goodreau, S. M., and Morris, M. (2008). 'Statnet: Software Tools for the Representation, Visualization, Analysis and Simulation of Network Data', *Journal of Statistical Software* 24/1: 1548–1560.

Hannerz, U. (2003). 'Being There . . . and there . . . and there! Reflections on multi-site ethnography', *Ethnography* 4/2: 201–216.

Howison, J., Wiggins, A., and Crowston, K. (2011). 'Validity issues in the use of social network analysis with digital trace data', *Journal of the Association for Information Systems* 12/12: 767–797.

Jarzabkowski, P., Bednarek, R., and Lê, J. K. (2014). 'Producing Persuasive Findings: Demystifying Ethnographic Textwork in Strategy and Organization Research', *Strategic Organization* 12/4: 274–287.

Jarzabkowski, P., Bednarek, R., and Spee, P. (2015). *Making a Market for Acts of God: The Practice of Risk-trading in the Global Reinsurance Industry*. Oxford University Press.

Jick, T. D. (1979). 'Mixing Qualitative and Quantitative Methods: Triangulation in Action', *Administrative Science Quarterly* 24/4: 602–611.

Jungherr, A. (2018). 'Normalizing Digital Trace Data', in Stroud, N. J., and McGregor, S. (eds.), *Digital Discussions. How Big Data Informs Political Communication*. Routledge, 19–45.

Kozinets, R. V. (2010). *Netnography: Doing Ethnographic Research Online*. Sage.

Latzko-Toth, G., Bonneau, C., and Millette, M. (2017). 'Small Data, Thick Data: Thickening Strategies for Trace-based Social Media Research', *The SAGE Handbook of Social Media Research Methods*. Sage, 199–214.

LeBaron, C., Christianson, M. K., Garrett, L., and Ilan, R. (2016). 'Coordinating Flexible Performance during Everyday Work: An Ethnomethodological Study of Handoff Routines', *Organization Science* 27/3: 514–534.

Maaradji, A., Dumas, M., La Rosa, M., and Ostovar, A. (2016). 'Fast and Accurate Business Process Drift Detection', *International Conference on Business Process Management*. Springer, 406–422.

Moody, J., McFarland, D., and Bender-Demoll, S. (2005). 'Dynamic Network Visualization', *American Journal of Sociology* 110/4: 1206–1241.

Neef, D. (2014). *Digital Exhaust: What Everyone Should Know about Big Data, Digitization and Digitally Driven Innovation*. Pearson Education.

Pentland, B. T., Hærem, T., and Hillison, D. (2010). 'Comparing Organizational Routines as Recurrent Patterns of Action', *Organization Studies* 31/7: 917–940.

Pentland, B. T., and Feldman, M. S. (2007). 'Narrative Networks: Patterns of Technology and Organization', *Organization Science* 18/5: 781–795.

Pentland, B. T., Recker, J., and Wyner, G. (2017). 'Rediscovering Handoffs', *Academy of Management Discoveries* 3/3: 284–301.

Pentland, B.T., Vaast, E., and Ryan Wolf, J. (2021). 'Theorizing Process Dynamics with Directed Graphs: A Diachronic Analysis of Digital Trace Data', *MIS Quarterly* 45/2: 967–984.

Pettigrew, A. M. (1990). 'Longitudinal field research on change: Theory and practice', *Organization Science* 1/3: 267–292.

Van Hulst, M., Ybema, S., and Yanow, D. (2017). 'Ethnography and Organizational Processes', in H. Tsoukas and A. Langley (eds), *The Sage Handbook of Process Organization Studies*, Sage, 223–236.

Van Maanen, J. (2011). *Tales of the Field: On Writing Ethnography*. University of Chicago Press.

Varis, P. (2016). 'Digital Ethnography', in Georgakopoulou, A., & Spilioti, T. (eds.), *The Routledge Handbook of Language and Digital Communication*. Routledge, 55–68.

Zheng, K., Hanauer, D. A., Weibel, N., and Agha, Z. (2015). 'Computational Ethnography: Automated and Unobtrusive Means for Collecting Data in Situ for Human–Computer Interaction Evaluation Studies', in *Cognitive Informatics for Biomedicine*. Springer, 111–140.

# 8
# Collaborating Using Digital Technologies

## The Role of Generative Memory

*Raghu Garud, Arun Kumaraswamy, and Philipp Tuertscher*

Digital technologies are ushering in fundamental changes in the ways we work (Hinds and Kiesler 2002; Gibson and Cohen 2003), and the ongoing Covid-19 pandemic has only hastened these changes. One such change is the possibility of collaboration among actors who are not co-located. Indeed, digital technologies can serve as platforms for groups of actors from different time zones, cultures, and practice domains to engage with one another to accomplish complex tasks, even in the absence of a hierarchy (Hinds and Kiesler 2002; Gibson and Cohen 2003; Raghuram, Hill, Gibbs, and Maruping 2019).

Consider Wikipedia, which employs the wiki digital technology. Begun in 2001 and written off as an unacceptable substitute for an encyclopedia, it has become an information powerhouse. Indeed, within a few years, its accuracy rating was as good or above those of reputable encyclopedias such as Encyclopedia Britannica (Giles 2005). This is a remarkable accomplishment given that the many articles on Wikipedia are not created and maintained by pre-appointed experts but, instead, by an army of users operating in an asynchronous and distributed manner.

How is it possible for such asynchronous, distributed collaboration to yield such outcomes? Although digital technologies play a role, technology by itself cannot explain how these groups work. In addition to technology, we must consider social dynamics (Orlikowski and Scott 2008; Leonardi and Barley 2010; Malhotra, Majchrzak, and Lyytinen 2021). Indeed, as Orlikowski and Scott (2008) pointed out, we must look not just at the social or the technical, but instead at the sociomaterial, i.e. the constitutive entanglement of the

Raghu Garud, Arun Kumaraswamy, and Philipp Tuertscher, *Collaborating Using Digital Technologies.* In: *Organizing in the Digital Age.* Edited by: Michael Barrett, Emmanuelle Vaast, Ann Langley, and Haridimos Tsoukas, Oxford University Press.
 DOI: 10.1093/oso/9780198899457.003.0008

two, to appreciate the process through which productive outcomes emerge through distributed processes.

This chapter explores the sociomaterial constitutive processes that enable asynchronous, distributed collaboration using digital technologies. Specifically, we examine Wikipedia articles to understand the mutually constitutive processes involved in their emergence. Our analysis reveals that Wikipedia uses the wiki digital technology to continually update and preserve emergent outcomes. It automatically keeps a digital trace of who contributed what, as well as the justifications, discussions, and negotiations that unfolded as these contributions were synthesized.

Along with features built into the wiki technology, this rich, multi-layered digital trace serves as a generative memory. Specifically, the availability of the digital trace makes it possible for an emergent group of actors to discern what happened in the past, draw new contextualized inferences, and contribute to an article's reconfiguration and development. Thereby, the digital trace shapes but does not determine the progression of outcomes seen on Wikipedia.

The chapter is organized as follows. First, we examine how the technical and the social are mutually constitutive to flesh out the challenges in collaborating using digital technologies. After introducing Wikipedia as a research site, we describe our research design and methodology. Then, we report our findings and theorize about what we can learn from the processes underlying the emergence and evolution of Wikipedia articles. Finally, we discuss the implications of our findings for asynchronous, distributed collaborative work using digital technologies.

## 8.1 Sociomateriality and Digital Collaboration

Orlikowski (2007) used the term 'sociomaterial' to acknowledge the mutually constitutive roles played by the technical (i.e. the material) and the social (see also Leonardi and Barley 2010). Instead of a dualism between 'technologies of work' and 'how we work with technology', there is a duality—a constitutive entanglement—between the two (see also Pickering 1993). This is the principle of symmetry between the social and the technical (Latour 1999) that sometimes is broken when people consider only the social (e.g. social networks) or the technical (e.g. digital knowledge repositories).

Several streams of research embrace this mutually constitutive view. One stream has its roots in the sociology of science and technology. For instance, Pickering (1993), studying high-energy physics, wrote about a 'mangle of practice', a series of incidents in which actors make accommodations to emergent resistances as they engage with nature. Likewise, Actor-Network Theory too adopts such an ontology (Callon 1986; Latour 2005), viewing actors as gaining agency by participating in 'heterogeneous' networks, i.e. assemblages of social and material elements that together constitute what Callon (2005) terms as 'agencements', i.e. agency in arrangements. A parallel stream of literature is exemplified by Hutchins's (1995) work on distributed cognition. According to Hutchins, we cannot ascribe agency to either the social or the material but the entire sociomaterial ensemble in place. An implication of such a perspective is that agency is distributed among multiple actors (see also Weick and Roberts 1993) and constituted by sociomaterial arrangements. When actors interact, they do so from their own sociomaterial arrangements, and therefore possess different agentic orientations (see also Dunbar and Garud 2009).

These considerations bring into sharper relief the challenges in using digital technologies to facilitate distributed collaboration (cf. Hinds and Kiesler 2002; Gibson and Cohen 2003). For instance, how can multiple and distributed actors who interact using digital technologies coordinate their activities? Coordination challenges, present in even co-located actors, are amplified by virtuality (Gibson and Cohen 2003: 7). Specifically, digital technologies increase the fluidity of participation and the number of potential interactions possible (Wiesenfeld et al. 1999; Faraj et al. 2011; Ransbotham and Kane 2011). The sheer amount of information generated by digital technologies in-use (Zuboff 1988) may overwhelm actors, given that information is a scarce resource (Hansen and Haas 2001). Moreover, especially in emergent groups without predetermined structures, questions such as 'Who knows what?' and 'Who does what and when?' become all the more important but difficult to answer (Majchrzak et al. 2007; Leonardi 2014). Also, as Mark (2002) reported, distributed actors confront difficulties in establishing 'conventions'. These challenges are exacerbated because the use of digital technologies dampens the availability of contextual knowledge and cues (Cramton 2001).

Cooperation, too, is an important aspect of organizing (March and Simon 1993). Cooperation is difficult to engender because actors may operate from different sociomaterial arrangements that shape their agentic orientations (Callon 2005; Dunbar and Garud 2009; Barrett et al. 2016). Conflicts may arise, especially when actors are distributed (Hinds and Bailey 2003; Hinds and Mortensen 2005), have diverse backgrounds and perspectives (Cramton 2001; Carlile 2002; Majchrzak et al. 2012), or interact virtually using asynchronous communication technologies (Montoya-Weiss et al. 2001;

Gibson and Cohen 2003). The potential for conflict increases further when members of a group possess diverse expertise and the mix of expertise changes over time due to changing membership (Kane et al. 2014). How can such conflict be addressed, and what is the nature of cooperation that ensues?

To address these questions, we examine the collaborative processes that unfold during the co-creation of articles in Wikipedia by an emergent group of actors who are distributed, have different interests and expertise, and interact asynchronously with one another using the wiki digital technology.

## 8.2 Research Design and Methods

Ours is a process study (Mohr 1982) that identifies the driving mechanisms underlying manifest phenomena (Tsoukas 1989; Pettigrew 1992), so that they may be applied to other domains (Tsoukas 1989). Our research site is Wikipedia, a free, multilingual online encyclopedia that uses a digital technology called the wiki. Launched in 2001, Wikipedia (as of April 2021) contains over 56 million articles in over 300 languages written collaboratively by volunteers; the English language version alone contains over 6.28 million articles and has nearly 140,000 active contributors. What renders Wikipedia a strategic research site (Merton 1959) for our study is that it is characterized by distributed, non-hierarchical, and emergent collaborative processes.

### 8.2.1 Data Access

Wikipedia's wiki technology makes it possible to recreate earlier versions of every Wikipedia article and track its evolution right from its inception. All Wikipedia articles have a history page that automatically keeps a record of earlier versions, including the date and time of any change, the username or IP address of the contributor who made the change, and a summary of the change. Also associated with each article is a discussion page that serves as a forum for contributors to discuss improvements and changes.

The presence of the history and discussion pages holds both theoretical and methodological implications. Theoretically, they serve as a digital trace that is created in-use by contributors and constitute a generative memory that helps address challenges associated with coordination and cooperation.

Methodologically, the digital trace serves as a valuable source of data. Accordingly, we used the history and discussion pages of randomly chosen Wikipedia articles to reconstruct how contributors interacted using the wiki technology. Besides, we downloaded the content of these five articles into a database for analysis. We also used the various built-in tools that Wikipedia offers to procure various usage- and interaction-related statistics for all these articles.

### 8.2.2 Data Analysis

We used a process of analytical induction (e.g. Znaniecki 1934; Glaser and Strauss 1999) to guide our overall theorization from the data. As per analytical induction, researchers observe a phenomenon of interest to generate provisional insights. Examining other similar phenomena then progressively refines these insights. Consistent with this approach, we analysed five randomly chosen articles on Wikipedia ('Daylight Saving Time', 'Cryptography', '1981 Irish Hunger Strike', 'Durian', and 'Tulip Mania').

We conducted both qualitative and quantitative analyses of data obtained from these digital traces. Specifically, we examined the history pages, read through the discussion pages, and followed the emergence of the articles over time. We wrote scripts to automatically download data (e.g. who had done what) and created several plots (e.g. flow diagrams, see Viègas et al. 2004). We also calculated simple statistics such as correlations between the number of changes to the article page and the number of justifications on the discussion page or the rapidity with which contributors responded to changes made to the article to gain more confidence in our qualitative observations. Our analysis revealed essentially similar underlying patterns and mechanisms across all five articles that we analysed. Given space consideration and the similarity of sociomaterial dynamics across the articles we analysed, we report findings on only one article (Cryptography) to provide a deep and rich understanding of the dynamics at play.

## 8.3 Findings

The first screen that one encounters when visiting the Cryptography page is the 'article' page. This page includes textual and multimedia content as well as citations, hypertext links, and categories. Visitors may be motivated to contribute to the article, a task that the simple and easy-to-use wiki technology facilitates by inviting everyone to edit or contribute otherwise to articles. For instance, editing an article is as simple as typing plain text into the article's editing window. Also, by using the edit window's toolbar, contributors can enhance the format of the text and embed non-textual content such as images, audio and video files, and links to other sources. However, as with the Cryptography article and especially after damaging events (e.g. indiscriminate editing of the article), a page may be protected by administrators so that edits made by unregistered or first-time contributors are reviewed first before being included in the article.

To obtain a bird's-eye view of the collaborative process that unfolded in the emergence of the Cryptography article, we first created a history flow diagram (Viègas et al. 2004) covering the period December 2001 to December 2009, a time during which the article went through a significant evolution, was promoted to a featured article[1], and eventually stabilized (Figure 8.1). As this figure shows, some contributions were additions within existing topics represented by the increasing size of a block of text marked as (a), some were deletions for clarity and focus represented by a shrinking of the text blocks marked as (b), and yet others were links to additional topics represented by additions of tiny blocks at the bottom of the article marked as (c).

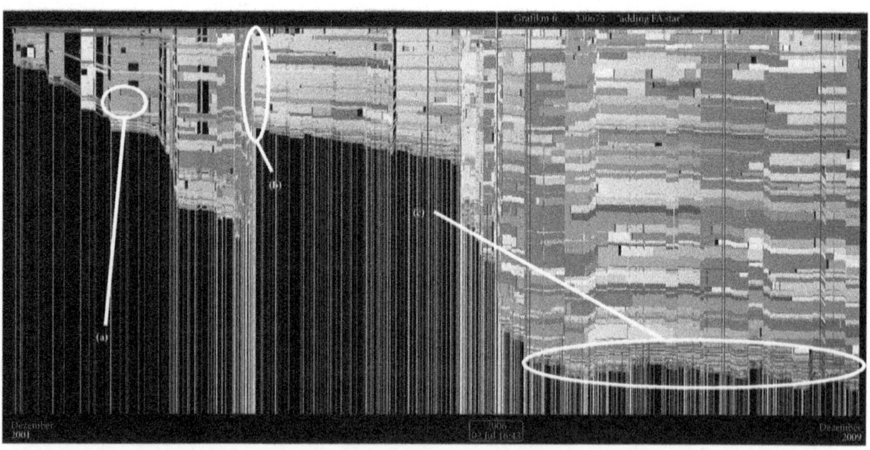

**Figure 8.1** History flow diagram of Cryptography article

The X axis of the diagram shows the sequence of edits made to the article over time, and the Y axis shows how much of these individual edits were retained, rearranged, or deleted from version to version (Viegas et al. 2004). Edits made by each contributor are represented by a distinct shade of grey. Text accepted and retained over time is represented by horizontal layers, along with who had made these edits as is indicated by the streak that runs across the flow diagram. Edit wars exhibit a zigzag pattern on the horizontal axis, whereas the black gaps between different versions represent massive deletions. Please note that this diagram was originally created in color and the full color version is available from the authors on request.

### 8.3.1 Facilitating Coordination

A detailed analysis showed that altogether, 991 actors made 2,080 contributions during this period (Figure 8.2). How did so many actors coordinate their activities to co-create the Cryptography article?

To answer this question, we conducted several analyses. A distribution plot of the number of contributions made by each contributor revealed that most contributors accounted for just one or two changes, with 12 contributors accounting for nearly 30% of the 2,080 contributions. The participation of even these 12 most active contributors waxed and waned over time (Figure 8.3). For instance, after an anonymous contributor initiated the article in December 2001, *Ww* then became its lead contributor during 2003 and 2004, with *Arvindn*, *Imran*, and *Matt Crypto* helping him. *Matt Crypto*

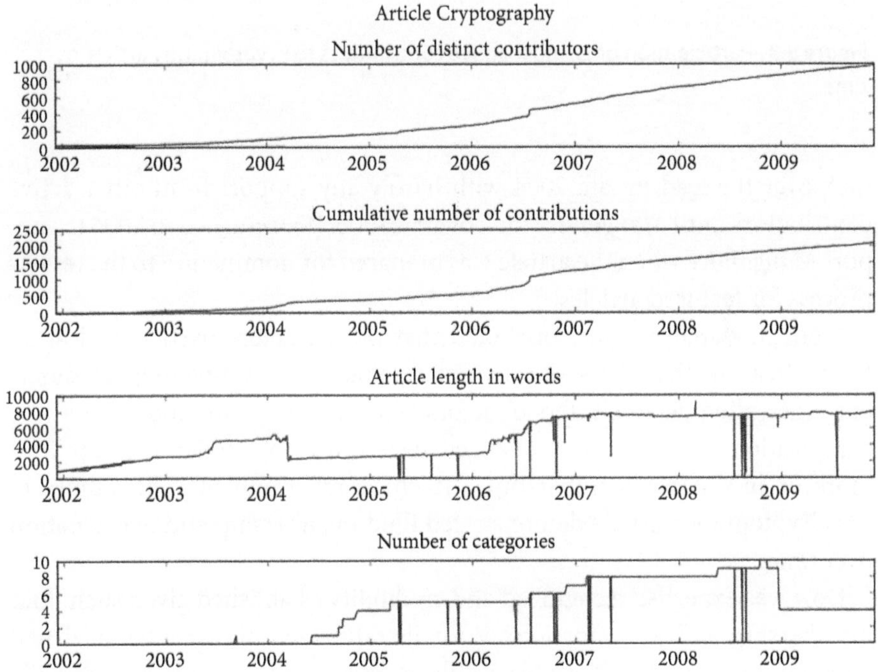


**Figure 8.2** Key statistics of the Cryptography article over time

These statistics show that the number of contributions and the length of the article increased as more and more contributors became involved towards mid-2006. An earlier spike in contributions had occurred during the first quarter of 2004, but these, instead of adding new content, aimed to reorganize and improve the article's quality. During this reorganization, the article was integrated into Wikipedia's emerging category system. The vertical lines in the 'article length' and 'number of categories' graphs indicate vandalism (i.e. mass deletion) that were instantly repaired by the community.

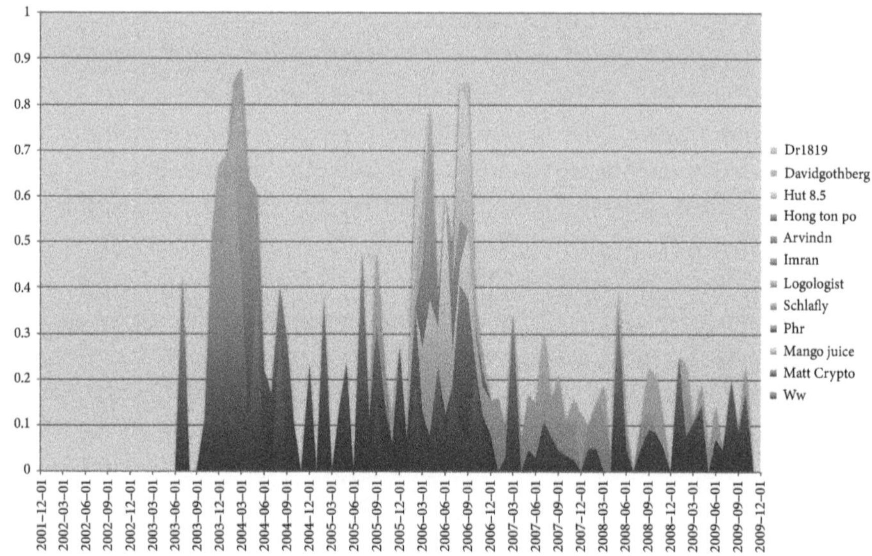


**Figure 8.3** Participation of 12 most active contributors to Cryptography article over time.

took over the lead in late 2004 with hardly any support from other active contributors until *Mangojuice* took over in 2006. *Ww* returned in 2006 to support *Mangojuice* when the article was prepared for nomination to the review process for featured articles.

From this analysis, we concluded that not all actors participated at all times. Instead, there was selective engagement. More precisely, at different times, there were clusters of actors who performed in tandem, and the composition of the clusters changed over time. So, unlike a group with more or less stable membership, the emergent group of contributors to the Cryptography article demonstrated fluid membership and participation over time.

How was expertise recognized and credibility established given such fluid membership and participation? Prior literature has shown how a virtual community comes to associate specific contributions to actors with specific usernames and also identifies these actors as integral community members who share the same purpose and goals (also, see Bryant et al. 2005 for the significance of registration as a means for contributors to identify with the Wikipedia community). In turn, identification with the community can generate 'swift trust', a form of trust that has been observed in emergent groups and virtual communities even in the absence of prior interactions (Meyerson et al. 1996; Jarvenpaa and Leidner 1999; Majchrzak et al. 2007).

Consistent with these observations, on the history and discussion pages of the Cryptography article, contributors referred to each other by their respective usernames. They also appeared to use these usernames to infer other contributors' track records.[2] For instance, when an anonymous (i.e. unregistered) contributor changed the spelling from 'cypher' to 'cipher' throughout the Cryptography article,[3] a registered contributor (*Jdforrester*) reverted the spelling to 'cypher' several times, discounting the evidence offered by the anonymous contributor on the discussion page that the spelling 'cypher' was rarely used. This was in contrast to the more measured response to *Imran* that occurred later on. From the article's history page, *Imran* was easily identifiable as a frequent contributor during that period. *Imran*, too offered several cites that 'cipher' was the more accepted spelling and removed references to the alternative spelling from the article, advising others not to reinstate it without providing sufficient evidence. *Jdforrester* and *Ww* still argued for their view that 'cypher' was the preferred spelling but conceded the point and refrained from reverting *Imran*'s changes.

In another instance, when a newcomer (*Larsholmjensen*) suggested a change after noting a potential error in the article,[4] *Mangojuice*, a very active contributor, disagreed. However, when *Skippydo*, who also appeared to be contributing for the first time to the cryptography article, agreed with *Larsholmjensen* and made a change to the article, *Mangojuice* allowed the change to stand without further discussion. Intrigued, we probed deeper to find that *Skippydo* had contributed significantly to technically challenging articles, including one related to cryptography. From *Skippydo*'s user page, we found out that this contributor was a member of the *Wikiproject Cryptography*. These illustrations indicate that the wiki technology enables community members to track and consider a contributor's track record of contributions to a particular article and overall Wikipedia to establish their credibility.

In addition, contributors seemed to establish a reputation beyond their direct contributions to a specific article. For instance, *Ww*, *Matt Crypto*, and *Mangojuice* assumed responsibilities as administrators to help shape Wikipedia articles besides Cryptography, mentored newcomers, praised valuable contributions made by others, and helped contributors start new Wikipedia articles and projects. Contributors with established track records for trustworthiness and constructive collaboration were 'promoted' to mentorship roles as administrators or reviewers by the Wikipedia community. In these roles, they developed an understanding of the interests and expertise of contributors across Wikipedia, and sometimes invited others (as *Ww* did) to help co-construct an article.

**Table 8.1** Response time to changes made to the Cryptography article

| Response to | Mean response time |
|---|---|
| Minor change | 56,7 hr |
| Major change | 39,3 hr |
| Changes by the 12 most active contributors | 46,7 hr |
| Changes by 489 registered occasional contributors | 38,0 hr |
| Changes by 467 anonymous contributors | 33,2 hr |

In general, we found that contributions by newcomers were scrutinized more rapidly by active contributors (see Table 8.1). Besides, newcomers typically had to first engage in minor roles until they had created track records, thereby enabling legitimate peripheral participation (Lave and Wenger 1991) in virtual communities (e.g. Wikipedia) (Bryant et al. 2005). Responses were also faster in the case of 'major' changes made to the article than in the case of 'minor' changes.

The mean response time was calculated by measuring the time elapsed between a contribution and the next contribution made by another user. Individual response times were grouped by type of changes (minor or major) and the mean for each group was calculated.

Our analysis also revealed additional mechanisms to focus attention and engage selectively. One such mechanism is the use of 'bots' (automated software programs) written by contributors. These bots are designed to specialize in tasks such as standardizing references or cross-linking Wikipedia articles and categories. By performing these tasks automatically, bots relieve contributors of the need to attend to mundane maintenance-related tasks and facilitate selective engagement.

Another such mechanism is a watchlist that registered contributors can set up to monitor articles of interest (Viègas et al. 2004; Bryant et al. 2005). In the Cryptography article case, we found 351 contributors 'watching' it and keeping track of recent changes. Contributors also can set their watchlist preferences to selectively track only major changes or those made by occasional or anonymous contributors, thereby ignoring any changes flagged as being minor or those made by bots.

Another mechanism that enables selective engagement is the possibility of contributors using the wiki technology to compare and contrast the current version of the article with earlier versions. This feature works just like the 'track changes' feature common in word processing software by highlighting portions of text that have been added or removed and focusing attention on the specific changes made. The preservation of earlier versions thereby facilitates interactive editing by many contributors. When changes made to an article are unsatisfactory, contributors can easily revert the article to an earlier version and negate these changes. This ability to revert allows contributors (whether registered or not) to experiment with changes without fear of destroying the coherence and integrity of the article beyond repair. The ability to revert also enables an article to be recreated when 'vandals' deliberately delete, destroy, or make inappropriate changes. In the Cryptography article, for instance, we found an incident in June 2006 where *Ww* asked why a large block of text had been deleted by a contributor, *Scircle*, without justification. Later, *Ww* reverted the article to its previous state, with *Scircle* noting that the deletion was an error due to his/her status as a new contributor.[5]

In sum, our analysis revealed how actors coordinated their activities despite emerging structures and evolving ownership. First, Wikipedia's technology made it possible for a relevant group of actors to coordinate their activities by selectively engaging with contributions made to the article depending on issues deemed pertinent at any given time. Second, a digital trace of contributors and contributions enabled actors to establish track records while other interested actors could appreciate their earlier contributions. Third, when actors engaged in collaboratively writing the article, features of the wiki technology enabled selective attention to specific contributions or issues.

## 8.3.2 Fostering Cooperation

Selective engagement enables the coordination of this distributed, emergent group of actors over time. Though, what is the nature of the cooperation among these actors with different interests and expertise, and how are conflicts among them resolved? What role does the wiki technology play in fostering cooperation?

We found answers to these questions on the article's discussion page, highlighting that justification is a part and parcel of the 'communication genre' (Yates and Orlikowski 1992) on Wikipedia. Upon noticing a change (or a proposal for a change), community members posted questions on the discussion page seeking justification for the change. In many cases, however, contributors making a change proactively posted justifications on the discussion page. In turn, these justifications led to comments and counterpoints from others, thereby generating a discussion on the appropriateness of the change. Such discussions eventually led to temporary settlements whereby contributors agreed to either let the change stand in its entirety, circumscribe its scope, or even negate it by reverting to an earlier article version. In cases where the contributor who made the change did not respond to a query seeking justification, reversions occurred, thereby negating the change.

Literature has noted the critical role that justification plays in such change processes (Tilly 2006; Tuertscher, Garud, and Kumaraswamy 2014). For instance, justification is essential to institutionalize modifications to social facts (Green 2004). To the extent that a rationale is available, others can also appreciate why a change has been proposed and respond appropriately.

Besides offering an opportunity to justify changes, our analysis revealed that the discussion page also offers contributors the opportunity to enter into a dialogue. Literature has recognized the importance of such dialogical processes, noting how new frames and innovative insights may emerge in and through dialogue between actors who have commonalities and differences (Boden 1994; Tsoukas 2009). In this regard, Wilkinson and Huberman (2007) found that the quality of Wikipedia articles increases with the amount of dialogue unfolding on discussion pages.

In addition to dialogue on the discussion page, we found 'spontaneous communication' (Hinds and Mortensen 2005) that occurred on the personal 'talk' pages of contributors. For instance, entries on *Ww*'s talk page include conversations with several contributors (such as queries for *Ww* or responses to *Ww*'s messages on their talk pages) in addition to those contributing to the Cryptography article. Overall, these personal talk pages appear to serve as message boards for contributors to engage in one-on-one dialogue. Such spontaneous communication helps strengthen shared identity and shared context (Hinds and Mortensen 2005) and creates a bond between individual contributors (Ren et al. 2007).

Yet another purpose of the dialogue on the discussion page was to resolve conflict. A difference in opinion between two contributors would quickly prompt others who would offer their opinions. In the Cryptography discussion pages, we found several occasions when discussions unfolded around differences in opinion amongst contributors. One such instance was a discussion by contributors to the Cryptography article on whether 'cryptology' was a subset or a superset of 'cryptography' and what the title of the article ought to be.[6] After a wide-ranging dialogue among contributors with knowledge of different languages, etymology, usage, and previous discussions on this issue, a settlement was reached on the appropriate categorization of the article and its links to related articles; additionally, two topics in the article were merged.[7] Such a discussion transformed what might quickly have become a battle between entrenched contributors into a dialogical process that harnessed the insights and memories of an emergent and interested group to eventually generate a synthesis. Indeed, as Boden (1994: 164) noted: 'People build layers of discussion, debate and eventual decision on a given topic or activity, diffusing possible disagreements while moulding decision through multiple occasions of interaction. Their conversational collusion is a matter of weaving, turn by turn, one agenda into another.'

Based on rhetorical theory (Green 2004), we would expect dialogue on the discussion page to occur when changes are made to the article. Accordingly, we calculated the correlation between the number of entries on the discussion page and the number of changes made to the article per month. This correlation (0.345) was positive and significant at 1% level. To visualize what was happening, we plotted the number of entries on the discussion page against the number of contributions made to the article page (see Figure 8.4). This figure shows that the number of entries on the discussion page ebbed and flowed with the number of contributions.

In particular, major changes generated intense discussions. For instance, the first peak in Figure 8.4 corresponds to the restructuring of the entire article undertaken when *Matt Crypto*, a newcomer, made fundamental changes to the article in March 2004 and set off intense discussions between regular contributors. A series of minor changes followed this significant transformational change to the article's architecture. Some changes brought back content from previous versions to fill in gaps (see Figure 8.1), while others involved reformatting, re-categorizing, or adding links to references. Equally important were the changes made to assimilate new content by repositioning it within the article so that overall coherence was not lost.

The other two peaks in Figure 8.4 indicate increased activity to prepare the article for nomination as a featured article during the first half of 2006. This preparation was spearheaded by regular contributors such as *Mangojuice, Phr,* and *Ww*. Also, these changes were made to improve the quality of the article without changing its vision or underlying structure. Discussions, in this instance, were meant more to coordinate the flurry of editorial activities than to resolve conflicts. Accordingly, we observed that these changes, though cumulatively significant in their impact, did not generate as much discussion as the transformational change initiated by *Matt Crypto* in March 2004.

Green (2004) pointed out that justification around a change subsides once it has become institutionalized and taken for granted. Our analysis of

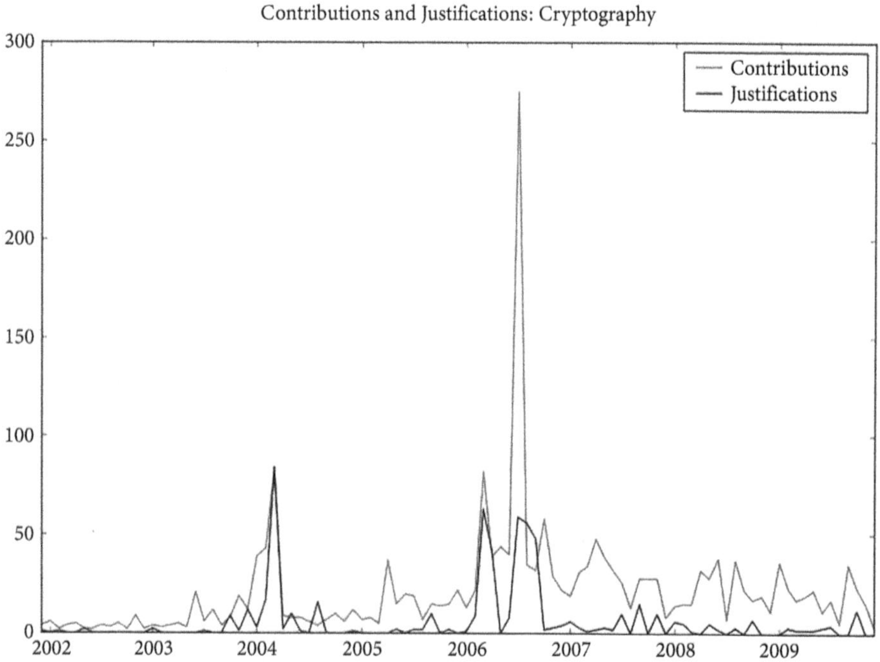


**Figure 8.4** A plot of contributions and justifications to the Cryptography article.

Wikipedia articles suggests a twist to this observation. Specifically, these justifications are always available as part of the digital trace and are transparent to all. Therefore, they offer the community of contributors an opportunity to work with a common fabric of knowledge and the context of its creation. This digital trace allows contributors to even 'forget' the past because they can reconstruct the memory of what happened and why it happened when required.

Contributors to the Cryptography article appeared to realize the role of the digital trace, referring each other to past discussions (sometimes, even to those on the discussion pages of other Wikipedia articles) when contesting or justifying a change. For instance, an explicit understanding of the value of the digital trace in shaping future interactions is well captured by this request made by *Ww* on his personal 'talk' page:[8]

> Please do not delete or substantially change edits made on this page, whether they were made by you or not. This page can be a (semi) official record of actions and reactions. I am an admin, and they may be of import at some future time. Thank you. *Ww*

In sum, our analysis showed how the discussion page allows contributors to post or receive justifications for any changes made. In addition, it facilitates dialogue between contributors with different perspectives, thereby mitigating conflict. Equally important, the digital trace of all justifications and discussions serves as a memory of what happened and why a particular choice was made.

Overall, the ability to coordinate (through selective engagement) and to cooperate (through justification, dialogue, and temporary settlements) resulted in the Cryptography article being accepted as a 'featured article' with all of the hallmarks of quality determined by Wikipedia. At each stage of the process, the wiki technology and the digital trace that it generated offered contributors a forum to explore and negotiate potential directions for the future. The technology allowed contributors easy access to emerging outcomes and one another. As a result, multiple distributed actors with different interests could engage selectively with the article. As significant changes were made, justifications also emerged. All this was automatically recorded, creating a multi-layered digital trace that allowed members of the emergent group to infer each other's areas of expertise, coordinate their interactions and cooperate in the creation of a high-quality outcome.

## 8.4 Discussion

In their book entitled *The Emergent Organization*, Taylor and Van Every (2000) noted how organizing occurs as actors co-orient themselves towards an objective through their conversations around texts that serve as structuring devices. In this chapter, we have explored how digital technologies can facilitate such conversations by harnessing the efforts of multiple actors who operate asynchronously and in a distributed manner. Specifically, we show how the new medium facilitates such conversations while preserving a digital trace of who were involved as well as the justifications that were given as contributions are interwoven into text, which manifests itself as a palimpsest.

Yet, along with such possibilities come challenges. To obtain productive outcomes, contributions must be coordinated, and conflicts resolved. Our detailed analysis of the Cryptography article suggests how these challenges can be addressed. For instance, the wiki technology's ease of use invites even casual readers to make contributions. A digital trace of who contributed what, when and why, along with tools integrated into the wiki technology (such as the watchlist, the ability to generate a track record of contributors, and the ability to compare different versions of the article and revert to earlier versions), facilitate selective engagement by contributors, thereby mitigating the challenge of coordination. The discussion page serves as a forum for contributors to question and justify their contributions, enter into dialogues, and negotiate temporary settlements to address conflicts that arise due to contributions informed by different perspectives. These discussions and resulting contributions, in turn, automatically become an integral part of the digital trace and form the basis for future interactions and contributions.

Overall, the multi-layered digital trace plays a constitutive role by shaping interactions among distributed actors with different perspectives, but without determining these interactions or their emergent outcomes. The source of such generativity is evident when we look at the mutually constitutive dynamics between the social and the material that unfold across the different layers of the digital trace. For instance, the multi-layered digital trace generated by Wikipedia is similar to digital repositories that organizations use to explicate and store knowledge for future reference and reuse (Massey et al. 2002; Miller 2002; Sambamurthy et al. 2003; Kankanhalli et al. 2005). However, knowledge stored in such repositories may not be easily accessible. Even when accessible, a user may find it difficult to understand or reuse the knowledge because it has been codified without any reference to the context within which it was created (see Davenport and Prusak 1998; Markus 2001; Majchrzak et al. 2004).

Unlike the codified knowledge devoid of context and sub-text stored in digital repositories—what Anand et al. (1998: 797) refer to as 'soft knowledge'—the various layers of the digital trace generated by Wikipedia provide a more holistic account of what had transpired. For instance, the text of the article page serves as a core source of knowledge. In addition, Wikipedia also provides knowledge of who contributed what and when (serving as the context) and the justifications and discussions surrounding these contributions (serving as the sub-text). Given that this is accessible to all, the entire digital trace becomes a holistic 'community narrative' (Boland and Tenkasi 1995) or a 'meta-conversation' (Robichaud et al. 2004) by offering actors a record of the reasoning behind past decisions and an opportunity to generate a larger picture of the emergent structure.

From a community narrative perspective, it becomes possible to see how and why this digital trace in-use is generative. Narratives are more readily comprehensible to those (even casual users and newcomers) who engage with them, given the presence of text, context and sub-text (Czarniawska 2004; Bartel and Garud 2009). At the same time, they are pliable enough to let each actor contribute based on what is most personally relevant given their own individual contexts (Star 1989; Taylor and Van Every 2000; Bartel and Garud 2009) through a process of abductive reasoning (Peirce 1955). That is, when participants read these pages, they generate their own contextualized understanding of emergent outcomes and are able to contribute (Ricoeur 1984). To do so, they may even go back in time through this trace to abstract the rich and appropriate historical contexts and sub-texts surrounding prior outcomes. This is what contributes to the generativity of the memory.

Another way to understand the generativity is to consider the narrative structure offered by the digital trace as a dynamic transactive memory system (cf. Brandon and Hollingshead 2004). Transactive memory enables task groups, epistemic communities, and virtual teams within organizations to encode, store, and retrieve knowledge in the web of relationships that constitute these groups/communities without losing sight of the origins and contexts of creation (Wegner et al. 1985; Moreland 1999; Brandon and Hollingshead 2004; Griffith and Neale 2011). Such a memory emerges through interactive cueing as group members identify, negotiate, and then stabilize a mutual understanding of 'who knows what' over time. Once it emerges, a transactive memory enables the division of labour and an allocation of tasks within the group to those with relevant expertise. It is this cognitive and behavioural division of labour that generates many of the benefits that have been reported in groups with transactive memory compared to groups without such memory (see Moreland and Levine 1992; Moreland 1999).

Similarly, the digital trace generated by the wiki technology provides transparency of contributions and the conversations around them (Leonardi 2014). This is important because the community of contributors to Wikipedia articles is far more fluid than traditional groups operating with fixed boundaries and stable membership (Faraj et al. 2011). Such fluidity in group membership could potentially disrupt transactive memory systems by changing the distribution of task-relevant knowledge within a group (Moreland 1999). However, the digital trace as transactive memory is less disrupted by fluid membership because it preserves the rationale for every contribution (or change) and facilitates the socialization of newcomers (Moreland 1999). It also offers old-timers an ability to refresh their respective memories, reflect upon their collective knowledge at any given time, and then adjust their roles accordingly—a mechanism that has been found to mitigate process inefficiencies due to partial changes in group membership (Lewis et al. 2007).

To summarize our central thesis, a digital trace created in use can bring together two systems of organizational memory—the digital repository and transactive memory. By combining the material (a wiki technology-based digital repository) and the social (a transactive memory), the digital trace serves as a generative memory offering all actors the ability to experiment with new possibilities and contribute to the Wikipedia article's future development. As such, it transcends the limitations of either system and facilitates evolving ownership of an emergent structure. The resultant memory is generative because it reconfigures the sociomaterial elements in use, thereby transcending the divide between knowledge as outcome and knowledge as process (Ackerman and Halverson 2000).

## 8.5 Conclusion

We close by highlighting the significance of virtual collaborative spaces that digital technologies enable. A debate continues amongst scholars on how we should refer to collectives of individuals working together—as organizations with fixed boundaries, or as temporary scaffoldings facilitating work-in-progress. The former perspective (i.e. organizations) takes an entitative view on phenomena wherein actors occupy fixed positions/identities and the artifacts they use possess specific functionalities (Rescher 1996). The latter perspective (i.e. organizing) takes a processual view on phenomena wherein actors' positions/identities and the artifacts they use are materialized in and through the intra-actions (Rescher, 1996; Barad, 2003). In this regard, digital technological platforms such as Wikipedia overcome dualisms between phenomena as entities and phenomena as process. These platforms have built in affordances that generate digital traces which facilitate temporary settlements in the very process of becoming. Thereby, they enable a new way to organize as an emergent yet fragile journey.

## Acknowledgement

We thank Ann Langley for her inputs on an earlier version of this chapter.

## Notes

1. Please see http://en.wikipedia.org/wiki/Wikipedia:Featured_article_criteria for a complete list of criteria used by the Wikipedia community to select featured articles. Also, see Wilkinson and Huberman (2007) for an in-depth analysis of the differences between featured and non-featured articles on Wikipedia.

2. By accessing the 'Revision history statistics' tool on the history page, any interested person can find out the cumulative number of contributions made by specific contributors to the Cryptography page, indicating whether they were active or occasional contributors. Furthermore, anyone can easily identify the extent and diversity of contributions made by a contributor to Wikipedia articles by clicking on the link titled 'Contribs' (on the history page) associated with the contributor. This information offers a potential window into the interests and expertise of each contributor, thereby enabling others to judge his/her credibility.
3. See http://en.wikipedia.org/wiki/Talk:Cryptography/Archive_1#.22Cypher.22_vs_.22Cipher.22.
4. See http://en.wikipedia.org/wiki/Talk:Cryptography/Archive_5#Trivially_breakable.
5. http://en.wikipedia.org/wiki/Talk:Cryptography/Archive_3#large_block_deleted._Why.3F.
6. For the complete discussion, please see: http://en.wikipedia.org/wiki/Talk:Cryptography/Archive_2#Cryptology_.3D_cryptography_.2B_cryptanalysis_.3F and http://en.wikipedia.org/wiki/Talk:Cryptography/Archive_2#.22Crypto.22-proliferation.
7. Conflict also led to 'edit wars' or sustained attempts by uncompromising actors to revert changes made by others. In instances when a settlement cannot be reached, rules embedded in the wiki technology limited the number of reversions any actor can make to three in any 24-hour period. In addition, after a review, administrators can block the editing privileges of disruptive contributors for longer periods.
8. See http://en.wikipedia.org/wiki/User_talk:Ww.

## References


Ackerman, M. S., and C. A. Halverson. (2000). 'Reexamining Organizational Memory', *Communications of the ACM* 43/1: 58–64.

Anand, V., Manz, C. C., and Glick, W. H. (1998). An Organizational Memory Approach to Information Management, *Academy of Management Review* 23: 796–809.

Barad, K. (2003). 'Posthumanist Performativity: Toward an Understanding of How Matter Comes to Matter', *Signs: Journal of Women in Culture and Society* 28/3: 801–831.

Barrett, M., E. Oborn, and W. Orlikowski. (2016). 'Creating Value in Online Communities: The Sociomaterial Configuring of Strategy, Platform, and Stakeholder Engagement', *Information Systems Research* 27/4: 704–723.

Bartel, C. A., and R. Garud. (2009). 'The Role of Narratives in Sustaining Organizational Innovation', *Organization Science* 20/1: 107–117.

Boden, D. (1994). *The Business of Talk: Organizations in Action*. Polity Press.

Boland, R. J., and R. V. Tenkasi. (1995). 'Perspective Making and Perspective Taking in Communities of Knowing', *Organization Science* 6/4: 350–372.

Brandon, D. P., and A. B. Hollingshead. (2004). 'Transactive Memory Systems in Organizations: Matching Tasks, Expertise, and People', *Organization Science* 15/6: 633–644.

Bryant, S. L., A. Forte, and A. Bruckman. (2005). 'Becoming Wikipedian: Transformation of Participation in a Collaborative Online Encyclopedia', *GROUP'05. ACM, Sanibel Island, FL.*

Callon, M. (1986). 'Some Elements of a Sociology of Translation: Domestication of the Scallops and the Fishermen of St. Brieuc Bay', in J. Law (ed.), *Power, Action and Belief: A New Sociology of Knowledge?* Routledge & Kegan Paul.

Callon, M. (2005). 'Why Virtualism Paves the Way to Political Impotence', *Economic Sociology* 6: 3–20.

Carlile, P. R. (2002). 'A Pragmatic View of Knowledge and Boundaries: Boundary Objects in New Product Development', *Organization Science* 13: 442–455.

Cramton, C. D. (2001). 'The Mutual Knowledge Problem and Its Consequences for Dispersed Collaboration', *Organization Science* 12/3: 346–371.

Czarniawska, B. (2004). *Narratives in Social Science Research.* Sage Publications.

Davenport, T. H., and L. Prusak. (1998). *Working Knowledge: How Organizations Manage What They Know.* Harvard Business School Press.

Donahue, K. B. (2001). 'Knowledge Management: Beyond Databases', *Harvard Management Update* 6/5: 6–7.

Dunbar, R. L. M., and R. Garud. (2009). 'Distributed Knowledge and Indeterminate Meaning: The Case of the Columbia Shuttle Flight', *Organization Studies* 30/4: 397–421.

Faraj, S., S. L. Jarvenpaa, and A. Majchrzak. (2011). 'Knowledge Collaboration in Online Communities', *Organization Science* 22/5: 1224–1239.

Gibson, C. B., and S. G. Cohen. (2003). *Virtual Teams that Work: Creating Conditions for Virtual Team Effectiveness.* Jossey Bass.

Giles, J. (2005). 'Internet Encyclopaedias Go Head to Head', *Nature* 438/7070: 900–901.

Glaser, B. G., and A. L. Strauss. (1999). *The Discovery of Grounded Theory: Strategies for Qualitative Research.* Aldine de Gruyter.

Green, S. E., Jr. (2004). 'A Rhetorical Theory of Diffusion', *Academy of Management Review* 29: 653–669.

Hackbarth, G., and V. Grover. (1999). 'The Knowledge Repository: Organizational Memory Information Systems', *Information Systems Management* 16/3: 21–30.

Hansen, M. T., and M. R. Haas. (2001). 'Competing for Attention in Knowledge Markets: Electronic Document Dissemination in a Management Consulting Company', *Administrative Science Quarterly* 46/1: 1–28.

Hinds, P. J., and D. E. Bailey. (2003). 'Out of Sight, Out of Sync: Understanding Conflict in Distributed Teams', *Organization Science* 14/6: 615–632.

Hinds, P. J., and S. Kiesler (eds). (2002). *Distributed Work*. The MIT Press.

Hinds, P. J., and M. Mortensen. (2005). 'Understanding Conflict in Geographically Distributed Teams: The Moderating Effects of Shared Identity, Shared Context, and Spontaneous Communication', *Organization Science* 16/3: 290–307.

Hutchins, E. (1995). *Cognition in the Wild*. MIT Press.

Jarvenpaa, S. L., and D. E. Leidner. (1999). 'Communication and Trust in Global Virtual Teams', *Organization Science* 10/6: 791–815.

Kankanhalli, A., B. C. Y. Tan, and K. K. Wei. (2005). 'Contributing Knowledge to Electronic Knowledge Repositories: An Empirical Investigation', *MIS Quarterly* 29/1: 113–143.

Kane, G. C., J. Johnson, and A. Majchrzak. (2014). 'Emergent Life Cycle: The Tension between Knowledge Change and Knowledge Retention in Open Online Coproduction Communities', *Management Science* 60/12: 3026–3048.

Latour, B. (1999). *Pandora's Hope. Essays on the Reality of Science Studies*. Harvard University Press.

Latour, B. (2005). *Reassembling the Social*. Oxford University Press.

Lave, J., and E. Wenger. (1991). *Situated Learning: Legitimate Peripheral Participation*. Cambridge University Press.

Leidner, D. E. (2000). Editorial, *Journal of Strategic Information Systems* 9: 101–105.

Leonardi, P. M. (2014). 'Social Media, Knowledge Sharing, and Innovation: Toward a Theory of Communication Visibility', *Information Systems Research* 25/4: 796–816.

Leonardi, P. M., and S. R. Barley. (2010). 'What's Under Construction Here? Social Action, Materiality, and Power in Constructivist Studies of Technology and Organizing', *Academy of Management Annals* 4: 1–51.

Lewis, K., M. Belliveau, B. Herndon, and J. Keller. (2007). 'Group Cognition, Membership Change, and Performance: Investigating the Benefits and Detriments of Collective Knowledge', *Organizational Behavior and Human Decision Processes* 103/2: 159–178.

Majchrzak, A., L. P. Cooper, and O.E. Neece. (2004). 'Knowledge Reuse for Innovation', *Management Science* 50/2: 174–188.

Majchrzak, A., S. L. Jarvenpaa, and A. B. Hollingshead. (2007). 'Coordinating Expertise among Emergent Groups Responding to Disasters', *Organization Science* 18/1: 147–161.

Majchrzak, A., P. H. More, and S. Faraj. (2012). 'Transcending Knowledge Differences in Cross-Functional Teams', Organization Science 23/4: 951–970.

Malhotra, A., Majchrzak, A., and Lyytinen, K. (2021). 'Socio-Technical Affordances for Large-Scale Collaborations: Introduction to a Virtual Special Issue', *Organization Science* (in press). https://doi.org/10.1287/orsc.2021.1457.

March, J. G., and H. A. Simon. (1993). *Organizations*, Second ed. Blackwell Publishers.

Mark, G. (2002). 'Conventions and Commitments in Distributed CSCW Groups', *Computer Supported Cooperative Work: The Journal of Collaborative Computing* 11/3–4: 349–387.

Markus, M. L. (2001). 'Toward a Theory of Knowledge Reuse: Types of Knowledge Reuse Situations and Factors in Reuse Success', *Journal of Management Information Systems* 18/1: 57–93.

Massey, A. P., M. M. Montoya-Weiss, and T. O'Driscoll. (2002). 'Knowledge Management in Pursuit of Performance: Insights from Nortel Networks', *MIS Quarterly* 26/3: 269–289.

Merton, R. K. (1959). 'Problem-finding in Sociology', in R. K. Merton, L. Broom, and L. S. Cottrell (eds). *Sociology Today*. Basic Books.

Meyerson, D., K. E. Weick, and R. M. Kramer. (1996). 'Swift Trust and Temporary Groups', in R. M. Kramer and T. R. Tyler (eds), *Trust in Organizations: Frontiers of Study and Research*. Sage Publications.

Miller, K. (2002). 'Knowledge Inventories and Managerial Myopia', *Strategic Management Journal* 23: 689–706.

Mohr, L. B. (1982). *Explaining Organizational Behavior: The Limits and Possibilities of Theory and Research*. Jossey-Bass.

Montoya-Weiss, M. M., Massey, A. P., and Song, M. (2001). 'Getting it Together: Temporal Coordination and Conflict Management in Global Virtual Teams', *Academy of Management Journal* 44: 1251–1262.

Moreland, R. L. (1999). 'Transactive Memory: Learning Who Knows What in Work Groups and Organizations', in L. Thompson, D. Messick, and J. Levine (eds), *Shared Cognition in Organizations: The Management of Knowledge*. Erlbaum, 3–31.

Moreland, R. L., and J. M. Levine. (1992). 'Problem Identification by Groups', in S. Wrochel, W. Wood, and J.A. Simpson (eds), *Group Process and Productivity*. Sage, 17–47.

Orlikowski, W. J. (2007). 'Sociomaterial Practices: Exploring Technology at Work', *Organization Studies* 28/9: 1435–1448.

Orlikowski, W. J., and S. V. Scott. (2008). 'Sociomateriality: Challenging the Separation of Technology, Work and Organization', *Academy of Management Annals* 2: 433–474.

Peirce, C. S. (1955). 'Abduction and Induction', in J. Buchler (ed.), *Philosophical Writings of Pierce*. Dover Books.

Pettigrew, A. M. (1992). 'The Character and Significance of Strategy Process Research', *Strategic Management Journal* 13/S2: 5–16.

Pickering, A. (1993). 'The Mangle of Practice—Agency and Emergence in the Sociology of Science', *American Journal of Sociology* 99/3: 559–589.

Raghuram, S., Hill, N. S., Gibbs, J. L., and Maruping, L. M. (2019). Virtual Work: Bridging Research Clusters', *Academy of Management Annals* 13/1: 308–341.

Ransbotham, S., and G. C. Kane. (2011). 'Membership Turnover and Collaboration Success in Online Communities: Explaining Rises and Falls from Grace in Wikipedia', *MIS Quarterly*, 613–627.

Ren, Y. Q., R. Kraut, and S. Kieier. (2007). 'Applying Common Identity and Bond Theory to Design of Online Communities', *Organization Studies* 28/3: 377–408.

Rescher, N. (1996). *Process Metaphysics: An Introduction to Process Philosophy.* SUNY Press.

Ricoeur, P. (1984). *Time and Narrative.* University of Chicago Press.

Robichaud, D., H. Giroux, and J. R. Taylor. (2004). 'The Metaconversation: The Recursive Property of Language as a Key to Organizing', *Academy of Management Review* 29/4: 617–634.

Sambamurthy, V., A. Bharadwaj, and V. Grover. (2003). 'Shaping Agility through Digital Options: Reconceptualizing the Role of Information Technology in Contemporary Firms', *MIS Quarterly* 27/2: 237–263.

Star, S. L. (1989). 'The Structure of Ill-Structured Solutions: Heterogeneous Problem-Solving, Boundary Objects and Distributed Artificial Intelligence', in M. Hans and L. Gasser (eds), *Distributed Artificial Intelligence.* Morgan Kauffman.

Taylor, J. R., and E. J. Van Every. (2000). *The Emergent Organization: Communication as the Site and Surface.* Lawrence Erlbaum Associates.

Tilly, C. (2006). *Why? What Happens When People Give Reasons . . . and Why.* Princton University Press.

Tsoukas, H. (1989). 'The Validity of Idiographic Research Explanations', *Academy of Management Review* 14/4: 551–561.

Tsoukas, H. (2009). 'A Dialogical Approach to the Creation of New Knowledge in Organizations', *Organization Science* 20/6: 941–957.

Tuertscher, P., R. Garud, and A. Kumaraswamy. (2014). 'Justification and Interlaced Knowledge at ATLAS, CERN', *Organization Science* 25/6: 1579–1608.

Viègas, F., M. Wattenberg, and K. Dave. (2004). 'Studying Cooperation and Conflict between Authors with History Flow Visualizations', Proceedings of the *SIGCHI Conference on Human Factors in Computing Systems. ACM, Vienna, Austria,* 575–582.

Walsh, J. P., and G. R. Ungson. (1991). 'Organizational Memory', *Academy of Management Review* 16/1: 57–91.

Wegner, D. M., T. Giuliano, and P. T. Hertel. (1985). 'Cognitive Interdependence in Close Relationships', in W. J. Ickes (ed.), *Compatible and Incompatible Relationships*. Springer-Verlag, 253–276.

Weick, K. E., and K. H. Roberts. (1993). 'Collective Mind in Organizations: Heedful Interrelating on Flight Decks', *Administrative Science Quarterly* 38: 357–381.

Wiesenfeld, B. M., S. Raghuram, and R. Garud. (1999). 'Communication Patterns as Determinants of Organizational Identification in a Virtual Organization', *Organization Science* 10/6: 777–790.

Wilkinson, D. M., and B. A. Huberman. (2007). 'Cooperation and Quality in Wikipedia', in *Proceedings of the 2007 International Symposium on Wikis*, 157–164.

Yates, J., and W. J. Orlikowski. (1992). 'Genres of Organizational Communication: A Structurational Approach to Studying Communication and Media', *Academy of Management Review* 17: 299–326.

Znaniecki, F. (1934). *The Method of Sociology*. Farrar and Rinehart.

Zuboff, S. (1988). *In the Age of the Smart Machine*. Basic Books.

# 9

# Blockchain and the Performativity of Emerging Technology Theories

*Moritz J. Kleinaltenkamp and Shaz Ansari*

## 9.1 Introduction

'Performativity' describes the phenomenon of theories not only *describing*, but at times also *producing* social reality (Callon 1998; MacKenzie and Millo 2003; Ferraro et al. 2005; Gond et al. 2016). Over recent years, management and strategy scholars have increasingly appreciated the role of discursive performativity in shaping organizational realities. Scholars have stressed the performative dimensions of a variety of organizational concepts (e.g. Feldman and Pentland 2003; Vaara et al. 2010; Gehman et al. 2013; Guérard et al. 2013) as well as scientific theories of organizing (e.g. Cabantous and Gond 2010; Carter et al. 2010; D'Adderio and Pollock 2014). The performativity perspective has contributed to these fields of study by showing how practitioners' and scholars' theories can become self-reinforcing and self-fulfilling (Marti and Gond 2017), and how they can impact social welfare (Marti and Scherer 2016) on basis of their ethical dimensions (Ferraro et al. 2009), thus opening new avenues for productive critique and research into organizational change, strategy, and public policymaking.

One area of practitioner and scholarly theorizing that is garnering increasing attention revolves around emerging technologies; innovations characterized by radical novelty and impact, yet also uncertainty (Rotolo et al. 2015). Technological change has been a key topic of organizational research and practice for decades (e.g. Zammuto et al. 2007; Orlikowski and Scott 2008). Over the last decade in particular, technologies such as social media (e.g. Dutta 2010; Gaines-Ross 2010; Treem and Leonardi 2013), artificial intelligence (e.g. McAfee and Brynjolfsson 2012; Faraj et al. 2018; Mahidhar and Davenport 2018) and blockchain (Gupta 2017; Seidel 2018; Lumineau et al. 2021), have captured the imaginaries of organizational practitioners and

Moritz J. Kleinaltenkamp and Shaz Ansari, *Blockchain and the Performativity of Emerging Technology Theories.* In: *Organizing in the Digital Age.* Edited by: Michael Barrett, Emmanuelle Vaast, Ann Langley, and Haridimos Tsoukas, Oxford University Press.
 DOI: 10.1093/oso/9780198899457.003.0009

researchers. This has resulted in vocal theorization about these (once) emerging technologies' potential organizational and societal impacts. Such theories tend to extrapolate organizational outcomes in the future from technological features observed in the present. Frequently, this link is forged by (explicitly or implicitly) theorizing affordances (Gibson 1979): imagined action potentials that would arise as a consequence of the emerging technology being subjected to organizational use (Faraj and Azad 2012; Majchrzak et al. 2013; Leidner et al. 2018).

Such theorizing of the potential organizational impacts of emerging technologies has not only inspired insightful research, but also provided welcome guidance for practitioner decision-making and pilot projects. However, some have noted that emerging technology theories at times tend to exaggerate outcomes (e.g. Ramiller 2006) as well as 'muddle' the distinction between what is an inherent *technological feature*, what is a *contextual affordance*, and what *respective outcomes* are associated with these categories (Leidner et al. 2018: 4). These critiques are important as emerging technology theories and the organizational outcomes they posit are a powerful driver of organizations' engagement with the technologies in question.

From a performativity perspective, inspiring organizational pilot projects is a hallmark of self-fulfilling theories (Marti and Gond 2017). However, the question of whether theories of emerging technology impacts may in fact have a performative dimension, and the conditions under which they do so, has not received adequate attention in extant management research. Answering this question is crucial, as it promises to uncover a hitherto disregarded yet potentially powerful driver of organizational change. From a practical perspective, it could also help foster more reflective discourses on emerging technologies, creating a foundation for informed resource allocation and public policymaking vis-à-vis uncertain innovations that could enhance social welfare just as well as diminish it.

In this chapter, we explore the performativity of emerging technology theories conceptually and through illustrative examples. Synthesizing existing literature from the fields of performativity as well as technological and organizational change, we develop an analytical vocabulary for conceptualizing the performativity and performative consequences of emerging technology theories. Based on this, we propose that the performativity of emerging technology theories will be more pronounced the more those theories conflate the categories of technology feature use and affordances, and their respective organizational outcomes. Using blockchain as an exemplary emerging technology, we provide two illustrative examples from our past empirical research in which emerging technology theories have become performative.

In each of the examples we discuss, organizational actors started to enact blockchain's widely theorized impact of trust-building *before* blockchain was yet materially present at the site of organizing. We subsequently use these examples as an opportunity to further develop our proposition, discussing how different degrees of conceptual 'muddling' can lead emerging technology theories to exhibit different degrees of performativity.

In the rest of the chapter, we first explain the concepts of 'performativity' and 'emerging technology theories', developing our proposition and analytical vocabulary. Then, we briefly explain blockchain technology and describe the theories around this emerging technology's organizational impacts that dominated public discourse between 2016 and 2019. Third, we discuss two illustrative examples of organizational blockchain use from 2019 and, fourth, offer an answer to our motivating research question. Finally, we discuss how this answer contributes to research on technological and organizational change, and how it can help build more reflective emerging technology discourses benefitting management practice and public policymaking.

## 9.2 Performativity

In 1962, Austin observed that 'to *say* something is to *do* something' (p. 12, original emphasis). This phenomenon—today referred to as performativity—went on to find wide appeal in philosophy (Butler 1997; Derrida 1979; Barad 2007), sociology (Callon 1998; MacKenzie and Millo 2003), and most recently management and strategy research (e.g. Feldman and Pentland 2003; Ferraro et al. 2005; Carter et al. 2010; Vaara et al. 2010; Guérard et al. 2013; D'Adderio and Pollock 2014; Garud et al. 2018). While always coming back to Austin's original observation, scholars across these fields have taken the concept of performativity into a variety of directions. In a review of performativity literature in organization research, Gond and colleagues (2016) identified five different, prevalent perspectives upon the concept: (1) 'performativity as doing things with words', (2) 'performativity as efficiency', (3) 'performativity as actors' constituting the self', (4) 'performativity as bringing theory into being', and, (5) 'performativity as socio-materiality mattering' (p. 445). In exploring whether and how emerging technology theories can be performative, this chapter is most closely aligned with the fourth of these perspectives ('performativity as bringing theory into being').

This conceptualization of performativity as bringing theory into being originated with science and technology sociologists, in particular Hacking (1983), Pickering (1995), Latour (1993), and Callon (1998). Building on

Hacking's, Pickering's, and Latour's critiques of representationalism, Callon in *The Law of Markets* (1998) argued that the science of 'economics, broadly defined, performs, shapes and formats the economy, rather than observing how it functions' (p. 2). This view was further popularized by MacKenzie and Millo's (2003) striking empirical analysis of the Black-Scholes' formula becoming able to predict derivative market prices by shaping traders' practices. A few years later, MacKenzie (2006) refined the analytical tools of this particular conception of performativity by distinguishing between three hierarchically related types of performativity: 'generic' (corresponding to the use of a theory), 'effective' (corresponding to the use of a theory making a difference in the world), and 'Barnesian' (corresponding to the use of a theory making a difference in the world that moves the world closer to how it is depicted in the theory).

These conceptual foundations have since inspired management and strategy scholars to theorize the performative dimensions of organizational concepts such as routines (Feldman and Pentland 2003), labels (Learmonth 2005), strategic plans (Vaara et al. 2010), performance (Guérard et al. 2013), and values (Gehman et al. 2013). In addition, there is a growing management and strategy literature specifically investigating the performativity of scientific theories. For example, scholars have investigated Porter's competitive strategy framework (Carter et al. 2010), rational choice theory (Cabantous and Gond 2010), and modularity theory (D'Adderio and Pollock 2014) through the performative lens offered by Callon and MacKenzie. In all of these cases, the understanding that theories do more than simply describe the world facilitated sophisticated critiques, thereby refining existing management and strategy concepts and opening up new research avenues. Most recently, Marti and Gond (2017) built on this body of research to conceptualize the conditions under which theories can exhibit 'Barnesian' performativity. They argued that theories became self-fulfilling when they first motivated experimentation, that experimentation then produced anomalies, and those anomalous outcomes finally induced shifts in organizational practices. They further proposed mechanisms fostering this chain of events. For example, as regards the first phase, they posit that theories will be better at motivating practitioners to experiment when they, (1) challenge existing practices in culturally resonant ways, (2) identify material devices that make theoretical concepts visible, and (3) by doing so, can garner the support of powerful initial backers (Marti and Gond 2017: 16–19). As regards the second phase, they define anomalies as 'observable events that (1) violate widely shared expectations about how certain actors or entities will behave, while (2) conforming with expectations that result from the new theory' (p. 11).

We now discuss how this performativity lens relates to emerging technology theories.

## 9.3 Emerging Technology Theories

Even though the term 'emerging technology' is enjoying increasing popularity among practitioners and scholars alike (e.g. Bailey et al. 2019), a definition has remained elusive. A literature review (Rotolo et al. 2015) of emerging technology research concluded that academic conceptualizations of the term gravitated around five key attributes of technologies: '(i) radical novelty, (ii) relatively fast growth, (iii) coherence, (iv) prominent impact, [and] (v) uncertainty and ambiguity' (p. 13). Accordingly, the authors define an emerging technology as:

> a radically novel and relatively fast growing (sic) technology characterised by a certain degree of coherence persisting over time and with the potential to exert a considerable impact on the socio-economic domain(s) which is observed in terms of the composition of actors, institutions and patterns of interactions among those, along with the associated knowledge production processes. Its most prominent impact, however, lies in the future and so in the emergence phase is still somewhat uncertain and ambiguous.
>
> **(Rotolo et al. 2015: 13)**

This definition reveals an intimate relationship between emerging technologies and theorization: in the general understanding, theories ascribing 'considerable impact' (taking forms such as changed actor compositions, institutions, and interaction patterns) to a particular technology are inherently necessary for that technology to be considered an 'emerging technology'. Simply put, emerging technologies cannot exist without theories ascribing considerable future impact to them, and the existence of such theories for a particular technology is a good indicator that the technology will be considered as 'emerging' by a majority of observers.

Accordingly, there is a rich landscape of practitioner and scientific theories ascribing at times drastic organizational impacts to the latest technological advancements. Over the last decades, contributions in practitioner-oriented journals such as *Harvard Business Review* ascribed far-reaching organizational impacts to digital technologies considered emerging at the time, and ranging from social media (e.g. Dutta 2010; Gaines-Ross 2010), via big data and artificial intelligence (e.g. Davenport and Patil 2012; McAfee and Brynjolffson 2012; Bean 2016; Mahidhar and Davenport 2018; Fountaine et al. 2019) to blockchain (e.g. Gupta 2017; Iansiti and Lakhani 2017; Choudary et al. 2019). This is neither a new phenomenon—contributions to *Harvard Business Review* with striking titles such as 'Telecom: hook up or lose out' (Clemens and McFarlan 1986) have a history of more than 40 years—nor a phenomenon confined to a single outlet. Scholarly journals, too, have been platforms for theorizing the impacts of emerging digital technologies ranging from internet-enabled information technology (e.g. Zammuto et al. 2007), to social media (e.g. Treem and Leonardi 2013), artificial intelligence (e.g. Faraj et al. 2018), and blockchain (e.g. Seidel 2018).

While providing crucial guidance to practitioners and scholars facing a radically new phenomenon, emerging technology theories such as the above have also faced criticism for exaggerating organizational impacts by amplifying the value of innovations, glossing over organizational variation, and amplifying the urgency of organizational response (e.g. Ramiller 2006). Further, Leidner and colleagues (2018: 4) recently pointed out that technological feature use, affordances (i.e. action potentials arising in context of feature use), and their respective organizational outcomes were frequently 'muddled' in academic theorizing of technology impacts. Using the example of a train ride, Leidner and colleagues (p. 4) emphasize the distinction between feature use, affordances, and their respective organizational outcomes as they envision it:

> Riding the train is the direct use of the object [the train] whereas working, sleeping, meditating, or conversing are not uses of the train itself, but affordances made possible by the train ride. One might be tempted to say that the outcome is that the individual arrives at work, but this is the outcome of riding the train, not the outcome of the affordances produced by riding the train. An outcome of affording the ride on the train to work, for example, may be that the individual completes more work in a given day than he would if he drove to work.

This example reveals a number of important aspects about emerging technology theories. First and foremost, it highlights that affordances, being action potentials opened up by technology use, are naturally more relational and precarious than inherent technology features (Shotter 1983, Faraj and Azad 2012; Fayard and Weeks 2014). Where the outcomes of feature use can more or less be expected to manifest so long as one meets the use requirements ('buying a ticket' in the case of the train ride), the outcomes of affordances will manifest only if use requirements are met *and* the circumstances of use support actualizing the affordance ('being motivated to work during the commute' in case of the train ride). Thus, secondly, where emerging technology theories do not sufficiently distinguish between feature use and affordances, they are also less likely to distinguish between the degrees of attainability that are associated with outcomes of feature use on the one hand ('arriving at work'), and the outcomes of affordances ('getting more work done in a single day') on the other.

Consequently, leaving implicit the differences between feature use and affordances 'muddles' the distinction between the straightforward use of an emerging technology's features and the contextual action potentials afforded by the use of those features. This portrays a simplified relationship in which far-reaching but conditional organizational outcomes can be reaped with certainty and little effort. Returning to Ramiller's (2006) critique, such 'muddling' amplifies the portrayed value of the technology relative to its costs, glosses over organizational variation that might powerfully mediate outcomes, and thereby amplifies the urgency of organizational response.

## 9.4 Conceptionalizing the Performativity of Emerging Technology Theories

Based on the above considerations, we propose that a lack of differentiation between the explicit or implicit categories of feature use and affordances as well as their respective outcomes in the theorizing of emerging technology impacts will amplify the extent, attainability, and immediateness of the technologies' impacts. These theories' simplified narratives will be better at challenging existing practices in culturally resonant ways and at garnering the support of powerful backers (see Marti and Gond 2017). Uninhibited by the conditionality of actual organizational praxis, they are able to craft an enticing link between a single material device (the emerging technology in question) and far-reaching organizational outcomes that include both, the straightforward outcomes of feature use *and* the 'anomalies' (Marti and Gond 2017) stemming from affordances. In this vein, they will be better at inducing experimentation, the first phase of theories becoming self-fulfilling. We thus propose that emerging technology theories leaving implicit the categorial differences between technology feature use and affordances, and thus their respective organizational outcomes, will be more likely to exhibit general, effective, and Barnesian performativity.

With this proposition, we have also arrived at an analytical vocabulary that facilitates a deeper look into when and how emerging technology theories become performative. Based on our reading of the literature, the search for answers to these questions should proceed by analysing how emerging technology theories differentiate (or not) between the categories of feature use and affordances as well as their respective outcomes, and whether their application in practice meets the requirements of general, effective, and Barnesian performativity.

We now turn to blockchain, an exemplary emerging technology. Against this backdrop, we discuss two examples from our past empirical research that serve to illustrate and enhance our proposition.

## 9.5 Blockchain as an Exemplary Emerging Technology

We chose blockchain as an exemplary emerging technology because it was considered a novel and fast-growing technology in 2019 (Deloitte 2019), for which practitioners and scholars alike had theorized considerable organizational impacts (Tapscott and Tapscott 2016; Underwood 2016; Gupta 2017; Iansiti and Lakhani 2017; Seidel 2018; Choudary et al. 2019). It is also a technology that exhibited coherence across socio-economic domains at the time—with blockchain applications being observable in private business sectors ranging from manufacturing to financial services, energy, and healthcare (Deloitte 2019), in development NGOs, and in public administration (Allessie et al. 2019)—while at the same time still being characterized by conceptual ambiguity (Jeffries 2018). In this vein, blockchain in 2019 was an archetypical example of emerging technology.

From a technology features perspective, blockchain facilitates the maintenance of data across a network of computers (Nakamoto 2008). Rather than storing records on central servers, blockchain uses encryption methods to allow peer-to-peer connected computers to store, update, and verify such records on distributed digital ledgers, which are sometimes also referred to as 'global spreadsheets' (Swan 2015). Blockchain transactions are verified, cleared, and stored in digital blocks of data connected to preceding blocks, thereby creating the eponymous 'chain'. The first blockchain application, Bitcoin, was developed in 2008 (Nakamoto 2008). In 2014, the blockchain application 'Ethereum' (Buterin 2014) iterated upon this foundation to enhance its potential through so-called 'smart contracts'. Simply put, smart contracts represent computer programs that are automatically executed by the computer network maintaining the blockchain when the records meet certain conditions. For example, if blockchain is used to store financial data, one might devise a smart contract that, at the start of every month, automatically distributes 5 $US to all accounts.

From an organizational outcomes perspective, the features of blockchain technology outlined above were theorized to facilitate radical organizational decentralization (Tapscott and Tapscott 2016; Gupta 2017; Seidel 2018; Choudary et al. 2019). Satoshi Nakamoto, the creator of blockchain, designed the technology with the intention of making obsolete central third parties such as banks, which have created lucrative intermediary positions for themselves by garnering the trust of unacquainted actors and, on the basis of that trust, maintaining and verifying transactional data (Nakamoto 2008: 1). Before blockchain, maintaining and verifying such data without such an intermediary would have been difficult, because malicious actors could have cheated (e.g. double-spending money). As the cryptographic methods employed by blockchain networks counteract cheating while maintaining equal authority for all members of the network, practitioners and scholars alike theorized that the use of blockchain would create trust between unacquainted actors, making them able and willing to transact even in the absence of third parties and centralized authority. In this vein, the abolition of intermediaries and hierarchical structures has been portrayed as the natural, even inevitable, result of the 'trust machine' (The Economist 2015) that is blockchain (e.g. Tapscott and Tapscott 2016; Gupta 2017; Seidel 2018; Choudary et al. 2019).

In such theories about the organizational impacts of blockchain technology, the affordances of the technology tend to remain implicit. As a result, such theories present a straightforward narrative according to which simple use of the features of blockchain directly produces the far-reaching organizational outcomes: feature use outcomes such as the storage and maintenance of data across a network of computers, and affordance outcomes such as the building of trust between parties, the automation of interdependent activities based on the blockchain data, and the decentralization of organizational/market structures. However, as previously discussed, affordances are mere action *potentials* that are more precarious and context-dependent than technology features. Thus, when not clearly separating affordances from feature use, blockchain theories tend to disregard the many material and social contingencies mediating the appealing affordance outcomes of inter-party trust, algorithmic coordination, and organizational/market decentralization. For example, there may be reasons other than a lack of mutual trust and ability to coordinate—such as legislation, contractual obligations, and normative institutions—that explain why incumbent intermediaries and hierarchies exist. Consequently, predominant blockchain theories amplify the extent, attainability, and immediateness of the technology's impacts, increasing their performative quality by inducing experimentation.

We now offer two examples of organizations using blockchain technology in which the performativity of simplified blockchain theories came to the fore.

## 9.6 Illustrative Examples of Organizational Blockchain Use

The data supporting these two examples stems from past research into organizational blockchain use. In Spring 2019, we conducted a primary interview with a top manager of each case organization. In addition, we gathered publicly available archival materials on the case organizations (three secondary interviews and 35 blog posts) available online.

### 9.6.1 Illustration 1: Standards Org

Standards Org (a pseudonym) is an international NGO working on the development and maintenance of supply chain standards. In 2017, Standards Org's innovation department concluded that blockchain was likely to have a 'strong future impact on trade and industry' (Pilot Project Head, primary interview). In 2018, the organization's management decided that 'alright, blockchain, the hype existing around that should be captured and we should simply test, in a pilot project ..., what you can and can't do with that technology' (Pilot Project Head, primary interview). Searching for a viable context for the pilot project, they identified an appropriate use case in the field of lorry delivery.

Lorry delivery is one of the primary methods by which goods are transported along the supply chain. To make this process more efficient, collaborating as well as competing European producers, retailers, and providers of transport services have long agreed upon a standardized shipping container: wooden pallets. As of 2019, more than 500 million such pallets were in use. These pallets were bought by organizations individually but were frequently traded in a routinized exchange system—the sum of them changing hands around 2.5 billion times a year. The process works as follows: as warehouse staff receive goods from lorry drivers, they would sign an exchange form indicating the number of laden pallets received, and empty pallets given in exchange. When an organization received less pallets than it delivered, it was able to use this exchange form as a voucher to claim additional pallets at a later point. But in the run up to 2017, this paper-based exchange routine had come under increasing scrutiny. Retailers, producers, and logistics companies alike had criticized the paper forms for being error-prone and cumbersome. At the same time, previous efforts to digitize the pallet exchange forms had been held back by the sensitivity of the data represented on them. Because pallets have intrinsic value, and sales volumes can be read off from the number of containers exchanged, organizations seeking to protect their competitive positions were loath to share pallet exchange information or store it under the lone jurisdiction of any individual actor.

As the pilot project's head reflected:

> You have a use case with a lot of transactions, with many parties involved; you have a lack of transparency and a lack of trust, and you have a highly manual task, because around 95% of these transactions are still being handled manually today .... So that was a use case that practically cried for testing whether blockchain can deliver trust, security ..., distributed data. And blockchain also provides the opportunity to abolish intermediaries, and we at [Standards Org] of course also wanted to see: does that work? Because we are also a kind of intermediary.
>
> **(Pilot Project Head, primary interview)**

Thus, in 2018, Standards Org gathered 35 national and multinational businesses around a pilot project aimed at using blockchain to digitize the exchange of wooden pallets. These businesses included competing as well as collaborating producers, retailers, and logistics companies, as well as IT service providers, who engaged in a series of workshops in order to collectively design the blockchain solution. They decided on aspects such as what data should be stored on the blockchain, and how visible that data should be to all parties. Over the course of these workshops, almost half of the initial partnering businesses dropped out of the project. Thus, the pilot project ended in late 2018 with 17 businesses testing the viability of a blockchain-based solution in a two-week practical experiment where lorry drivers and warehouse staff used a mobile app to register the exchange of pallets on a blockchain. The experiment was deemed a success by all parties that participated. Ultimately, however, the pilot project revealed also surprising aspects about blockchain:

> The biggest problem is that blockchain itself does not create trust. Rather, I have to build trust between the parties as a foundation. ... And so we found that, especially in the beginning of such a project, a neutral third party or intermediary can foster the use of a blockchain architecture.
>
> **(Pilot Project Head, primary interview)**

Standard Org's pilot project thus provides an example of emerging technology theories becoming performative. As the pilot project head's comments reflect, the organization was driven to initiate the pilot project on the basis of emerging technology theories that had ascribed considerable future impacts to blockchain based on the simplified argument that use of its features would 'deliver trust' and 'abolish intermediaries' (even though these are actually affordance outcomes). Connecting the material device of blockchain to drastic organizational impacts in this straightforward way resonated with the key decision-makers at Standards Org and resulted in experimentation. These aspects of the example illustrate the potential for emerging technology theories to, (1) exhibit *generic performativity* (the theories arguing that blockchain can deliver trust and abolish intermediaries were being used by decision-makers) and, (2) *effective performativity* (the theories arguing that blockchain can deliver trust and abolish intermediaries were motivating experiments that would not happen in absence of these theories).

Strikingly, in order to follow through with the experiment, Standards Org found itself building trust between the parties involved (through a series of workshops) in order to even *create* a situation where blockchain could be used (the field test). This aspect of the example illustrates also the potential for emerging technology theories to exhibit *Barnesian performativity*, where the theories arguing that blockchain can deliver trust were driving the building of trust and the use of blockchain, even if the former was not materially tied to the latter.

## 9.6.2 Illustration 2: Energy Org

Energy Org (a pseudonym) is a technology start-up in the energy industry. In 2015, a co-founder of Energy Org was working at a professional services firm and encountered blockchain technology while doing desk research. At the time, she perceived the technology as an opportunity to address pressing issues in energy markets:

> So, it was only when I heard about blockchain ..., I came across a single slide, when I was at [a professional services firm], on the Ethereum white paper ... And for me, it was really like the missing piece in the coordination of this new decentralizing energy industry. There was an 'aha' moment—actually, I was like Cassandra. I kind of picked up the sheet and was running around the energy floor being like: 'Do you realize what this means!?'
>
> **(Co-founder, archival interview)**

She went on to co-found Energy Org together with an experienced energy industry CEO in 2016. The mission of Energy Org was to provide a blockchain-based platform that would provide different actors in the energy industry with a better visibility of energy generation and demand, creating a market that could allocate resources more efficiently. At the time, Energy Org's strategy director informed us, energy transmission companies did not 'actually have visibility of 50% of [energy] generation that's on the network ... They can't see that it's there, let alone what it's doing' (Strategy Director, primary interview). Energy Org believed that this problem would only be exacerbated in the future, by cheap renewables enabling private individuals to generate and sell electric energy on their own. Moreover, previous efforts that sought to counteract the fragmentation of energy markets by establishing centralized platforms had failed, because they could not do so without creating exploitable information asymmetries and conflicts of interest. Such outcomes were deemed unacceptable for platforms that fundamentally sought to bring together competitors lacking mutual trust.

Energy Org believed that blockchain would provide the solution. A 'blockchain-based platform would allow different products to be traded in one central location without having a central authority with privileged visibility and access over that market' (Strategy Director, primary interview). Energy Org believed blockchain to have this capacity because it 'fosters transparency and trust by guaranteeing the execution of certain processes (pre-programmed through "smart contracts")' (Co-founder, archival blog post), and thus 'can stand in for many of the trust functions for which we have typically looked to large, established & expensive corporates' (Co-founder, archival blog post).

Since its foundation, Energy Org's efforts to realize such blockchain-based platforms in various national contexts have moved forward by approaching the biggest actors, 'taking them through proof-of-concept, into pilots, and into deployment' (Strategy Director, primary interview). One of the start-up's biggest projects faced different energy system operators and started in early 2018, when Energy Org got those system operators to agree to participate in a proof-of-concept. In this project, Energy Org sought to create the foundation for an efficient energy market by using blockchain as a means for data sharing. However, a year later, the project was still in its infancy, and blockchain far from being deployed:

> [*Laughs*] Well, the project's been running 12 months, and we have just gotten to the point where we can start the project, because it's taken 12 months to negotiate the contract which defines what [the participating system operators'] involvement in

> the project is going to be. So that just goes to show how difficult that coordination is between the parties. Even having agreed to do the project, it's taken 12 months to actually get to the start. So that's precisely the issue, that there's a lack of trust . . .
>
> **(Strategy Director, primary interview)**

In this vein, Energy Org, too, exemplifies the performative quality that emerging technology theories can take on. The co-founders' comments indicate that Energy Org was founded based on the theory that blockchain could 'foster trust' in a fragmenting energy industry. This motivating theory, conflating feature use and affordances, created an '"aha" moment' and spurred the co-founder to seek opportunities to test the theory through experiments with groups of large corporate actors. Once more, these aspects of the example illustrate the potential for emerging technology theories to exhibit *generic performativity* (the theories arguing that blockchain can foster trust are being used by the co-founder) and *effective performativity* (the theories arguing that blockchain can foster trust motivated the founding of an organization and engaging in experimentation to test its promise). While seeking opportunities to engage in experimentation, Energy Org found that it first had to spend considerable time and effort building initial levels of trust between corporate actors through negotiation, before it could even begin conducting proofs-of-concept and field tests in which blockchain would be deployed. Thus, this example, too, illustrates also the potential for emerging technology theories to exhibit *Barnesian performativity*, where the theories arguing that blockchain can foster trust were driving the building of trust and the use of blockchain, even if the former was not materially tied to the latter.

## 9.7 Reflections on the Illustrations

Both Energy Org and Standards Org found themselves building trust between unacquainted actors *in order to use* blockchain technology, as opposed to this process being an *outcome* of blockchain use. At both sites, the trust-building efforts happened *before* blockchain was even yet materially present. In this vein, the examples provide an opportunity to further clarify our proposition of how emerging technology theories may become performative.

As we previously proposed, a lack of differentiation between feature use, affordances, and their respective organizational outcomes is likely to induce experimentation by amplifying the extent, attainability, and immediateness of emerging technology impacts. Where such experimentation actually happens on the basis of emerging technology theories, generic, and effective performativity are enacted. However, when it comes to Barnesian performativity (theories becoming self-fulfilling), experimentation is merely the first stage. For a theory to exhibit Barnesian performativity, experimentation on the basis of a theory in the next phase also has to produce observable events that violate widely shared expectations and were predicted by the theory (Marti and Gond 2017). The examples of Energy Org and Standards Org show how this may happen for emerging technology theories. Simplified narratives disregarding the different conditionalities of feature use and affordances may be so inspiring that actors feel compelled to force the anomalous outcomes predicted for the emerging technology (e.g. trust building)—which are actually outcomes of implicit affordances—*before* the technology is even yet being used. In such cases, actors *imitate* the affordances theorized for the emerging technology even in the absence of the material device, producing the theorized anomalies and practice shifts even though the underlying causality has been reversed ('blockchain itself does not create trust. Rather, I have to build trust between the parties as a foundation' to use blockchain).

Regarding the question of how emerging technology theories may become performative, we thus propose: (1), the less that emerging technology theories differentiate between feature use, affordances, and their respective organizational outcomes, the more simplified their narrative will be and the more likely they will be to enact generic and effective performativity; (2), the most simplified of these theories will be so inspiring that actors force the occurrence of the theorized anomalies by imitating the implicit affordances (even in the absence of the material devices in question), thereby inducing practice shifts and enacting Barnesian performativity.

## 9.8 Discussion

In this chapter, we have sought to extend the burgeoning discussion on the performativity of scientific and practitioner theories to the field of technological and organizational change. Examining emerging technologies as a key area in this field of research, we have argued that emerging technologies cannot exist without theories ascribing considerable impact to them. Synthesizing insights from the research on performativity as well as technological and organizational change, we have proposed that emerging technology theories conflating the implicit or explicit categories of feature use and affordances as well as their respective outcomes will be more likely to enact all three types of performativity—generic, effective, and Barnesian performativity—offered explanations for why this may be the case, and we have discussed examples illustrating this logic.

We thus view this chapter as a first step towards recognizing the performativity of emerging technology theories that opens the door for systematic and empirical investigations of this issue. In this vein, we believe that we make a number of contributions to the existing scholarly discourse and open up a promising research agenda.

First, our conceptual examination of the performativity of emerging technology theories reinforces and extends research on the sociomaterial (Orlikowski and Scott 2008) nature of technological and organizational change, that is, the insight that organizational transformations are never single-handedly 'driven' or 'produced' by new and emerging technologies. Where previous research has especially focused on the sociomaterial entanglement of technological artefacts and their developers and users (e.g. Leonardi 2011; Barrett et al. 2012; Mazmanian et al. 2013), our performative perspective on emerging technology theories brings a new type of actor to the fore: scholars and experts whose theorizing attracts an audience in organizational and field-level discourses. Moreover, where longitudinal, empirical research on technological and organizational change has tended to view the adoption or internal development of a new technology as the 'starting point' of the change process (e.g. Heracleous and Barrett, 2001; D'Adderio, 2003; Leonardi, 2011; Barrett et al., 2012; Orlikowski 2013), our performative perspective on emerging technology theories shows that it is crucial to also consider how managerial decision-making and exposure to certain theories set the ground for and frame that change process.

Second, our conceptual examination of the performativity of emerging technology theories calls for deeper inquiry into the extensive, unforeseen, but hitherto disregarded organizational consequences of conceptual work and theories, and how these theories may potentially amplify the organizational impacts of emerging technologies. How different emerging technologies have been co-constituted in discourses ascribing 'considerable impact' to them, how those discourses have gone on to exhibit different types of performativity, and what consequences these performative outcomes have had for practitioners and scholars (e.g. attaining a thought-leader image, misallocating financial resources) all appear as promising, new research questions.

In the meantime, we believe that our conceptualization of how emerging technology theories can exhibit different types of performativity creates an opportunity to more critically engage with the existing practitioner and scholarly discourse on emerging technologies and their impacts on organizations. Reflecting on the clarity with which prominent emerging technology theories distinguish between feature use, affordances, and their respective outcomes, how much space those distinctions leave for also considering the contingencies of outcomes, and whether the direction of causality implied is realistic, may produce discourses that are less prone to hype cycles and more attuned to the capabilities and needs of real organizations.

Finally, performative theories do not only shape social reality in terms of managerial decision-making, they also affect social welfare (Marti and Scherer 2016) and have 'ethical consequences' (Ferraro et al. 2009: 673). Recognizing these dimensions of emerging technology theories is particularly important given how drastic some of the impacts they ascribe to technologies are. To consider just one example, the on-going practitioner and scholarly discourse surrounding artificial intelligence is rich with speculation of just how many jobs the technology is likely to replace. Being sensitive to the performativity of such theories could help public policymakers consider the extent, attainability, and immediateness of their theorized impacts, thus supporting their efforts to minimize social harm and maximize social welfare in the context of this emerging technology. In this vein, policymakers, scholars, and practitioners must recognize that, due to performative dynamics, their discoursive theorizing of AI-driven work replacement can contribute to the real 'loss of jobs' just as well as the technological features of actual AI artefacts.

## References


Allessie, D., Sobolewski, M., and Vaccari, L. (2019). 'Blockchain for Digital Government'. JRC Science for Policy Report. https://publications.jrc.ec.europa.eu/repository/bitstream/JRC115049/blockchain_for_digital_government_online.pdf (accessed 19.5.20).

Bailey, D., Faraj, S., Hinds, P., von Krogh, G., and Leonardi, P. (2019). 'Call for Papers: Special Issue of Organization Science: Emerging Technologies and Organizing', *Organ. Sci.* 642–646. https://doi.org/10.1287/orsc.2019.1299.

Barad, K. (2007). *Meeting the Universe Halfway*. Duke University Press.

Barrett, M., Oborn, E., Orlikowski, W. J., and Yates, J. (2012). 'Reconfiguring Boundary Relations: Robotic Innovations in Pharmacy Work', *Organ. Sci.* 23/5: 1448–1466.

Bean, R. (2016). 'Just Using Big Data Isn't Enough Anymore', *Harv. Bus. Rev.* February 2016. https://hbr.org/2016/02/just-using-big-data-isnt-enough-anymore (accessed 19.5.20).

Buterin, V. (2014). White Paper: 'A Next-Generation Smart Contract and Decentralized Application Platform'. https://blockchainlab.com/pdf/Ethereum_white_paper-a_next_generation_smart_contract_and_decentralized_application_platform-vitalik-buterin.pdf (accessed 19.5.20).

Butler, J. (1997). *Excitable Speech: A Politics of the Performative*. Psychology Press.

Cabantous, L., and Gond, J.-P. (2010). 'Rational Decision Making as Performative Praxis: Explaining Rationality's Éternel Retour', *Organ. Sci.* 22/3: 573–586. https://doi.org/10.1287/orsc.1100.0534.

Callon, M. (1998). *The Laws of the Markets*. Blackwell Publishers.

Carter, C., Clegg, S., and Kornberger, M. (2010). 'Re-Framing Strategy: Power, Politics and Accounting', *Account. Audit. Account. J.* 23/5: 573–594. https://doi.org/10.1108/09513571011054891.

Choudary, S. P., Alstyne, M. W. V., and Parker, G. G. (2019). 'Platforms and Blockchain Will Transform Logistics', *Harv. Bus. Rev.*, June. https://hbr.org/2019/06/platforms-and-blockchain-will-transform-logistics (accessed 19.5.20).

Clemens, E. K., and McFarlan, F. W. (1986). 'Telecom: Hook Up or Lose Out', *Harv. Bus. Rev.* 64: 91–97.

D'Adderio, L. (2003). 'Configuring Software, Reconfiguring Memories: The Influence of Integrated Systems on the Reproduction of Knowledge and Routines', *Ind. Corp. Change* 12/2: 321–350. https://doi.org/10.1093/icc/12.2.321.

D'Adderio, L., and Pollock, N. (2014). 'Performing Modularity: Competing Rules, Performative Struggles and the Effect of Organizational Theories on the Organization', *Organ. Stud.* 35/12: 1813–1843. https://doi.org/10.1177/0170840614538962.

Davenport, T. H., and Patil, D. J. (2012). 'Data Scientist: The Sexiest Job of the 21st Century', *Harv. Bus. Rev.* October. https://hbr.org/2012/10/data-scientist-the-sexiest-job-of-the-21st-century (accessed 19.5.20).

Deloitte (2019). 'Deloitte's 2019 Global Blockchain Survey'. https://www2.deloitte.com/content/dam/Deloitte/se/Documents/risk/DI_2019-global-blockchain-survey.pdf (accessed 19.5.20).

Derrida, J. (1979). 'Signature Event Context', *Glyph* 1: 172–197.

Dutta, S. (2010). 'Managing Yourself: What's Your Personal Social Media Strategy?', *Harv. Bus. Rev.* November 2010. https://hbr.org/2010/11/managing-yourself-whats-your-personal-social-media-strategy (accessed 19.5.20).

Faraj, S., and Azad, B. (2012). 'The Materiality of Technology: An Affordance Perspective', in Leonardi, P. M., Nardi, B. A., and Kallinikos, J. (eds), *Materiality and Organizing: Social Interaction in a Technological World*. Oxford University Press.

Faraj, S., Pachidi, S., and Sayegh, K. (2018). 'Working and Organizing in the Age of the Learning Algorithm', *Inf. Organ.* 28/1: 62–70. https://doi.org/10.1016/j.infoandorg.2018.02.005.

Fayard, A.-L., and Weeks, J. (2014). 'Affordances for Practice', *Inf. Organ.* 24/4: 236–249. https://doi.org/10.1016/j.infoandorg.2014.10.001.

Feldman, M. S., and Pentland, B. T. (2003). 'Reconceptualizing Organizational Routines as a Source of Flexibility and Change', *Adm. Sci. Q.* 48/1: 94–118. https://doi.org/10.2307/3556620.

Ferraro, F., Pfeffer, J., and Sutton, R. I. (2005). 'Economics Language and Assumptions: How Theories Can Become Self-Fulfilling', *Acad. Manage. Rev.* 30/1: 8–24. https://doi.org/10.5465/amr.2005.15281412.

Ferraro, F., Pfeffer, J., and Sutton, R. I. (2009). 'How and Why Theories Matter: A Comment on Felin and Foss (2009)', *Org. Sci.* 20/3: 669–675.

Fountaine, T., McCarthy, B., and Saleh, T. (2019). 'Building the AI-Powered Organization', *Harv. Bus. Rev.* July–August. https://hbr.org/2019/07/building-the-ai-powered-organization (accessed 19.5.20).

Gaines-Ross, L. (2010). 'Reputation Warfare', *Harv. Bus. Rev.* December. https://hbr.org/2010/12/reputation-warfare (accessed 19.5.20).

Garud, R., Gehman, J., and Tharchen, T. (2018). 'Performativity as Ongoing Journeys: Implications for Strategy, Entrepreneurship, and Innovation'. *Long Range Planning* 51/3: 500–509.

Gehman, J., Treviño, L. K., and Garud, R. (2013). 'Values Work: A Process Study of the Emergence and Performance of Organizational Values Practices', *Acad. Manage. J.* 56/1: 84–112. https://doi.org/10.5465/amj.2010.0628.

Gibson, J. J. (1979). *The Ecological Approach to Visual Perception*, 1st ed. Houghton-Mifflin.

Gond, J.-P., Cabantous, L., Harding, N., Learmonth, M. (2016). 'What Do We Mean by Performativity in Organizational and Management Theory? The Uses and Abuses of Performativity', *Int. J. Manag. Rev.* 18/4: 440–463. https://doi.org/10.1111/ijmr.12074.

Guérard, S., Langley, A., and Seidl, D. (2013). 'Rethinking the Concept of Performance in Strategy Research: Towards a Performativity Perspective', *M@n@gement* 16/5: 566–578.

Gupta, V. (2017). 'The Promise of Blockchain Is a World Without Middlemen', *Harv. Bus. Rev.* March. https://hbr.org/2017/03/the-promise-of-blockchain-is-a-world-without-middlemen (accessed 19.5.20).

Hacking, I. (1983). *Representing and Intervening: Introductory Topics in the Philosophy of Natural Science*. Cambridge University Press.

Heracleous, L., and Barrett, M. (2001). 'Organizational Change as Discourse: Communicative Actions and Deep Structures in the Context of Information Technology Implementation', *Acad. Manage. J.* 44/4: 755–778. https://doi.org/10.5465/3069414.

Iansiti, M., and Lakhani, K. R. (2017). 'The Truth about Blockchain', *Harv. Bus. Rev.* January–February. https://hbr.org/2017/01/the-truth-about-blockchain (accessed 19.5.20).

Jeffries, A. (2018). '"Blockchain" Is Meaningless', *The Verge*. https://www.theverge.com/2018/3/7/17091766/blockchain-bitcoin-ethereum-cryptocurrency-meaning (accessed 19.5.20).

Latour, B. (1993). *We Have Never Been Modern*. Harvard University Press.

Learmonth, M. (2005). 'Doing Things with Words: The Case of "Management" and "Administration"', *Public Adm.* 83/3: 617–637. https://doi.org/10.1111/j.0033-3298.2005.00465.x.

Leidner, D. E., Gonzalez, E., and Koch, H. (2018). 'An Affordance Perspective of Enterprise Social Media and Organizational Socialization', *J. Strateg. Inf. Syst.* 27/2: 117–138. https://doi.org/10.1016/j.jsis.2018.03.003.

Leonardi, P. (2011). 'When Flexible Routines Meet Flexible Technologies: Affordance, Constraint, and the Imbrication of Human and Material Agencies', *MIS Q.* 35/1: 147–167. https://doi.org/10.2307/23043493.

Lumineau, F., Wang, W., and Schilke, O. (2021). 'Blockchain Governance—A New Way of Organizing Collaborations?' *Organ. Sci.* 32/2: 500–521.

Mackenzie, D. (2006). 'Is Economics Performative? Option Theory and the Construction of Derivatives Markets', *J. Hist. Econ. Thought* 28/1: 29–55. https://doi.org/10.1080/10427710500509722.

MacKenzie, D., and Millo, Y. (2003). 'Constructing a Market, Performing Theory: The Historical Sociology of a Financial Derivatives Exchange', *Am. J. Sociol.* 109/1: 107–145. https://doi.org/10.1086/374404.

Mahidhar, V., and Davenport, T. H. (2018). 'Why Companies that Wait to Adopt AI May Never Catch Up', *Harv. Bus. Rev.* December. https://hbr.org/2018/12/why-companies-that-wait-to-adopt-ai-may-never-catch-up (accessed 19.5.20).

Majchrzak, A., Faraj, S., Kane, G. C., and Azad, B. (2013). 'The Contradictory Influence of Social Media Affordances on Online Communal Knowledge Sharing', *J. Comput.-Mediat. Commun.* 19/1: 38–55. https://doi.org/10.1111/jcc4.12030.

Marti, E., and Gond, J.-P. (2017). 'When Do Theories Become Self-Fulfilling? Exploring the Boundary Conditions of Performativity', *Acad. Manage. Rev.* 43/3: 487–508. https://doi.org/10.5465/amr.2016.0071.

Marti, E., and Scherer, A. (2016). 'Financial Regulation and Social Welfare: The Critical Contribution of Management Theory', *Acad. Manage. Rev.* 41/2: 298–323. http://dx.doi.org/10.5465/amr.2013.0469.

Mazmanian, M., Orlikowski, W. J., and Yates, J. (2013). 'The Autonomy Paradox: The Implications of Mobile Email Devices for Knowledge Professionals', *Organ. Sci.* 24/5: 1337–1357. https://doi.org/10.1287/orsc.1120.0806.

McAfee, A., and Brynjolfsson, E. (2012). 'Big Data: The Management Revolution', *Harv. Bus. Rev.* October. https://hbr.org/2012/10/big-data-the-management-revolution (accessed 19.5.20).

Nakamoto, S. (2008). 'Bitcoin: A Peer-to-Peer Electronic Cash System'. https://bitcoin.org/bitcoin.pdf (accessed 19.5.20).

Orlikowski, W. J., and Scott, S. V. (2008). 'Sociomateriality: Challenging the Separation of Technology, Work and Organization', *Acad. Manag. Ann.* 2/1: 433–474. https://doi.org/10.1080/19416520802211644.

Pickering, A. (1995). *The Mangle of Practice*. University of Chicago Press.

Ramiller, N. C. (2006). 'Hype! Toward a Theory of Exaggeration in Information Technology Innovation', *Acad. Manag. Proc. 2006*: A1–A6. https://doi.org/10.5465/ambpp.2006.27169062.

Rotolo, D., Hicks, D., and Martin, B. R. (2015). 'What Is an Emerging Technology?', *Res. Policy* 44/10: 1827–1843.

Seidel, M.-D. L. (2018). 'Questioning Centralized Organizations in a Time of Distributed Trust', *J. Manag. Inq.* 27/1: 40–44. https://doi.org/10.1177/1056492617734942.

Shotter, J. (1983). '"Duality of Structure" and "Intentionality"', *Ecological Psychology.J. Theory Soc. Behav.* 13/1: 19–44. https://doi.org/10.1111/j.1468-5914.1983.tb00460.x.

Swan, M. (2015). *Blockchain: Blueprint for a New Economy*. O'Reilly Media Inc.

Tapscott, D., and Tapscott, A. (2016). *Blockchain Revolution: How the Technology Behind Bitcoin Is Changing Money, Business, and the World*. Portfolio.

The Economist (2015). 'The Trust Machine', *The Economist*. https://www.economist.com/leaders/2015/10/31/the-trust-machine (accessed 19.5.20).

Treem, J. W., and Leonardi, P. M. (2013). 'Social Media Use in Organizations: Exploring the Affordances of Visibility, Editability, Persistence, and Association', *Ann. Int. Commun. Assoc.* 36/1: 143–189. https://doi.org/10.1080/23808985.2013.11679130.

Underwood, S. (2016). 'Blockchain beyond Bitcoin', *Commun. ACM* 59: 15–17.

Vaara, E., Sorsa, V., and Pälli, P. (2010). 'On the Force Potential of Strategy Texts: A Critical Discourse Analysis of a Strategic Plan and Its Power Effects in a City Organization', *Organization* 17/6: 685–702. https://doi.org/10.1177/1350508410367326.

Zammuto, R. F., Griffith, T. L., Majchrzak, A., Dougherty, D. J., and Faraj, S. (2007). 'Information Technology and the Changing Fabric of Organization', *Organ. Sci.* 18/5: 749–762. https://doi.org/10.1287/orsc.1070.0307.

# 10

# Computer Workarounds or Expediting Work?

*Bijan Azad and Nelson King*

## 10.1 Introduction

In several recent reviews of empirical literature on organizational information technology (IT) workarounds (e.g. Lund-Jensen et al. 2016; Röder et al. 2016; Ejnefjäll and Par 2019), three trends stood out: (a) most research employs an instrumental view of IT use and workarounds; (b) the dominant theoretical template for the empirical study of organizational IT workarounds remains rule non-compliance, and (c) studies largely focus on identifying how and which specific IT functionalities are being worked around rather than addressing how and why workarounds emerge (i.e. their genesis).[1] At the same time, scholars are increasingly recognizing that IT workarounds may arise from routine interactions with IT-enabled workflows rather than from the intention to avoid system use (e.g. Azad and King 2012; Malaurent and Karanasios 2020).

We aim to contribute to this stream of research by focusing on the work of clinicians facing anomalies in their workflow within an IT-enabled medical practice. Our proposed theoretical frame, tailored to the specific entwinement of medical practice and IT-enabled workflow, builds on the notions of pragmatism (Dewey 1938), interactionist sociology (Strauss 1993), phenomenology (Merleau-Ponty 1945–1962), and ecological psychology (Gibson 1950). Accordingly, we seek to move away from characterizing attempts to bypass IT as workarounds, a term with instrumental connotations (Mingers 2011; Røvik 2019) typically used to describe the intentional non-use of IT. Based on the actions of clinicians in the face of work anomalies, we propose a more nuanced picture of IT use within medical work practices, one characterized by a logic of expedience and thus more accurately portrayed as expediting work. Therefore, our research question asks: *How*

Bijan Azad and Nelson King, *Computer Workarounds or Expediting Work?*. In: *Organizing in the Digital Age*. Edited by: Michael Barrett, Emmanuelle Vaast, Ann Langley, and Haridimos Tsoukas, Oxford University Press. 
DOI: 10.1093/oso/9780198899457.003.0010

*does IT-enabled work get accomplished (expedited) in response to workflow anomalies?*

To empirically examine this question, we consider how key actors (e.g. nurses, attending physicians, interns, residents, pharmacists, infectious disease specialists, and hospital administrators) interacted with each other and responded to specific work practice anomalies in an accredited teaching hospital in the Eastern Mediterranean. Data are collected from observing the workflows of these clinicians and the actions they took to compensate for emergent work practice anomalies while attending to medication-dispensing processes—especially with regard to the use of a Medication Dispensing System (MDS) within a Health Information System/Electronic Health Record (HIS/EHR). This empirical context provides us with a unique opportunity to focus on a revelatory case to theorize the process through which an anomaly begets a compensating action that unintentionally bypasses the computer system and potentially may lead to subsequent anomalies—i.e. emergence of workarounds.

Our work contributes to the literature on the genesis of IT workarounds in three ways. First, we demonstrate that in routine IT-enabled work situations, anomalies trigger a distinct mechanism of *compensating* actions which attempt to restore the original workflow in three ways: through *performative procedures*, ad hoc *role crafting*, and *gaming the system*. Second, we show that these compensatory actions are governed by the logics of *expedience* and *satisficing*. Third, due to the predominance of expedience, the ensemble of logics and compensatory actions may be more accurately referred to as *expediting* work rather than as IT workarounds.

## 10.2 A Framework to Analyse Workaround Emergence

To begin laying out our theoretical framework, we first present a practical situation that can unfold in a hospital: a computer system is used for dispensing medications such that specialist physicians must approve restricted drugs by entering their signature on the screen before the medication can be dispensed (i.e. prior approval of a certain class of medications). Yet this practice invariably does not happen as specified by the formal hospital protocol for a variety reasons (e.g. specialists not being present during patient rounds). As a result, attending physicians, interns, nurses, pharmacists, and even other specialists may end up bypassing the computer system's prior approval function and dispensing drugs without it. They do so by adding a remark to the system's comment field and noting that the drug was dispensed but approval was missing.

This vignette demonstrates how clinicians routinely handle anomalies in their work practices and engage in compensatory actions—'ways of getting on' (Collins et al. 1997). Specifically, compensatory actions point to a tendency to maintain clinical activity and not stop just because an anomaly arose. In turn, this intent behind compensatory actions suggests that clinicians are not necessarily against the use of IT or the inscribed protocol; they just want to keep working. By drawing upon the theoretical frames of pragmatism, phenomenology, interactionism, and ecological psychology, we can explore the emergence and evolution of compensating actions and their corresponding underlying logics.

First, we link the compensatory action visible in the above medical work vignette with the pragmatist concept of situated 'problem-solving' in response to an anomaly (Dewey 1938). For Dewey, a process of situated problem-solving is often unleashed 'because of disturbance, which is indeterminate' (Dewey 1938: 34). In other words, compensatory actions emerge from ongoing work routines (Cohen 2007) running into anomalies. For compensatory actions, then, their situatedness is indeterminate compared to the certainty of prescribed organizational protocols.

However, the indeterminacy of compensatory actions as responses to anomalies does not imply that the flow of socio-material practices results in a chaotic disequilibrium. Crucially, a phenomenological dynamic 'motivates this *compensatory* activity' with an inherent movement towards the reduction of disequilibrium (Merleau-Ponty 1968–2003: 149, emphasis added). Thus, according to 'Merleau-Ponty's phenomenology', compensatory actions trigger a dynamic of 'reducing disequilibrium by moving towards' restoring a grip on the situation (Rietveld, Denys, and van Westen 2018)—referred to as the 'tendency towards grip' (Merleau-Ponty 1945–2002).

The combination of situated problem-solving and tendency towards grip does not guarantee that compensatory actions will result in the smooth restoration of an original workflow. Indeed, interactionist sociologists—and Strauss (1993), in particular—have identified two underlying mechanisms of compensatory actions: articulation work and professional stance. For Strauss (1993), articulation work involves the (re-) coordination of actions disturbed by anomalies, which in turn involves re-fitting joint actions among different actors within a disrupted workflow. This refitting is a negotiated[2] process, one that foregrounds how different organizational roles arrive at an arrangement alternative to their prescribed ones albeit rooted in their diverse role-based stances (Strauss 1978). As such, the resultant negotiated workflow arrangements often exhibit a logic or ethos which may be different from the action logic of the original workflow.

Finally, the ecological psychologist Gibson (1950) is credited with making the distinction between efficient action and proper action. For example, young children learn how certain things should be done with certain implements—for example, spoons and forks should be used for feeding oneself at the dinner table (Gibson 1950). In contrast, the efficient (quickest) ways are largely or primarily driven by more immediate functional considerations—for example, eating food with hands to satisfy a raw sense of hunger as quickly as possible despite the norms of social dining. In the context of an institutionalized medical work practice, dispensing medication as soon as possible may be efficient, yet doing so may oppose organizational rules prescribed as proper actions.

To construct our sensitizing theoretical frame of reference (Bowen 2006), we invoked situated problem-solving in the face of an anomaly. Here, situated problem-solving attempts to restore grip on the situation while necessitating articulation work across diverse actors and their different stances, which remain subject to the norms of proper action.

## 10.3 Research Methodology

### 10.3.1 Rationale for Choosing Case Study Method

Our interest in interpreting IT workarounds in a hospital organization motivated our decision to employ the case study method (Yin 2014). This method enabled us to examine compensatory activities amidst work practice anomalies that challenge existing workflows informed by prescribed protocols and thus lead to workarounds. Although case studies may be criticized for researchers' proximity to phenomena under examination, we took steps to reduce the potential for bias. The two authors formed an insider–outsider research team, as suggested by Evered and Louis (1981) and Gioia et al. (2010). While one author was deeply embedded in the organizational processes and practices, the other author functioned as a 'sceptic' (Eisenhardt 1989). Additionally, we sought feedback from individuals within the hospital organization who were familiar with the medication-dispensing processes. Specifically, we consulted with two clinician board members on the university's 'Evidence-based Health Management Group' (EHMG, a pseudo name) during the coding and conceptual development phases, as well as on an early draft of the chapter. We also asked two nurses and two physicians from other EHMG projects for feedback on the framework. In both cases, these consultants were supportive of the framework as a fairly accurate characterization of the 'situation on the ground'. Their ideas and comments were integrated into the final version of this chapter.

## 10.3.2 Case Background

Overuse or misuse of antibiotics contributes to antibiotic-resistant bacteria which, in turn, threatens patient safety. This hospital, among many others, embraces the institutional efforts of the World Health Organization and national health regulatory agencies to combat antibiotic resistance by advocating for the controlled use of antibiotics.

The hospital chose a prior-approval process for controlling the use of antibiotics such that all orders for restricted medications require approval from an infectious disease physician (hereafter referred to as the ID specialist). The stated protocol on the 'form'[3] for dispensing a restricted antimicrobial medication requires the attending physician (MD) to consult the ID specialist and obtain approval prior to writing the order for the medication. This form must be sent to the pharmacy along with the order (i.e. prescription, in outpatient terminology). The pharmacist uses an MDS within an HIS/EHR to input and process the order before printing the labels so the medications can be gathered, labelled, and delivered to units (e.g. intensive care ward) within the hospital. Nurses in the units administer the restricted medication once delivered by the pharmacy.

The case study hospital and most teaching hospitals commonly use patient rounds (or simply rounds), led by a senior physician, to create and communicate a daily patient care plan that the interns and medical students will follow (Satterfield et al. 2014; Blankenburg et al. 2018). While the participant list varies by hospital, rounds facilitate shared decision-making by encouraging each discipline to contribute their expertise. Rounds, due to the co-presence of clinical decision-makers, facilitate a highly efficient decision-making process by minimizing coordination burdens. Indeed, as we will see, the ostensive design of the antimicrobial prior-approval policy and MDS use depended heavily on the co-presence of key clinical decision-makers during rounds.

### 10.3.3 Data Collection

Our ongoing relationship with the hospital to improve its MDS workflow dates back to 2006 and continued in 2008. Subsequently, in 2012, our nursing graduate student examined the hospital's transition to a web-based restricted antimicrobial approval form. The data for this chapter builds upon these previous data collections and includes subsequent interviews and shadowing work in 2013 and 2014 to further understand the MDS workflow. A final round of data collection was conducted by another nursing student in Summer 2018 after the hospital went live with EPIC®, an enterprise HIS/EHR software. Permission was obtained from both the institutional review board and the hospital director to conduct these observational studies and interviews.

Members of the research team shadowed clinicians, especially nurses and the medical team, on the units that frequently ordered restricted medications. Initially, the subjects provided real-time commentary on their tasks and the steps taken to complete tasks. The subject's commentary quickly diminished once the observers (i.e. member of the shadowing team) demonstrated an understanding of the tasks and workflow. Over time, the observers became more knowledgeable and acquired an ostensive or formal understanding of the work. In turn, they began looking for anomalies or breaches as discussed previously in the theoretical section of the chapter. For example, an observer would ask, 'What did the pharmacy technician delivering medications mumble to you about some form for patient Y?' or, later in the study, 'Why is a sticky note [with written approval] taped to the computer screen?' The subject then explained what was happening in practice. The observers took field notes and developed process maps based on this shadowing work. The designed/ostensive and practiced/actual approval processes were verified through a nursing-sponsored quality workshop on process improvement during which 12 nurses from across the hospital dissected the observer's process maps.

Once the observers completed enough observations across multiple units in the hospital and obtained agreement from the nurses at the quality workshop, data collection acquired a more traditional qualitative approach, using interviews to gain insight into the motivation behind observed phenomena. During the shadowing process, a large number of clinical staff provided information. Different role-based perspectives on the approval process were obtained by interviewing 28 nurses, nine medical team members (fellows,

**Table 10.1** Clinical roles interviewed

| Role | Title | Number of Interviews | Task |
|---|---|---|---|
| Physician | medical team members (fellows, residents, interns) | 9 | Orders restricted medication |
| Physician | Attending physician | 4 | Orders restricted medication |
| Infectious disease specialist | Infectious disease physician | 3 | Consults and approves restricted medication order |
| Nurse | Nurse | 28 | Transcribes order and sends to pharmacy—administers restricted medications |
| Pharmacist | Pharmacist | 4 | Verifies ordered medication has approved form—dispenses |

residents, interns), three ID specialists, four pharmacists, and four attending physicians who did not have teaching responsibilities (i.e. not assigned a medical team). The list of informants interviewed is provided in Table 10.1. Each formal interview lasted on average 45minutes.

### 10.3.4 Data Analysis, Coding Process, and Key Themes/Categories

The context-rich data needed to perform processual analysis require us to pay attention to the nuances of process while analysing field notes and interview transcripts (e.g. Bidart, Longo, and Mendez 2013; Abbott 2016). As a first step, the interviews were recorded and transcribed. Subsequently, we started to code data and field notes with the aim of answering the research question: *How does IT-enabled work get accomplished (expedited) in response to workflow anomalies?*

We began analysing our data using the process recommended by Corbin and Strauss (2008) based on three types of data coding using NVIVO® 10 software: open, axial, and selective. Aided and sensitized (Bowen 2006) by the theoretical lenses of pragmatism, phenomenology, and interactionism, we looked for patterns in the data that corresponded to the following situations: anomaly-triggered workflow problem solving; subsequent compensatory actions that aimed to reduce disequilibrium with a tendency towards grip; and articulation work as refitting joint work to restore the original workflow according to each actor's perspective. Initial coding resulted in the following broad categories: compensatory activities to rectify anomalies and the distinctive types of compensatory activities employed; whether or not compensatory activities attempted to restore the original workflow and how; and the underlying logic or ethos that drove clinicians to engage in compensatory actions.

Next, we grouped codes together to detect conceptual and empirical similarities across the data. As is common in most coding processes, we started with a large number—29 codes. Then, we narrowed down the codes to 12 useful ones, each with more than one incidence of the code and in more than one text fragment.

Below, we describe in more detail the major themes and categories that emerged from our coding and analysis efforts. They are summarized in the Gioia et al. (2013) data structure diagram in Figure 10.1.

*1) Logic of Compensatory Actions in Response to Anomalies.* The operative logic of clinicians' work practices, in general, was an important factor in shaping their response to anomalies. Although we initially looked at more logics, most actions were re-classified under three main logics (largely inspired by the work Gibson (1950) and Cyert and March (1963)) through which the prior-approval policy was manifested in work procedures: (1) 'proper action', which satisfies both the letter and intent of the policy within the prescribed workflow (i.e. the default logic; as such, it will not be described in the findings or analysis); (2) 'satisficing action', whereby compensatory actions aim to satisfy the policy's intent; and (3) 'efficient action' or 'expedient action', according to which compensatory actions aim to dispense medication in the quickest way possible—without explicit regard for either the intent or letter of the prior-approval policy.

*2) Types of Compensatory Activities in Response to Anomalies.* The above coding process yielded the following three categories for compensatory activities undertaken by clinicians: (1) performative procedures that varied routines slightly in response to anomalous conditions; (2) ad hoc role crafting which refers to situated role-based responses to anomalies that are contrary to prescribed procedures; and (3) gaming the system, activities that 'dupe' the system into ignoring the actions based on conscious steps.

*3) Mechanism of Compensatory Actions as Expediting Work versus Working Around.* According to our coded data, the clinicians appeared not to oppose the use of the MDS. Notably, in the course of tackling anomalies, not once was the intention to bypass the MDS mentioned. More specifically, clinicians often responded to anomalies disrupting standard workflow steps involving

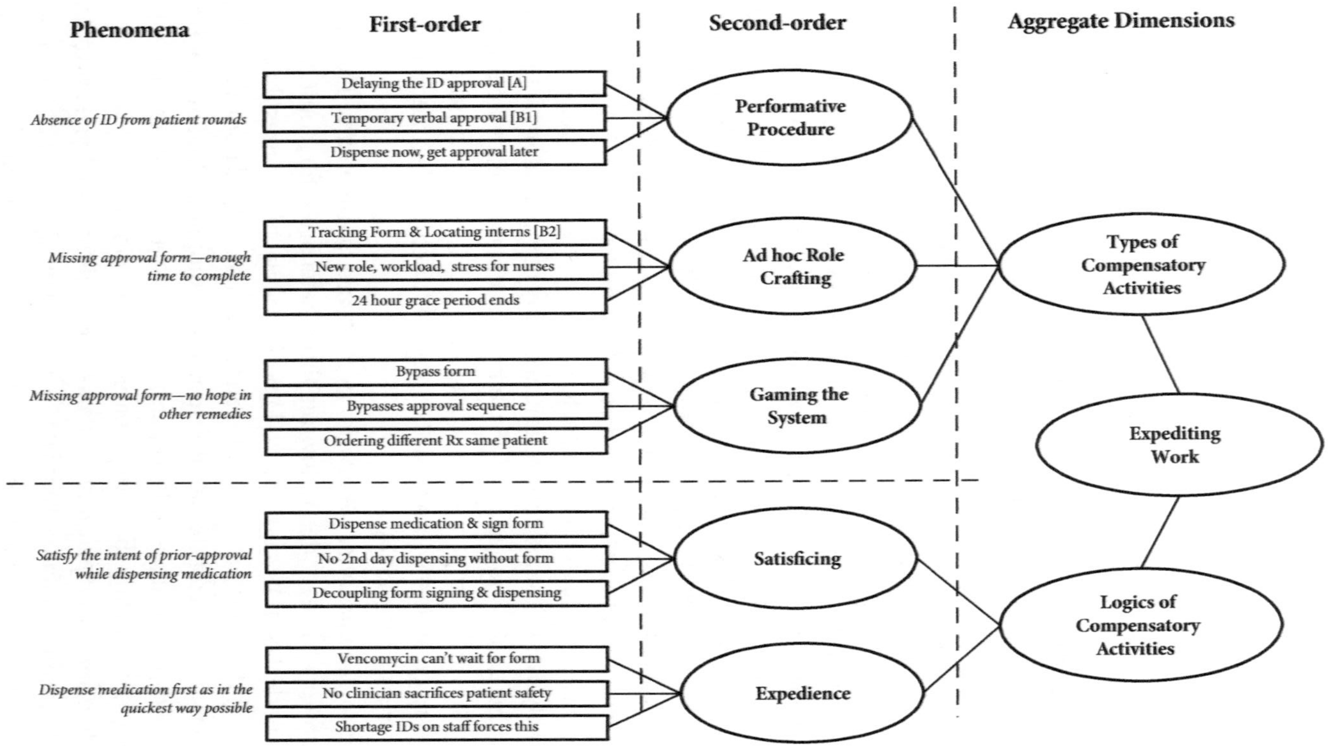


**Figure 10.1** Categories of Gioia et al. (2013) data structure resulting from the data analysis process

the MDS in two general ways: (a) in almost all cases, their responses ensured that medication was dispensed to the user expeditiously (expedience), and (b) less frequently, their responses attempted to satisfy the 'intent' of securing an approval (satisficing). Accordingly, we label the mechanism of these compensatory activities and their associated logics as 'expediting work', which appears to be a more accurate representation than workarounds.

## 10.4 Findings

Here, we present findings from two cycles of processual analyses. The initial cycle shows how the original workflow changes in the presence of anomalies with attempts to restore the workflow. The subsequent cycle shows how this restored workflow changes in the presence of new anomalies introduced from the first cycle via the restoration attempts. Finally, we present an analytical summary focusing on the categories of compensatory actions and their corresponding logics.

### 10.4.1 Original Workflow and Initial Anomalies

1) *Background.* The original workflow, prescribed by hospital policy, shows that the delivery of restricted medications to the units (e.g. once labels have been printed) occurs only after the completion of the sequential medication-dispensing workflow (Figure 10.2). The attending physician

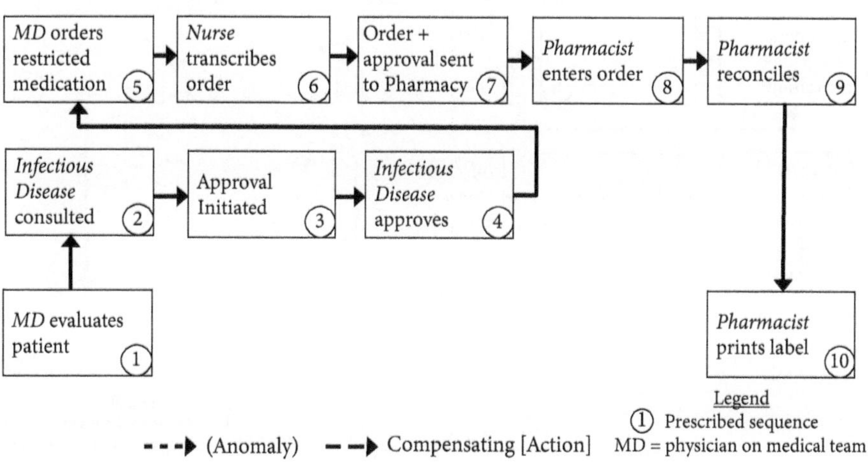


Figure 10.2 Original workflow sequence

and the accompanying medical team evaluate the patient (step 1) in the presence of the ID specialist. The clipboard (or its current digital version on the computer screen) with the form filled out by the intern can be 'passed' to the ID specialist who quickly scans the information to confirm that the written order matches the verbal instruction and that any lab results are properly considered. The ID specialist's presence during rounds makes for a seamless approval process (steps 2 to 4) before the team moves on to the next patient. The approval form is circulated among the clinicians and approved (signed) before the ordering process (steps 5 to 7) takes place. The nurse then transcribes the order, which is sent along with the completed approval to the pharmacist (step 8). The pharmacist, possessing both the order and the accompanying approval (step 9), has no further interaction with upstream actors and proceeds to dispense the medication (step 10).

The original workflow prescribes an approval process that can be potentially completed in a matter of minutes, often while the medical team walks down the hall to the next patient. Co-present clinicians know whose instructions should be recorded, the data required for the form, and the appropriate time to get a signature.

2) ***Disruption of Original Workflow Due to Initial Anomalies.*** Inherent to any workflow can be the unexpected Cycle A anomalies that transform the original state to an anomalous one. The first anomaly of the original state, identified as a dotted arrow A1 in parentheses in Figure 10.3,

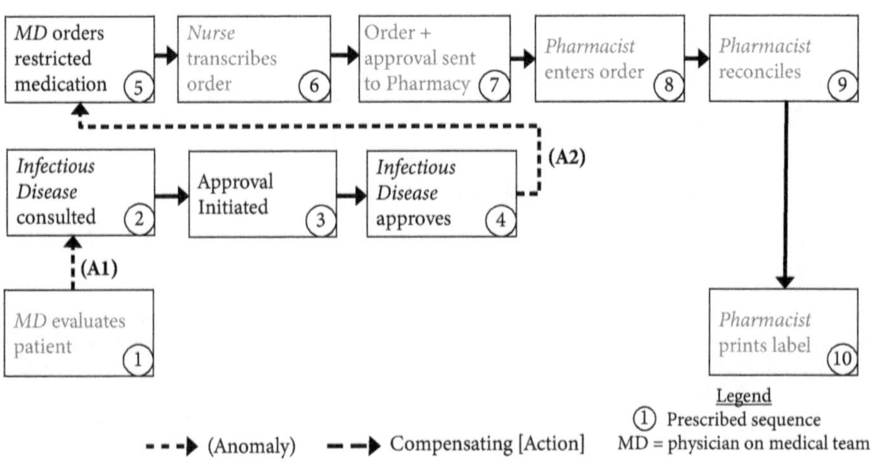


**Figure 10.3** Original workflow sequence with its anomalies

reflects the common situation wherein the ID specialist is not present during rounds. Without the ID specialist, the approval process (steps 2 to 4) cannot occur. The second anomaly, identified as A2, happens when the missing approval prevents the ordering (steps 5 to 7) and dispensing (steps 8 to 10) of medication.

The anomaly A1 and the resultant anomaly A2 can shut down the workflow if the sequence is followed to the letter of the policy. A common sentiment conveyed by one of our informants suggested that this outcome was not in patients' best interests: 'This has dire consequences to the patient who needs a restricted medication in hours rather than the next day. Nobody [clinician] would put a patient at risk merely to follow the prescribed prior approval protocol.'

3) ***Attempts to Restore Original Workflow.*** A solution to restore the original workflow, constrained by Cycle A anomalies, embodies several compensating actions, as shown in Figure 10.4. First, the physician can order a restricted medication without the immediate need for approval as indicated by the dashed arrow labelled CA1 in brackets. This action relieves the potential blockage caused by anomalies (A1) and (A2). The order, without the approval, can then be sent to the pharmacy (step 7) for immediate processing. The pharmacist, after entering the order (step 8), no longer needs to immediately check for an accompanying approval (step 9), since often it is missing. Instead, the pharmacist can invoke the second compensating action, labelled CA2, that allows the first day of doses to be dispensed (step 10) by merely setting a flag requiring reconciliation for the next day's doses. CA2

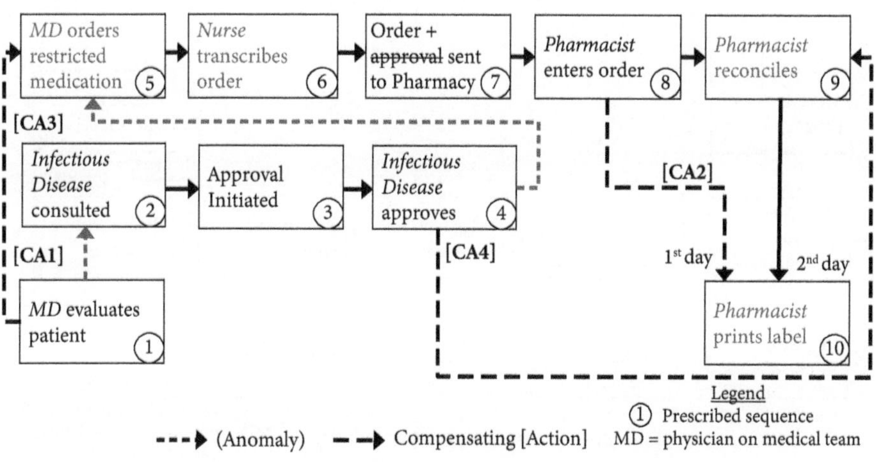


**Figure 10.4** Restoration of original workflow sequence with its compensating actions

compensates for this first-day-approval exemption by limiting its use to only the doses for the first day. In Figure 10.4, the steps that do not change are greyed out to highlight the steps that do change as a result of responding to the anomaly that occurs when prior approval is missing from the form.

While the medical team can now order a restricted medication without the prior approval of the ID specialist, we observed an operative norm calling for the approval to still be obtained even after the drug is ordered. The compensating action CA3 reflects the related action initiation by the medical team after writing an order. The fourth compensating action, labelled CA4, requires the ID specialist's approval to be received by the pharmacist before dispensing the medication on the second and subsequent day.

While CA1 relieves the blockage caused by anomalies A1 and A2 by delaying approval, both CA2 and CA4 facilitate the completion of the delayed approval on the first day. Whereas obtaining prior approval was presumed to be automatic during rounds in the original sequence, the restored sequence adds CA3 as an additional task for the medical team to compensate for the ID specialist's absence from rounds.

## 10.4.2 Restored Workflow and Subsequent Anomalies

1) ***Background.*** The attempt to restore workflow through compensatory actions CA1 to CA4 has been redrawn in Figure 10.5 to show the revised sequence of steps in the order that they are now conducted. The medical team can immediately order the medication (step 5) after the evaluation (step 1).

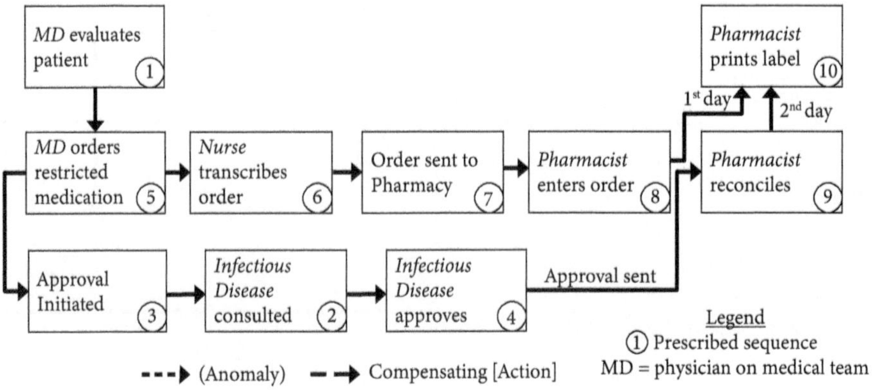


Figure 10.5 Restored workflow sequence

These step numbers refer to the original workflow for traceability and comparability. Rather than the sequential steps (1–10) in the original workflow, the restored workflow has the sequence 1-5-6-7-8-10-3-2-4-9-10. The medical team is also expected to initiate the approval outside of rounds (step 3) so the ID specialist can be consulted (step 2), which reverses the order of the original sequence.

The order now gets sent to the pharmacy without an approval (step 7) whereby the pharmacist takes on an ad hoc role serving as gatekeeper. When no approval accompanies the order, a 'note' must be made in the MDS (step 8), so only the first day of medications can be dispensed (step 10). While the pharmacist does not enforce the need for prior approval (step 9) for the first day, she often takes on this enforcer role before dispensing subsequent days of medication.

The order and approval steps are now in parallel with respect to the original sequence; as such, order reconciliation needs to be done twice before medication can be dispensed in the restored workflow sequence.

2) ***Disruption of Restored Workflow Due to Newly Introduced Anomalies.*** The restored workflow adds a step for explicit coordination between the now parallel ordering and approval paths, as shown in Figure 10.6. The medical team must remember to initiate the approval but often does not. This represents the first cycle B anomaly labelled B1a. Even if the approval is initiated, the medical team must also find the ID specialist for a consultation. Anomaly B1b reflects the difficulty of meeting up with an ID specialist in a timely manner. Even if the consultation takes place, the ID specialist must sign the form and notify someone at the nursing station to have the approval sent to the pharmacy: anomaly B2. If the approval form does not reach the pharmacist

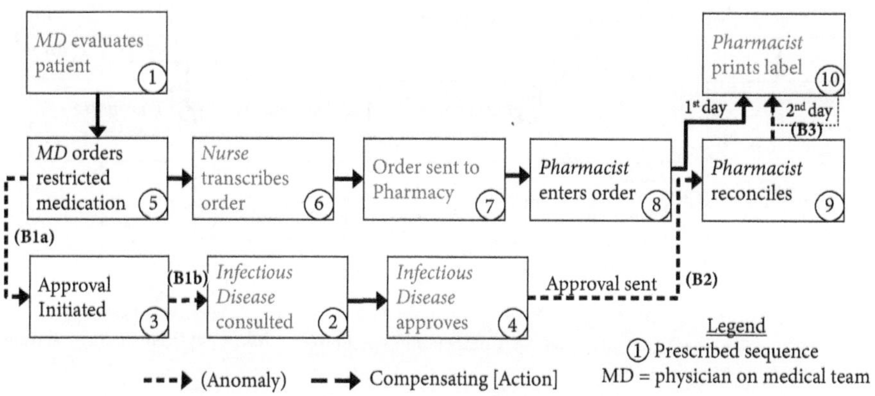


Figure 10.6 Restored workflow sequence with its newly introduced anomalies

in a timely manner, the gatekeeping pharmacist often will not release the second day of doses, which produces anomaly B3, one that has potentially serious consequences for the patient.

On the one hand, the parallel paths of the restored workflow allow for independent execution of steps; on the other hand, these parallel paths also render the urgency of each step invisible. In turn, an invisible urgent step that is delayed and then forgotten can hinder the smooth flow of work. Anomalies B1a, B1b, and B2 reflect procedural hindrances to a smoothly functioning workflow. According to a senior nursing informant, 'Unfortunately, the nursing staff report one of these anomalies occur at least once every ten medication orders.'

3) ***Attempts to 'Restore' the Previously Restored Workflow.*** With approval and ordering decoupled, anomalies B1a and B1b reflect the omission of a compulsory mechanism for the medical team to carry out the approval (step 3) and consult with the ID specialist (step 2). This type of anomaly allows these two steps to 'slip through the cracks' when the medical team is busy. To ensure forward progress, the compensating activity CB1 (see Figure 10.7) introduces a status-checking task/role to see if these steps are underway. Typically, this status check is done unofficially and in an ad hoc manner by nurses who worry that their patients may not get needed medication. Unfortunately, the ad hoc role of checking on the work of a physician by a clinician lower in the professional hierarchy can be problematic, so CB1 may or may not be carried out, depending on the relationship between the nurse and physician.

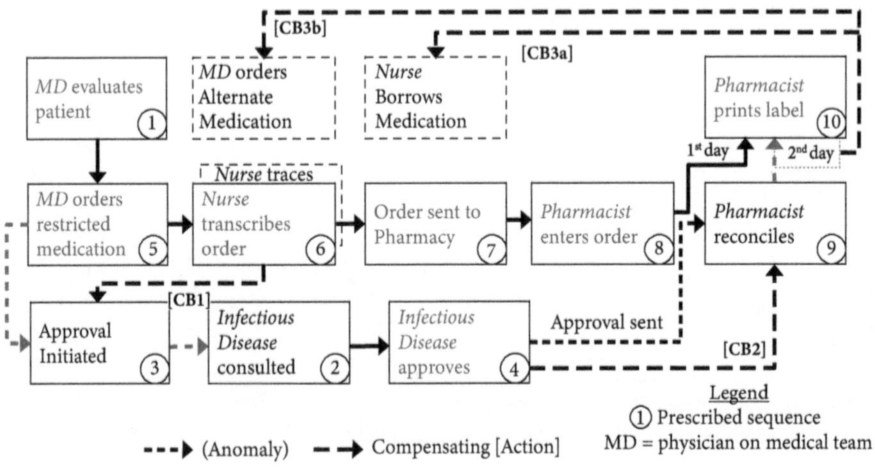


**Figure 10.7** 'Restoration' of previously restored workflow sequence and its compensating actions

Anomaly B2, failure to send the approval, occurs under several conditions. The medical team may have consulted with the ID specialist, but the ID specialist may not have actually signed the approval form. Alternatively, the ID specialist may have signed the approval form, but the form may have not been received by the time the pharmacy performs the approval reconciliation step. Compensating activity CB2 is invoked when the ID specialist can verbally convince the pharmacist that the approval has been made but the documentation—physical artifact or digital one in the online approval system—has been delayed.

Needless to say, most of our respondents were hesitant to specify how CB3a and CB3b take place. These compensating actions, however, were a deliberate effort to address the non-delivery of the original medication when attempts to restore workflow could not generate an approval in a timely manner.

### 10.4.3 Analytical Summary

So far, our analysis has focused on the manifestations of anomalies within existing medical work practices, the compensatory actions that attempt to restore workflow, and the new anomalies introduced as well as subsequent compensatory actions as a result of the restored workflow. Now, we elaborate a mechanism of response to anomalies that consists of a distinctive set of compensatory activities and a related set of motivating action logics.

1) ***Types and Mechanism of Compensating Activities.*** In Table 10.2, we summarize the observed compensating activities (column 2) discussed previously and their triggers (column 1). In addition, the key dynamic (column 3), or impact to the workflow, is provided. These triggers are primarily anomalies, marked in parentheses, and occasionally a compensating activity, shown in brackets and starting with the letter 'C'. Three of the eight compensating activities were triggered by a preceding compensating activity which points to a second-order effect—first-order compensatory actions triggering and compounding additional compensatory actions. For example, the absence of an ID specialist from patient rounds (i.e. A1) represents an anomaly that triggers CA1. Meanwhile, CA2 and CA3 are triggered by CA1, not by A1 directly. Next, we enumerate three more aggregated and general types of compensatory activities derived from Table 10.2 that appear to underpin the mechanism of restoring workflow in response to anomalies.

a) *Delaying ID specialist approval.* Postponing prior approval by the ID specialist can be seen in both the prescribed and practiced sequence (e.g. requesting temporary verbal approval). The anomaly in the prescribed

**Table 10.2** Triggers of compensating activities

| # | Trigger | Compensating Activity | Key Dynamic |
|---|---|---|---|
| 1 | Absence of ID from patient rounds (A1) | Delaying the ID approval [CA1] | Decouples approval from ordering |
| 2 | Delaying the ID approval [CA1] | Skip approval reconciliation for 24 hours [CA2] | Negotiated arrangement |
| 3 | Delaying the ID approval [CA1] | Get ID approval [CA3] | Restore approval into workflow relaxed by [CA1] |
| 4 | Absence of prior-order approval (A2) | Send approval directly to pharmacy [CA4] | Reconnect approval with order |
| 5 | Missing approval form—enough time to complete (B1a) | Status tracking form [CB1] | Adds unofficial role for nurses |
| 6 | Approval ready but not signed or sent (B2) | Requesting temporary verbal approval [CB2] | Convince pharmacist verbally |
| 7 | Missing approval form (B3) | Borrowing dose [CB3a] | Take chance that approval received by next shift |
| 8 | Unable to borrow doses [CB3a] | Ordering different drug [CB3b] | Bypass approval sequence |

sequence is addressed through a 'new' procedure: delaying approval. The practised sequence is largely performative; that is, each performance is slightly different when an ID specialist requests and a pharmacist accepts a temporary verbal approval. To generally characterize similar situations, we label this type of compensatory activity *performative procedure.*

b) *Tracking form and locating interns.* Decoupling the approval from the order means that someone must fill out the approval form. To dispense medication, the form needs to be tracked and interns need to be located to fill it. These two activities occur in the absence of a formal organizational procedure and typically fall to those lowest on the organizational hierarchy since they lack procedural specification. Interns, ranked lowest among the physicians, often forgot or conveniently ignored this tracking responsibility. In turn, ad hoc efforts beyond normal roles became critical, such as nurses reminding interns about a missing form or calling the pharmacy to see if a form has been received. We refer to this compensatory activity as ad hoc *role crafting,* whereby organizational roles are created on the fly to tackle the contingency at hand in a nonformal manner.

c) *Bypassing the form by ordering different drug.* Despite the seeming strangeness of borrowing medications from other patients, this situation can and does occur, most commonly in our study when the second day of medications did not arrive. Then, the nurses started borrowing medications temporarily until the form could be signed. At times, the form was bypassed entirely by ordering a different medication. Similarly, a patient's relatives might be asked to go to a local pharmacy and pick up the medication for the nurse. We refer to this type of compensating activity as *gaming the system.*

*2)* ***Logics that Govern Compensating Activities.*** For each of the three types of compensating activities described above, we suggest an underlying action logic that governs the attempt at workflow restoration, namely, *satisficing* or *expedience.* These logics are listed in Table 10.3.

For example, delaying the ID specialist's approval [CA1] is a performative procedure that can still lead to a restored workflow that satisfies the intent of the organization but follows a different task sequence. In other words, CA1 is satisficing and expedient. The satisficing element allows a delayed approval with the stipulation that an approval still should be obtained. The expedient logic recognizes that the limited numbers of ID specialists made the original workflow untenable in most instances. At the same time, skipping the reconciliation of an approval form to an order for the first 24 hours, done to accelerate access to first doses, goes against the prior-approval policy of the hospital. Indeed, the rule has not changed, but through negotiated agreement, stakeholders turn a blind eye to the rule by invoking the 'in case of an emergency' clause.

**Table 10.3** Mechanism of expediting work—compensating activities versus logics of action

| Compensating Activity | Logic of Action | |
|---|---|---|
| | Satisficing | Expedience |
| ***Performative Procedure*** | -Delaying the ID approval [CA1]<br>-Get ID approval [CA3]<br>-Send approval directly to pharmacy [CA4] | -Delaying the ID approval [CA1]<br>-Get ID approval [CA3]<br>-Send approval directly to pharmacy [CA4] |
| **Ad hoc *Role Crafting*** | -Tracking form status [CB1a]<br>-Requesting temporary verbal approval [CB2] | -Tracking form status [CB1a]<br>-Requesting temporary verbal approval [CB2] |
| ***Gaming the System*** | | -Skip approval reconciliation for 24 hours [CA2]<br>-Borrowing dose [CB3a]<br>-Ordering different drug [CB3b] |

Some compensating activities are merely done in the interest of saving time and expeditiously dispensing medication. Sending approval directly to the pharmacy [CA4] is one such procedural step. This activity has no bearing on role relationships for getting an approval. Similarly, tracking form status [CB1a] recognizes that those responsible for completing the approval form may forget to do so, and without a gentle reminder further delay is likely. The nurses who typically engage in this nudging can be reprimanded for completing any action related to the form itself, so their hands-off participation is ad hoc and depends on contextual factors, such as how soon doses will be needed and the track record of a particular physician for completing the form. Borrowing doses [CB3a] represents a last-ditch effort to help the patient. It is expedient as well as satisficing since the nurse knows that an approval will be coming but has yet to be sent to the pharmacy. In contrast, ordering a different drug [CB3b] intentionally bypasses (e.g. non-satisficing) the approval function of the original and restored workflows for the purpose of saving time (i.e. purely expedient).

## 10.5 Discussion and Conclusion

The novelty of our contribution derives from offering alternative explanations for the emergence of what are currently called computer workarounds. Here, we expound on why and how workarounds emerge.

First, why do actors engage in workarounds? At least in the context of our site (and others like it), the hospital's antimicrobial prior-approval policy inscribed within its MDS presumed the co-presence of key team members on patient rounds. This, however, was not an accurate assumption for the majority of cases. Based on our findings, the actors—including the ID specialists—admitted that the ostensive design of the prior-approval policy embedded within the MDS was not compatible with existing resource constraints: namely, very few ID specialists on staff. As a result, the lack of a co-present ID specialist was an anomaly that set in motion cycles of compensating actions that attempted to restore the original workflow. For these compensating actions, the operative action logic was largely dominated by the *expedience* of getting medication to the patient in the quickest way possible (all eight compensatory actions in Table 10.3), with little regard for the protocol's intent and/or letter. In certain other cases (five of the eight compensatory actions in Table 10.3), however, the action logic was characterized by *satisficing*, as well. That is, sometimes clinicians, while attempting to restore the original workflow, appeared to aim for not only expedience but also satisfying at least the intent of the prior-approval protocol. In practice, this meant that clinicians did their best to secure an approval though often not prior to dispensing medication. Due to the dominance of the expedience logic in almost all compensatory actions and the presence of the satisficing logic in some of these actions, we suggest that attempts at restoring the workflow can be labelled *expediting work*. Thus, expediting work appears to more accurately represent the compensatory activities described herein than IT workarounds, for IT was not bypassed intentionally but incidentally. The extant literature has acknowledged that some workarounds may be essential or caused by anomalies (e.g. Ferneley and Sobreperez 2006; Azad and King 2008). Our work, however, is among the first to provide a highly granular explanation for how action logics and compensatory actions together lead to the bypassing of protocols and their IT-based inscriptions in the face of work practice anomalies.

Second, how are compensatory actions enacted? In the face of work practice anomalies, compensatory actions are likely and common across a range of situations. In other words, regardless of the anomaly type even within a specialized workflow (e.g. clinical medication dispensing), a general pattern of compensatory actions is likely to be mobilized to assist in restoring the original workflow. Indeed, this case allowed us to enumerate a pattern of three compensatory activities: namely, *performative procedures*, ad hoc *role crafting*, and *gaming the system*. We suggest that these compensatory activities can be thought of as a preliminary palette or repertoire generically applicable to a range of contexts, beyond healthcare, facing anomalous situations—say, the use of Enterprise Resource Planning systems, for instance. Perhaps because the prior literature has focused more on classifying workarounds as instrumental and intentional IT-non-use, it has rarely theorized the mechanism and pattern of responses to anomalous IT-enabled work situations per se (e.g. Lund-Jensen et al. 2016; Ejnefjäll Röder et al. 2016; and Par 2019). Therefore, our work contributed by theorizing the existence of a general activity pattern that attempts to restore the flow of work, specifically through the three aforementioned activities.

In practical terms, by rooting the study of work practices and technology in pragmatism, phenomenology, interactionism, and ecological psychology, we can begin to identify systems and their embedded functions that depend unrealistically on assumptions about organizational processes (i.e. the co-presence of clinical team members making rounds in a hospital). Often, such IT-based protocols and workflow designs are devised by administrators and management as a shortcut to address underlying complex control and coordination processes.[4] Alternatively, the chapter's findings sensitize designers to develop systems that are 'ready' to expedite work through both expedience and satisficing action logics—which guide compensatory actions to restore the flow of work in the face of anomalies.

## Notes

1. Both authors contributed equally to this chapter's preparation. The research was in part supported by American University of Beirut, University Research Board, and Olayan School of Business OFFER grants.
2. A negotiated organizational arrangement here is used in the Straussian sense of being arrived at situationally.
3. In 2018, the hospital migrated to EPIC® which enabled digital forms. Thus for the remainder of the chapter, 'form' is used to refer to paper or digital form. Similarly, 'signature' can refer to paper or digital signature, etc.
4. Indeed, sometimes this is characterized as the 'folly of designing an artifact while hoping for a pattern of action' syndrome (Pentland and Feldman 2008).

## References

Abbott, A. (2016). *Processual Sociology*. University of Chicago Press.

Azad, B., and King, N. (2008). 'Enacting Computer Workaround Practices within a Medication Dispensing System', *European Journal of Information Systems* 17/3: 264–278.

Azad, B., and King, N. (2012). 'Institutionalized Computer Workaround Practices in a Mediterranean Country: An Examination of Two Organizations', *European Journal of Information Systems* 21/4: 358–372.

Bidart, C., Longo, M. E., and Mendez, A. (2013). 'Time and Process: An Operational Framework for Processual Analysis', *European Sociological Review* 29/4: 743–751.

Blankenburg, R., Hilton, J. F., Yuan, P., Rennke, S., Monash, B., Harman, S. M., ... and Satterfield, J. M. (2018). 'Shared Decision-Making during Inpatient Rounds: Opportunities for Improvement in Patient Engagement and Communication', *Journal of Hospital Medicine* 13/7: 453.

Bowen, G. (2006). 'Grounded Theory and Sensitizing Concepts', *International Journal of Qualitative Methods* 5/3: 12–23.

Cohen, M. D. (2007). 'Reading Dewey: Reflections on the Study of Routine', *Organization Studies* 28/5: 773–786.

Collins, H. M., de Vries, G. H., and Bijker, W. E. (1997). 'Ways of Going On: An Analysis of Skill Applied to Medical Practice', *Science, Technology, & Human Values* 22/3: 267–285.

Corbin, J., and Strauss, A. L. (2008). *Basics of Qualitative Research* (3rd ed). Sage Publications.

Cyert, R. M., and J. G. March. (1963). *A Behavioral Theory of the Firm.* Blackwell Publishers.

Dewey, J. (1938). *Logic: The Theory of Inquiry.* Henry Holt.

Eisenhardt, K. M. (1989). 'Building Theories from Case Study Research', *Academy of Management Review* 14/4: 532–550.

Ejnefjäll, T., and Ågerfalk, P. J. (2019). 'Conceptualizing Workarounds: Meanings and Manifestations in Information Systems Research', *Communications of the Association for Information Systems* 45/1: 20.

Evered, R., and Louis, M. R. (1981). 'Alternative Perspectives in the Organizational Sciences: "Inquiry from the Inside" and "Inquiry from the Outside"', *Academy of Management Review* 6/3: 385–395.

Ferneley, E. H., and Sobreperez, P. (2006). 'Resist, Comply or Workaround? An Examination of Different Facets of User Engagement with Information Systems', *European Journal of Information Systems* 15/4: 345–356

Gibson, J. J. (1950). 'The Implications of Learning Theory for Social Psychology', in J. G. Miller (eds), *Experiments in Social Process: A Symposium on Social Psychology.* McGraw-Hill: 147

Gioia, D. A., Corley, K. G., and Hamilton, A. L. (2013). 'Seeking Qualitative Rigor in Inductive Research: Notes on the Gioia Methodology', *Organizational Research Methods* 16/1: 15–31.

Gioia, D. A., Price, K. N., Hamilton, A. L., and Thomas, J. B. (2010). 'Forging an Identity: An Insider-Outsider Study of Processes Involved in the Formation of Organizational Identity', *Administrative Science Quarterly* 55/1: 1–46.

Lund-Jensen, R., Azaria, C., Permien, F. H., Sawari, J., and Bækgaard, L. (2016). 'Feral Information Systems, Shadow Systems, and Workarounds—a Drift in IS Terminology', *Procedia Computer Science* 100: 1056–1063.

Malaurent, J., and Karanasios, S. (2020). 'Learning from Workaround Practices: The Challenge of Enterprise System Implementations in Multinational Corporations', *Information Systems Journal* 30/4: 639–663.

Merleau-Ponty, M. (1945–2002). *Phenomenology of Perception.* Routledge.

Merleau-Ponty, M. (1968–2003). *Nature: Course Notes from the College de France* (trans. by R. Vallier). Northwestern University Press.

Mingers, J. (2011). 'The Truth, The Whole Truth, and Nothing but the Truth: High Quality Research in information Systems', in B. Galliers and W. Currie (eds), *The Oxford Handbook of Management Information Systems.* Oxford University Press, 67–86.

Pentland, B. T., and Feldman, M. S. (2008). 'Designing Routines: On the Folly of Designing Artifacts, while Hoping for Patterns of Action', *Information and Organization* 18/4: 235–250.

Rietveld, E., Denys, D., and Van Westen, M. (2018). 'Ecological-Enactive Cognition as Engaging with a Field of Relevant Affordances', in A. Newen, L. L. de Bruin and S. Gallagher (eds), *Oxford Handbook of 4E Cognition*. Oxford University Press, 41–70.

Röder, N., Wiesche, M., Schermann, M., and Krcmar, H. (2016, January). 'Toward an Ontology of Workarounds: A Literature Review on Existing Concepts', in *2016 49th Hawaii International Conference on System Sciences (HICSS)*. IEEE, 5177–5186.

Røvik, K. A. (2019). 'Instrumental Understanding of Management Ideas', in A. Sturdy, S. Heusinkveld, T. Reay, and D. Strang (eds), *The Oxford Handbook of Management Ideas*. Oxford University Press, 121–137.

Satterfield, J. M., Bereknyei, S., Hilton, J. F., Bogetz, M. A. L., Blankenburg, R., Buckelew, S. M., ... and Braddock III, C. H. (2014). 'The Prevalence of Social and Behavioral Topics and Related Educational Opportunities during Attending Rounds', *Academic Medicine: Journal of the Association of American Medical Colleges* 89/11: 1548.

Strauss, A. L. (1993). *Continual Permutations of Action*. Aldine Transaction.

Strauss, Anselm L. (1978). *Negotiations*. Jossey-Bass.

Yin, R. K. (2014). *Case Study Research: Design and Methods*. Sage Publications.

# Index

*For the benefit of digital users, indexed terms that span two pages (e.g., 52–53) may, on occasion, appear on only one of those pages.*

References to notes are indicated by a note suffix after the paragraph number, for example: 193 n.9

Tables and figures are indicated by an italic *t* or *f* following the page number.